W9-CCV-522

## BOOKS BY RONALD GROSS

**The Arts and the Poor** (with Judith Murphy)
**Learning by Television** (with Judith Murphy)
**Pop Poems**
**A Handful of Concrete** (portfolio of concrete poems, with Beatrice Gross)

### EDITOR

**The Teacher and the Taught: Education in Theory and Practice from Plato to Conant**
**The Revolution in the Schools** (with Judith Murphy)
**Radical School Reform** (with Beatrice Gross)
**Man in America** (with Paul Osterman)

# High School

EDITED BY
## Ronald Gross
AND
## Paul Osterman

SIMON AND SCHUSTER
*New York*

## ACKNOWLEDGMENTS

The editors wish to express their thanks and appreciation to the authors, editors and publishers who permitted us to use the following material:

"The Open Truth and Fiery Vehemence of Youth" by Peter Marin, copyright 1969 by The Fund for the Republic, Inc., by permission of the author, c/o International Famous Agency.

"If You're an Elephant Obviously You Need a Trunk, But That Doesn't Mean You Have to Be an Elephant" by Edgar Z. Friedenberg, permission of the author.

"Educating Contra Naturam" by Theodore Roszak, by permission of the author.

"Diary" by Daniel Hauben, by permission of the author.

"Wanted: A Humane Education," Montgomery County Student Alliance, with permission of Shannon Brubeck, Montgomery County Student Alliance.

"Andover: Even the Best Are Bad" by Thomas Doland, copyright © 1970 by Marc Libarle and Tom Seligson. Reprinted from High School Revolutionaries, edited by Marc Libarle and Tom Seligson, by permission of Random House, Inc.

"Students Work in a Classroom Maze" by Norman Soloman, by permission of the author.

"Two Straight Kids" by Jules Henry, from Culture Against Man by Jules Henry. Copyright © 1963 by Random House, Inc.

Reprinted by permission of the publisher.

"Boredom, Utopia, and 'Unprofessional Conduct'" by Joel Denker, by permission of the author.

"Teaching in Springville" by Jack Blodgett, by permission of the author.

"Schools for Scandal" by Ira Glasser, by permission of the author.

"Dangerous Saintly Tragic Brave Subversive" by Jonathan Kozol, from Isacs Bulletin, Winter 1970, reprinted by permission of the author.

"Murray Road: Beyond Innovations" by Evans Clinchy, by permission of the author.

"Parkway: The School Without Walls" by Henry Resnick, by permission of Cyrilly Abels Literary Agency.

"John Adams: Something for Everyone" by John Geurnsey, reprinted from American Education, U.S. Department of Health, Education, and Welfare.

"Harlem Prep: The Alternative System" by Ann M. Carpenter, by permission of the author.

"Shule Ya Uhuru: Freedom and Manhood" by Mamadou Lumumba, copyright by the Eastern High School Freedom Corporation, by permission of the author.

"Other Ways: Resource for a System" by Herbert Kohl, by permission of the author.

"LEAP: School Plus" by Michelle Cole, by permission of the author.

Copyright © 1971 by Ronald Gross and Paul Osterman
Published by Simon and Schuster
Rockefeller Center, 630 Fifth Avenue
New York, New York 10020

First printing

SBN 671–20838–1
Library of Congress Catalog Card Number: 71–139623
Designed by Irving Perkins
Manufactured in the United States of America
Printed by Mahony & Roese Inc., New York, N.Y.
Bound by H. Wolff Book Mfg. Co., Inc., New York, N.Y.

*To Henry and Esther, for their love*

*The editors are delighted to acknowledge
the invaluable help of four people:
Professor Edgar Friedenberg, Miss Shannon Brubeck,
Mrs. Leslie Shalen, and Mrs. Gail Shanks.*

# CONTENTS

7

# INTRODUCTION

The American high school is the most absurd part of an educational system pervaded by absurdity.

In elementary school, children clearly need some adult supervision to protect them from present dangers. In higher education young adults usually have enough freedom so that they can, if they choose, experiment and enjoy the pleasures and prospects of life. But high school . . .

The students are old enough to take care of themselves, old enough to reject the illegitimate authority of adults, old enough to love and fight and truly learn. To see these formidable creatures docilely submit to the indignities and boredom of the average high school is intolerably sad.

To keep the lid on, every form of persuasion has been used by educators, from cajolery to the harshest threats. The cajoling approach is given typical expression in Abraham Lass's *Success in High School*,[1] one of the most widely distributed guides for students. Here is some typical palaver by this principal of a leading New York City high school:

> High school is important business. You are America's business. . . . America needs trained people to keep us strong, prosperous, happy and free. This training starts in high school. That's why you and high school are so important.

> Study means doing well the things that may not interest you. You don't deserve any special credit for doing assignments that interest you.

[1] Abraham Lass, *Success in High School*, Scholastic Books, New York, 1967, pp. 12–13, 17, 60.

9

Anyone can do this. The successful student, the kind we're sure you want to be, gives his best to every assignment.

Good grades equal a good education. The higher your grades, the more you've learned and the more you know. It's true that some students with high grades haven't gotten very much out of their studies. But they are exceptions. The overwhelming majority of students with good grades are better educated than their friends with poor grades. Just "passing" (scoring about 65 percent) means that you haven't learned 35 percent of what you are supposed to know.

For students unamenable to such smarmy banalities, the hand is taken out of the velveteen glove; the threat becomes brutally harsh:

BOY

THAT'S WHAT THEY'LL CALL YOU

FOR THE REST OF YOUR LIFE

IF YOU DON'T FINISH SCHOOL

Now, sensing in their bones the inauthenticity of what they have been told about the purpose, meaning, and character of the education they are getting in high school, students throughout the country, supported by increasing numbers of teachers, parents, administrators, and writers are beginning to tell it like it is—and to act on their new knowledge.

> We've all been shit upon one way or another. But what did we do about it? Some of us dropped out. Others tore up bathrooms and desks and broke windows to tell them how we see the schools. Most of the kids still in school get out of it by using dope. This spring there may be more people outside the schools than inside. This spring we're going to begin the fight to make the buildings they call school useful.[2]

Such public language by high-school students would have been unthinkable ten years ago, but today students in the richest suburbs and in the inner cities are breaking the shackles. High-school student disorder has become as common a phenomenon as the unrest of their older brothers in college.

[2] New York High School Free Press, April, 1969.

To understand what is going on in the American high schools today, one must take into account the Conant Report, published in 1959, which expressed the conventional wisdom about high schools. Dr. Conant rightly recalls in his memoirs the occasion of the report's publication, the tenor of the findings, and the public reception which made it a watershed event in the history of the American high school.

The timing was perfect. A wave of public criticism of the high schools which has started after Sputnik has reached its crest. School board members all over the country were anxious for specific answers to such questions as: "How should we organize our schools?"; "What should the high schools teach?" We supplied the answers boldly and categorically in twenty-one specific recommendations. We also reported on what we had found, but this portion of the book went relatively unheeded except for the main conclusion:

The number of small high schools must be drastically reduced through district reorganization. Aside from this important change, I believe no radical alteration in the basic pattern of American education is necessary in order to improve our public high schools. If all the high schools were functioning as well as some I have visited, the education of all American youth would be satisfactory, except for the study of foreign languages and the guidance of the more able girls.

Those laymen who had been criticizing the public school most vigorously (and to my mind unfairly) cried "White-wash. . . ." My friends on the Educational Policies Commission, as well as most public school superintendents and high school principals, greeted the findings and recommendations with considerable enthusiasm. The parents liked the book. For several weeks it was high on the bestseller list. . . .[3]

The specific recommendations have a quaint ring now, with students demanding true autonomy and relevance in their schools. The first of the twenty-one recommendations, for example, was for a "fully articulated counseling system," and the last called for a "required twelfth-grade course in American problems or American government." In between, the recommendations were couched in compulsory terms, with students constrained to study a certain selection of academic subjects

[3] James B. Conant, *My Several Lives: Memoirs of a Social Inventor*, Harper & Row, New York, 1970, pp. 621–22.

to assure the "rigor" of their high-school experience. Academic honors lists were specifically extolled and six academic periods per day held out as a minimum. Yet, much of the list, stood on its head, could serve as a present manifesto of student discontents.

It became apparent by the late Sixties that Dr. Conant's recommendations had missed the mark, that his vision of school, though temporarily triumphant, could not last. By 1970 serious student disruptions had occurred in two-thirds of all city and suburban high schools and in more than half of all rural schools.

Most of us have gone through high school, but have forgotten what it was like. It took these students and the reports of observers to wake us up. The remembered misery of school was vividly evoked by Pauline Kael after she saw Fred Wiseman's film *High School*.[4]

> *High School* is so familiar and so extraordinarily evocative that a feeling of empathy with the students floods over us. How did we live through it? How did we keep any spirit? When you see a kid trying to make a phone call and being interrupted with "Do you have a pass to use the phone?" it all floods back—the low ceilings and pale-green walls of the basement where the lockers were, the constant defensiveness, that sense of always being in danger of breaking some pointless, petty rule. When since that time has one ever needed a pass to make a phone call? This movie takes one back to where, one discovers, time has stood still. Here is the girl humiliated for having worn a short dress to the Senior Prom, being told it was "offensive" to the whole class. Here it is all over again—the insistence that you be "respectful," and the teachers' incredible instinct for "disrespect," their antennae always extended for that little bit of reservation or irony in your tone, the tiny spark that you desperately need to preserve your *self*-respect. One can barely hear it in the way a boy says "Yes, sir" to the dean, but the dean, ever on the alert, snaps, "Don't give me that 'Yes sir' business! . . . There's no sincereness behind it." Here, all over again, is the dullness of high school education.

What are the complaints? What is it really like to be in a high school? The issues most frequently cited include:

[4] Pauline Kael, review of *High School* in *The New Yorker*, October 18, 1969, p. 199.

*Irrelevance:* The ideas espoused by Principal Lass—that study involves devoting oneself to boring or uninteresting subjects of the teacher's choosing, that good grades equal good education, and that studying hard to pass exam after exam is a worthwhile expenditure of energy and spirit—all are typical of the ideas which inform most high-school curricula. Equally outdated is the idea that there is a given body of knowledge all students should learn. The world has changed too much—there are too many facts and too many disciplines to make an arbitrary judgment about which are important.

Students are insisting that the curricula grow out of their own interests and concerns, that they be permitted to choose which path into learning to take. Perceptive observers agree that students do learn more and better when allowed to shape their own learning experience.

*Racism:* In New York City less than 25 percent[5] of the black high-school population ever finishes school, and many of those that do receive a virtually useless general diploma. New York is better than most cities. If schools seem irrelevant to the middle-class white student, they are not even within the sphere of comprehension for the black student facing the same curriculum. Add to this persistent rate of failure and irrelevant curriculum the contempt which many teachers and administrators feel toward black students, the fact that most inner city schools are controlled by whites, and the racial tension which pervades every aspect of our society—and the reason for the explosiveness of city high schools becomes apparent.

*Authoritarianism:* Herbert Kohl has identified this as a pervasive quality of American schools:

> My school happened to be in a black ghetto in New York City, and I thought for a while that it was a pathological case. In the last few years I have spoken with many teachers throughout the country and visited many schools—urban, suburban, black, white, integrated, segregated, elementary, secondary. There is the same obsession with power and discipline everywhere; for most American children there is essentially one public

[5] Charles Weingartner, "Relevance and Spirit," in *High School 1980* edited by Alvin C. Eurich, Pitman, 1970, p. 55.

school system in the United States, and it is authoritarian and oppressive. Students everywhere are deprived of the right to make choices concerning their own destinies.[6]

Naturally, the fight against authority is endemic in any high school which is not moribund. "All students, everywhere," writes Marvin Weisbord, "passionately resist rules, orders, decisions, policies which strike them as arbitrary, unfair, or punitive. So powerful is this drive among students that it transcends race conflict in many schools."[7]

These themes have been given broad resonance by the recent radical critics. A new breed of writers has emerged in the past five years, among them John Holt, Paul Goodman, Herbert Kohl, Peter Marin, Jonathan Kozol, Edgar Friedenberg, George Dennison, Marshall McLuhan, George Leonard and others. They have developed a devastating critique of prevailing practices and begun to articulate radical alternatives.

As critics, these writers have pointed out that the crises in American education goes beyond issues of underfinancing, poorly trained teachers, outdated curricula. To them, our schools don't merely fail to achieve their stated purposes. Rather, they argue, many schools are not even decent places for our children to be. Too many schools damage, thwart, stifle children's natural capacity to learn and to grow healthily.

True learning and healthy growth are sabotaged in most American schools today, these critics argue, because of an authoritarian atmosphere in which the emphasis is on the teacher teaching rather than on the student learning. The whole process of schooling is frozen into a rigid lock step through the grades, chopped up mechanically into blocks of time and different subjects, dominated by a curriculum fixed in advance and imposed from above. There is no real regard for the students as individual people, with real concerns of their own and inherent drives to know, understand, and create.

For John Holt, "To a very great degree, school is a place where

6 Herbert R. Kohl, *The Open Classroom: A Practical Guide to a New Way of Teaching,* New York Review/Vintage, 1970, pp. 11–12.

7 Danforth Foundation and Ford Foundation, *The School and the Democratic Environment,* Columbia University Press, 1970, p. 10.

children learn to be stupid." Paul Goodman "would not give a penny to the present administrators, and would largely dismantle the present school machinery." The high-school students who formed the Montgomery County (Maryland) Student Alliance testified that "From what we know to be true as full-time students . . . it is quite safe to say that the public schools have critically negative and absolutely destructive effects on human beings and their curiosity, natural desire to learn, confidence, individuality, creativity, freedom of thought and self-respect." [8]

Jonathan Kozol's ghastly metaphor perhaps says it most succinctly: Schools destroy the minds and hearts of our children.

It is almost too easy to catalogue these complaints; they have become commonplace. It is not enough simply to prove that the schools are damaging and boring. In order to find better ways for kids to grow up we must understand *why* the schools are like that. Why has America —and, for that matter, other advanced industrial societies—chosen to devise such rigid and mean-spirited institutions for the young? How did we come to devise a society in which the energies of youth had to be restrained so ruthlessly, in which young human beings so eager to explore and enjoy and invent and witness are so constrained?

Benjamin Franklin founded the first American Academy in Philadelphia in 1751, and the Phillips Academies were founded in New England during the Revolutionary War. But only in the past fifty years have compulsory-education laws served as a kind of enclosure legislation to round up, herd, and process this disturbing group who hitherto had been left more or less free to find its own way of growing up.

As late as 1893 an important study committee reported that the chief purpose of free public high schools was ". . . to prepare for the duties of life that small proportion of all the children in the country who show themselves able to profit by an education prolonged to the

[8] *Wanted: A Humane Education,* the Montgomery County Student Alliance, Spring 1969.

eighteenth year, and whose parents are able to support them while they remain so long in school."[9]

Yet, between 1890 and 1930 the academic high school became a comprehensive school designed to provide universal secondary education for "all American youth." Programs and purposes expanded while enrollments increased by an amazing 750 percent compared with a national population expansion of only slightly more than 60 percent. The resulting figures are familiar. Fifty years ago 35 percent of American seventeen-year-olds were in school; today, the corresponding figure is more than 70 percent. Ninety percent of the young people between fourteen and seventeen are in school.

Schooling thus has grown in recent years from a privilege for the few to a requirement for all. This transformation corresponded with the development of America from a rural to an industrial nation and with the influx of non-Anglo-Saxon immigrants from Europe. What purpose do schools serve modern industrial society and why are they so authoritarian and destructive?

A number of pieces in this book grapple with this issue and take somewhat different approaches. What emerges is a consensus that the basic reasons schools are so terrible is that they are not run for the benefit of children; they are run by adults for distinctively adult (and unsavory) purposes. As Jules Henry puts it, "The high school . . . is an institution run by adults for the entire community and, because of this, expresses the demands of the community and the idiosyncrasies of the adults who run the school."[10]

Two such purposes seem central: *stratification* and *socialization*. The schools are intended to channel kids into vocations and hence provide trained manpower for the economy and maintain the community's social class structure. The stratification function can be likened to the oil distillation process: Almost all children enter school in elementary school, but as they continue up the ladder they are dropped off at certain levels. Some drop out of high school, some receive a high-

[9] National Education Association, *Report of the Committee of Ten on Secondary School Studies*, American Book Company, 1893, pp 56–57.

[10] Jules Henry, *Culture Against Man*, Random House, New York, 1963, p. 183.

school diploma, others continue to junior colleges or vocational schools, some go on to college, and yet others continue to graduate school.

The schools thus act as a sieve, channeling manpower into the economy at each occupational level. The enforcement mechanism is, of course, the credential. Despite the fact that Ivar Berg's superb book *Education and Jobs: The Great Training Robbery*[11] shows that educational level is only marginally related to job performance, the credential remains the chief criterion for job acquisition. In this way the stranglehold of the school on the student is maintained, and the ability of the educational system to stratify the society is strengthened.

By what criteria do the schools select who achieves which level? Not by intelligence or merit but by social class. Generally speaking, it is the poor and the blacks who don't get the high-school diploma, the blue-collar kids who progress to junior college and vocational school, and the rich and middle class who go to college and beyond. In this way the schools maintain the community's social structure. This point, startling as it may seem, gains additional credence from Colin Greer's historical study of the purposes of the schools:

> The basic function of the schools is as the primary selector of the winners and losers in society. . . .
>
> The assumption that extended schooling promotes greater academic achievement or social mobility is . . . entirely fallacious. School performance seems consistently dependent upon the socio-economic position of the pupil's family. For example, of high school graduates who rank in the top fifth in ability among their classmates, those whose parents are in the top socio-economic status quartile are five times more likely to enter graduate or professional schools than those of comparable ability whose parents fall in the bottom quartile. Similarly, while American males born after 1900 spend more years in school than their nineteenth-century predecessors, federal and other estimates indicate no concomitant redistribution of economic and social rewards. . . .
>
> The pattern of school failure has been perennially uniform but concern for it was by no means as great as the concern on the part of educators to get more pupils into school. . . .

[11] Ivar Berg, *Education and Jobs: The Great Training Robbery*, Praeger, New York, 1970.

A close relationship obtained between various group designation (native-born with and without foreign parents, and foreign-born), which revealed that levels of school retention in any given group coincided with that group's adult employment rate. Drop-out rates for all groups, including the Negro, were in direct proportion to rates of adult unemployment. Further, the high degree of school achievement among Jews, which has confirmed our expectation of public schools, did not mean success for all Jews. Otherwise, why the remedial classes and drop-out panic in several of the schools on New York's Lower East Side with as much as 99 per cent "Hebrew" registration? Where the family was poor enough to take in boarders to cover rental costs, and desperate enough to join the city's welfare roles, then delinquency, prostitution, and child-labor were as much the burden of Jewish families, for whom such characteristics were real if not typical.

With rising industrial unemployment and an expanded technological economy, the school-leaving age increased so that the problem of caring for all grades of ability on the elementary school level escalated to the high school level. Vocational instruction programs were an inevitable corollary to the academic program and quickly became a symbol of the school's stratification role. Today, the junior college serves as the junior high school had served earlier, operating to a large extent as an extension of secondary education with back-seat status justified by the democratic rationale of monumental numbers to be catered to.[12]

The schools are not only designed to stratify society; they are also intended to socialize the youth in the society's mores. Every society must find ways to sustain itself, to pass on to its children the attitudes and beliefs which will lead them to accept their environment and recreate it as adults. In order to accomplish this socialization the society must devise appropriate mechanisms. The family, of course, has always played the key role, and so has the church. But with the development of a mass society in the early twentieth century, the influx of immigrants, the gradual abolition of child labor and the parallel expansion of compulsory education, the schools took on more of the burden of socialization.

As the society became more complex and the population more

[12] Colin Greer, "The Myth of the Melting Pot," *Saturday Review*, November 15, 1969, p. 84.

heterogeneous, it became more difficult and risky to leave this important task to the family, a small and private unit. It was much better to entrust the job to the schools, a governmentally controlled, large bureaucratic institution. Compulsory education assured that the schools had the opportunity to touch and shape the mind of virtually every child in the nation.

The resulting nature of schooling was inevitable. Modern American society depends on a high degree of conformity, materialism, and obedience, so these are qualities that schools encourage. The school develops these attitudes not through the formal curriculum but through the regulations, administrative arrangements, power structure, and adult attitudes which are pervasive.

As Edgar Friedenberg puts it, "What is learned in high school depends far less on what is taught than on what one actually experiences in the place." [13] And in high school students experience control, mistrust, and punishment. They have little privacy, little free time, little decision-making power. And, of course, they are forced to be there. In this way the schools succeed in teaching conformity, equation of power with legitimate authority, and a deficient sense of respect for dignity and privacy. Inculcation of these values are the second major purpose of the schools, and they succeed all too well at it. As Kurt Vonnegut, Jr., has written:

> When you get to be our age, you all of a sudden realize that you are being ruled by people you went to high school with. You all of a sudden catch on that life is nothing *but* high school . . . class officers, cheerleaders, and all. . . . High school is closer to the core of American experience than anything else I can think of.[14]

Boredom, irrelevant curriculum, uninspired teaching, and rigid authoritarianism pervade the nation's high schools. These are usually at the heart of student protest and most educational criticism.

[13] Edgar Z. Friedenberg, *Coming of Age in America*, Random House, New York, 1963, p. 40.

[14] Kurt Vonnegut, Jr., Introduction to *Our Time Is Now*, edited by John Birmingham, Praeger, New York, 1970.

Pressing further, to ask why society has created such institutions, leads to a deeper level of analysis. Schools are designed for distinctively adult needs—social stratification and socialization—and their inhumanity and destructiveness are really by-products of these purposes.

On the face of it, then, the logical position of radical educators should be to abolish high-school education and to set the kids free. Some do take this position. But a more widespread and influential development has been the creation of new schools which seek to fit education to the kids' needs, not the other way around. After all, young people do need help in growing up, and decent schools can play a major role. Harnessed properly, what George Dennison has called "the natural authority of adults" can do the trick. What is crucial, however, is to make sure that the schools serve the real needs of kids. From this principle it follows that the schools should have a curriculum that grows out of student interests, that students should play a large role in running the school, that arbitrary regulations be abolished, that free and critical thinking be encouraged, that the pressures of grades, exams, getting into college, etc., be ended. In short, the schools should unleash the spirits and impulses of the young, not dam them.

RONALD GROSS
PAUL OSTERMAN

# WHY WE HAVE THEM

The great secret of education is that there is no such thing. There is only the lives of children. In the keynote piece Peter Marin examines the central figure in high-school education, the adolescent.

Adolescence is "second infancy," a time when "what is growing inside the adolescent demands expression, requires it, and must . . . be received by the world and given form—or it will wither or turn to rage." The adolescent's tragedy, and ours, is that society does not provide opportunities for him to explore his environment and culture and to make sense of the churning ideas, emotions, and hopes inside him. Instead we have established a school system to restrain and diminish him.

"Schools are his natural enemies," writes Marin. "They don't help, as they might, to make that bridge between his private and social worlds; they insist, instead, upon their separation. . . . Thus the young, in that vivid confrontation with the thrust of nature unfolding in themselves, are denied adult assistance."

This is the central conflict which gives substance and form to what

21

is happening in the high schools today as students and critics join to find some way of making education help, not hinder, growing up. And this is the conflict which shapes this book and finds repeated expression in its pages. Marin's essay prefigures all the themes which other essays expand upon: the authoritarian and lifeless curriculum, the growing rebellion, the schools as producers of manpower and mass socializers, and the experiments with new forms of education.

What are schools really for? That is the perplexing question posed by Edgar Friedenberg. He finds that the most important function of school is to define youth as a social class, to constrain and limit them. The second purpose is to provide trained manpower and channel kids into certain occupations. And finally, says Friedenberg, the schools socialize students to understand and accept the disparity between American ideals and reality. "The function of school is to teach you about the unofficial sanctions, to prepare you for the blacklist, to make sure you understand the implications of being labeled a troublemaker; which is the worst thing a school can call you."

Theodore Roszak picks up these themes and the note struck by Peter Marin—that education today contravenes the nature of the adolescent, that it is *Contra Naturam*. Starting from the striking image of Age applying the scissors to the Wings of Youth, Roszak goes on to analyze why society devises institutions to do this. He finds that a large bureaucratic establishment is the natural product of a society unsure of its culture. "When a society begins to fear that its culture is not interesting or important to the young—that indeed its culture violates nature—then it concludes that education must be *made* to happen; must be organized strenuously into existence and enforced by professionals." Our clumsy, bureaucratic, repressive school system is the result.

# The Open Truth and Fiery Vehemence of Youth

## BY PETER MARIN

Peter Marin directed an experimental high school in California before becoming a Visiting Fellow of the Center for the Study of Democratic Institutions in 1967–68. He has recently been living in Europe, and is co-author of *Understanding Drug Use*.

IT IS midnight and I am sitting here with my notes, enough of them to make two books and a half and a volume of posthumous fragments, trying to make some smaller sense of them than the grand maniacal design I have in my mind. I don't know where to begin. Once, traveling in summer across the country with a friend from Hollywood and my young son in a battered green Porsche, I stopped for lunch somewhere in Kansas on a Sunday morning. As we walked into the restaurant, bearded, wearing dark glasses and strange hats, and followed by my long-haired boy, one Kansas matron bent toward another and whispered: "I bet those two men have kidnapped that little girl." I took a deep breath and started to speak, but I did not know where to begin or how to explain just how many ways she was mistaken. Now, trying to write clearly about education and adolescence, I feel the same way.

For that reason I have chosen an eccentric method of composition, one that may seem fragmentary, jumpy, and broken. This article will be more like a letter, and the letter itself is an accumulation of impressions and ideas, a sampling of thoughts at once disconnected but related. There is a method to it that may disappear in its mild madness, but I do not know at this juncture how else to proceed. Shuffling through my notes, I feel like an archeol-

23

ogist with a mass of uncatalogued shards. There is a pattern to all this, a coherence of thought, but all I can do here is assemble the bits and pieces and lay them out for you and hope that you can sense how I get from one place to another.

An entire system is hiding behind this, just beginning to take form, and these notes are like a drawing, a preliminary sketch. I feel comfortable with that notion, more comfortable than with the idea of forcing them together, cutting and pasting, to make a more conventional essay. I can perceive in myself at this moment what I also see in the young: I am reluctant to deal in sequence with my ideas and experience, I am impatient with transition, the habitual ways of getting "from here to there." I think restlessly; my mind, like the minds of my students, works in flashes, in sudden perceptions and brief extended clusters of intuition and abstraction—and I have stuck stubbornly to that method of composition. There is still in me the ghost of an apocalyptic adolescent, and I am trying to move it a few steps toward the future.

One theme, as you will see, runs through what I have written or thought: we must rethink our ideas of childhood and schooling. We must dismantle them and start again from scratch. Nothing else will do. Our visions of adolescence and education confine us to habit, rule perception out. We make do at the moment with a set of ideas inherited from the nineteenth century, from an industrial, relatively puritanical, repressive, and "localized" culture; we try to gum them like labels to new kinds of experience. But that won't do. Everything has changed. The notions with which I began my job as a high-school director have been discarded one by one. They make no sense. What emerges through these children as the psyche of this culture is post-industrial, relatively unrepressed, less literate and local: a new combination of elements, almost a new strain. Adolescents are, each one of them, an arena in which the culture transforms itself or is torn between contrary impulses; they are the victims of a culture raging within itself like man and wife, a schizoid culture—and these children are the unfinished and grotesque products of that schism.

They are grotesque because we give them no help. They are forced to make among themselves adjustments to a tension that must be unbearable. They do the best they can, trying, in increasingly eccentric fashions, to make sense of things. But we adults seem to have withdrawn in defeat from that same struggle, to have given up. We are enamored, fascinated, and deluded by adolescence precisely because it is the last life left to us; only the young rebel with any real passion against media, machines, the press of circumstance itself. Their elders seem to have no options, no sense of alternative or growth. Adult existence is bled of life and we turn in that vacuum toward children with the mixed repulsion and desire of wanton Puritans toward life itself.

As for me, an adult, I think of myself as I write as an observer at a tribal war—an anthropologist, a combination of Gulliver and a correspondent sending home news by mule and boat. By the time you hear of it, things will have changed. And that isn't enough, not enough at all. Somebody must step past the children, must move into his own psyche or two steps past his own limits into the absolute landscape of fear and potential these children inhabit. That is where I am headed. So these ideas, in effect, are something like a last message tacked to a tree in a thicket or tucked under a stone. I mean: we cannot *follow* the children any longer, we have to step ahead of them. Somebody has to mark a trail.

Adolescence: a few preliminary fragments . . .

( FROM MY STUDENT, V): *yr whole body moves in a trained way & you know that youve moved this way before & it contains all youve been taught its all rusty & slow something is pushing under that rusted mesh but STILL YOU CANNOT MOVE you are caught between 2 doors & the old one is much closer & you can grab it all the time but the other door it disappears that door you cant even scratch & kick (like the early settlers were stung by the new land) but this new land doesnt even touch you & you wonder if youre doing the right thing to get in.*

(FROM FRANZ KAFKA): *He feels imprisoned on this earth, he feels constricted; the melancholy, the impotence, the sicknesses, the feverish fancies of the captive afflict him; no comfort can comfort him, since it is merely comfort, gentle headsplitting comfort glazing the brutal fact of imprisonment. But if he is asked what he wants he cannot reply. . . . He has no conception of freedom.*

(FROM TAPES RECORDED IN PACIFIC PALISADES, 1966, SEVERAL BOYS AND GIRLS AGED 12–14): *Things are getting younger and younger. Girls twelve will do it now. One guy said I fuck a girl every Friday night. What sexual pleasure do you get out of this (he's very immature, you know) and he would say, I don't know, I'm just going to fuck.*

or

How old are you? —*Twelve.* —Will you tell us your first experience with drugs, how you got into it? —*Well, the people I hung around with were big acid-heads. So one day my friend asked me if I wanted to get stoned and I said yes. That was about five months ago and I've been getting on it ever since. Started taking LSD about one month ago. Took it eleven times in one month. I consider it a good thing. For getting high, smoking grass is better, or hashish—it's about six times stronger than marijuana.*

(FROM PAUL RADIN, Primitive Man As Philosopher): *It is conceivably demanding too much of a man to whom the pleasures of life are largely bound up with the life of contemplation and to whom analysis and introspection are the self-understood prerequisites for a proper understanding of the world, that he appreciate . . . expressions which are largely non-intellectual—where life seems, predominatingly, a discharge of physical vitality, a simple and naive release of emotions or an enjoyment of sensations for their own sake. Yet . . . it is just such an absorption in a life of sensations that is the outward characteristic of primitive peoples.*

Can you see where my thought leads? It is precisely at this point, adolescence, when the rush of energies, that sea-sex, gravitation, the thrust of the ego up through layers of childhood, makes itself felt, that the person is once more like an infant, is swept once more by energies that are tidal, unfamiliar, and unyielding. He is in a sense born again, a fresh identity beset inside and out by the rush of new experience. It is at this point, too—when we seem compelled by a persistent lunacy to isolate him—that what is growing within the adolescent demands expression, requires it, and must, in addition, be received by the world and given form—or it will wither or turn to rage. Adolescence is a second infancy. It is then that a man desires solitude and at the same time contact with the vivid world; must test within social reality the new power within himself; needs above all to discover himself for the first time as a bridge between inner and outer, a maker of value, a vehicle through which culture perceives and transforms itself. It is now, ideally, that he begins to understand the complex and delicate nature of the ego itself as a thin skin between living worlds, a synaptic jump, the self-conscious point at which nature and culture combine.

In this condition, with these needs, the adolescent is like a primitive man, an apocalyptic primitive; he exists for the moment in that stage of single vision in which myth is still the raw stuff of being, he knows at first hand through his own energies the possibilities of life—but he knows these in muddled, sporadic, contradictory ways. The rush of his pubescent and raw energy seems at odds, with public behavior, the *order* of things, the tenor of life around him, especially in a culture just emerging—as is ours—from a tradition of evasion, repression, and fear.

The contradictions within the culture itself intensify his individual confusion. We are at the moment torn between future and past: in the midst of a process of transformation we barely understand. The development of adolescent energy and ego—difficult at any time—is complicated in our own by the increase in early sexuality, the complicated messages of the media, and the effects of strong and unfamiliar drugs. These three elements are, in themselves, the salient features of a culture that is growing more permissive, less repressive. They are profound, complex, and strong: heavy doses of experience demanding changes in attitude, changes in behavior. The direction and depth of feeling responds accordingly; the adolescent tries—even as a form of self-defense against the pressure of his own energies—to move more freely, to change his styles of life, to "grow." But it is then that he finds he is locked into culture, trapped in a web of ideas, laws, and rituals that keep him a child, deprive him of a chance to test and assimilate his newer self. It is now that the culture turns suddenly repressive. His gestures are evaded or denied; at best he is "tolerated," but even then his gestures, lacking the social support of acknowledgment and reward, must seem to him lacking in authenticity—more like forms of neurosis or selfishness than the natural stages in growth.

He is thrust back upon himself. The insistent natural press within him toward becoming whole is met perpetually by unbudging resistance. Schools, rooted as they are in a Victorian century and seemingly suspicious of life itself, are his natural enemies. They don't help, as they might, to make that bridge between his private and the social worlds; they insist, instead, upon their separation. Indeed, family, community, and school all combine—especially in the suburbs—to isolate and "protect" him from the adventure, risk, and participation he needs; the same energies that relate him at this crucial point to nature result in a kind of exile from the social environment.

Thus the young, in that vivid confrontation with the thrust of nature unfolding in themselves, are denied adult assistance. I once wrote that education through its limits denied the gods, and that they would return in the young in one form or another to haunt us. That is happening now. You can sense it as the students gather, with their simplistic moral certainty, at the gates of the universities. It is almost as if the young were once more possessed by

Bacchanalian gods, were once again inhabited by divinities whose honor we have neglected. Those marvelous and threatening energies! What disturbs me most about them is that we lack rituals for their use and balance, and the young—and perhaps we ourselves —now seem at their mercy. The young have moved, bag and baggage, into areas where adults cannot help them, and it is a scary landscape they face, it is crowded with strange forms and faces, and if they return from it raddled, without balance and pitched toward excess, who can pretend to be surprised—or blameless?

At times they seem almost shell-shocked, survivors of a holocaust in which the past has been destroyed and all the bridges to it bombed. I cannot describe with any certainty what occurs in their minds, but I do know that most adults must seem to the young like shrill critics speaking to them in an alien language about a Greek tragedy in which they may lose their lives. The words we use, our dress, our tones of voice, the styles of adult lives—all of these are so foreign to that dramatic crisis that as we approach them we seem to increase the distance we are trying to cross. Even our attention drives them further away, as if adolescents perceived that adults, coming closer, diminish in sense and size.

The inner events in an adolescent demand from what surrounds him life on a large scale, in a grand style. This is the impulse to apocalypse in the young, as if they were in exile from a nation that does not exist—and yet they can sense it, they know it is there—if only because their belief itself demands its presence. Their demand is absolute and unanswerable, but it exists and we seem unable at this point in time to suppress or evade it. For one reason or another massive shifts in cultural balances, the lessening of repression for whatever reasons—economic, technological, evolutionary—those energies, like gods, have appeared among us again. But what can we make of them? The simple problem is that our institutions are geared to another century, another set of social necessities, and cannot change quickly enough to contain, receive, or direct them—and as we suppress or refuse them they turn to rage.

Primitive cultures dealt with this problem, I think, through their initiation rites, the rites of passage; they legitimized and accepted these energies and turned them toward collective aims; they were merged with the life of the tribe and in this way acknowledged, honored, and domesticated—but not destroyed. In most initiation rites the participant is led through the mythical or sacred world (or a symbolic version) and is then returned, transformed, to the secular one as a new person, with a new role. He is introduced through the rites to a dramatic reality coexistent with the visible or social one and at its root; he is put in direct touch with the sources of energy, the divinities of the tribe. In many cultures the symbolic figures in the rites are unmasked at the end, as if to reveal to the initiate the interpenetration of the secular and sacred worlds. Occasionally the initiate is asked at some point to don the ritual mask himself—joining, as he does, one world with another and assuming the responsibility for their connection. This shift in status, in *relation*, is the heart of the rite; a liturgized merging of the individual with shared sources of power.

Do you see what I am driving at? The rites are in a sense a social contract, a binding up; one occurring specifically, profoundly, on a deep psychic level. The individual is redefined in the culture by his new relation to its mysteries, its gods, to one form or another of nature. His experience of that hidden and omnipotent mythical world is the basis for his relation to the culture and his fellows, each of whom has a similar bond—deep, personal, and unique, but somehow shared, invisibly but deeply. These ritualized relationships of each man to the shared gods bind the group together; they form the substance of culture: an invisible landscape that is real and felt, commonly held, a landscape which resides in each man and in which, in turn, each man resides.

I hope that makes sense. That is the structure of the kaleidoscopic turning of culture that Blake makes in *The Crystal Cabinet*, and it makes sense too, in America, in relation to adolescents. What fascinates me is that our public schools, designed for adolescents—who seem, as apocalyptic men, to demand this kind of drama, release, and support—educate and "socialize" their students by depriving them of everything the rites bestow. They manipulate them through the repression of energies; they isolate them and close off most parts of the community; they categorically refuse to make use of the individual's private experience. The direction of all these tendencies is toward a cultural schizophrenia in which the student is forced to choose between his own relation to reality or the one demanded by the institution. The schools are organized to weaken the student so that he is forced, in the absence of his own energies, to accept the values and demands of the institution. To this end we deprive the student of mobility and experience; through law and custom we make the only legal place for him the school, and then, to make sure he remains dependent, manipulable, we empty the school of all vivid life.

We appear to have forgotten in our schools what every primitive tribe with its functional psychology knows: allegiance to the tribe can be forged only at the deepest levels of the psyche and in extreme circumstance demanding endurance, daring, and awe; that the participant must be given *direct* access to the sources of cultural continuity—by and in himself; and that only a place in a coherent community can be exchanged for a man's allegiance.

I believe that it is precisely this world that drugs replace; adolescents provide for themselves what we deny them: a confrontation with some kind of power within an unfamiliar landscape involving sensation and risk. It is there, I suppose, that they hope to find, by some hurried magic, a new way of seeing, a new relation to things, to discard one identity and assume another. They mean to find through their adventures the *ground* of reality, the resonance of life we deny them, as if they might come upon their golden city and return still inside it: at home. You can see the real veterans sometimes on the street in strange costumes they have stolen from dreams: American versions of the Tupi of Brazil, who traveled thousands of miles each year in search of the land where death and evil do not exist. Theirs is a world totally alien to the one we discuss in schools; it is dramatic, it enchants them; its existence forms a strange brotherhood among them and they cling to it—as though they alone had been to a fierce land and back. It is that which draws them together and makes of them a loose tribe. It is, after all, some sort of shared experience, some kind of foray into the risky dark; it is the best that they can do.

When you begin to think about adolescence in this way, what sense can you make of our schools? None of the proposed changes makes sense to me: revision of curriculum, teaching machines, smaller classes, encounter groups, redistributions of power —all of these are stopgap measures, desperate attempts to keep the young in schools that are hopelessly outdated. The changes suggested and debated don't go deeply enough; they don't question or change enough. For what needs changing are not the methods of the school system but its aims, and what is troubling the young and forcing upon their teachers an intolerable burden is the *idea* of childhood itself; the ways we think about adolescents, their place in the culture itself. More and more one comes to see that changes in the schools won't be enough; the crisis of the young cuts across the culture in all its areas and includes the family and the community. The young are displaced; there seems no other word for it. They are trapped in a prolonged childhood almost unique.

In few other cultures have persons of fifteen or eighteen been so uselessly isolated from participation in the community, or been deemed so unnecessary (in their elders' eyes), or so limited by law. Our ideas of responsibility, our parental feelings of anxiety, blame, and guilt, all of these follow from our curious vision of the young; in turn, they concretize it, legitimize it so that we are no longer even conscious of the ways we see childhood or the strain that our vision puts upon us. That is what needs changing: the definitions we make socially and legally of the role of the young. They are trapped in the ways we see them, and the school is simply one function, one aspect, of the whole problem. What makes real change so difficult in the schools is only in part their natural unwieldiness; it is more often the difficulty we have in escaping our preconceptions about things.

In general the school system we have inherited seems to me based upon three particular things:

What Paul Goodman calls the idea of "natural depravity": our puritanical vision of human nature in which children are perceived as sinners or "savages" and in which human impulse or desire is not to be trusted and must therefore be constrained or "trained."

The necessity during the mid-nineteenth century of "Americanizing" great masses of immigrant children from diverse backgrounds and creating, through the schools, a common experience and character.

The need in an industrialized state for energy and labor to run the machines: the state, needing workers, educates persons to be technically capable but relatively dependent and responsive to authority so that their energies will be available when needed.

These elements combine with others—the labor laws that make childhood a "legal" state, and a population explosion that makes it necessary now to keep adolescents off both the labor market and the idle street—to "freeze" into a school system that resists change even as the culture itself and its needs shift radically. But teachers can't usually see that, for they themselves have been educated in this system and are committed to ideas that they have never clearly understood. Time and again, speaking to them, one hears the same questions and anguish:

"But what will happen to the students if they don't go to school?" "How will they learn?" "What will they do without adults?"

What never comes clear, of course, is that such questions are, at bottom, statement. Even while asking them teachers reveal their unconscious and contaminating attitudes. They can no longer imagine what children will do "outside" schools. They regard them as young monsters who will, if released from adult authority or help, disrupt the order of things. What is more, adults no longer are capable of imagining learning or child-adult relationships outside the schools. But mass schooling is a recent innovation. Most learning—especially the process of socialization or acculturation—has gone on outside schools, more naturally, in the fabric of the culture. In most cultures the passage from childhood to maturity occurs because of social necessity, the need for responsible adults, and is marked by clear changes in role. Children in the past seem to have learned the ways of the community or tribe through constant contact and interchange with adults, and it was taken for granted that the young learned continually through their place close to the heart of the community.

We seem to have lost all sense of that. The school is expected to do what the community cannot do and that is impossible. In the end, we will have to change far more than the schools if we expect to create a new coherence between the experiences of the child and the needs of the community. We will have to rethink the meaning of childhood; we will begin to grant greater freedom and responsibility to the young; we will drop the compulsory-schooling age to fourteen, perhaps less; we will take for granted the "independence" of adolescents and provide them with the chance to live alone, away from parents and with peers; we will discover jobs they can or want to do in the community—anything from mail delivery to the teaching of smaller children and the counseling of other adolescents. At some point, perhaps, we will even find that the community itself—in return for a minimum of work or continued schooling—will provide a minimal income to young people that will allow them to assume the responsibility for their own lives at an earlier age, and learn the ways of the community outside the school; finally, having lowered the level of compulsory schooling, we will find it necessary to provide different *kinds* of schools, a wider choice, so that students will be willing voluntarily to continue the schooling that suits their needs and aims.

All these changes, of course, are aimed at two things: the restoration of the child's "natural" place in the community and lowering the age at which a person is considered an independent member of the community. Some of them, to be sure, can be made in the schools, but my sense of things, after having talked to teachers and visited the schools, is that trying to make the changes in schools *alone* will be impossible.

One problem, put simply, is that in every school I have visited, public or private, traditional or "innovational," the students have only these two choices: to drop out (either physically or mentally) or to make themselves smaller and smaller until they can act in ways their elders expect. One of my students picked up a phrase I once used, "the larger and smaller worlds." The schools we visit together, he says, are always the smaller world: smaller at least than his imagination, smaller than the potential of the young. The students are asked to put aside the best things about themselves—their own desires, impulses, and ideas—in order to "adjust" to an environment constructed for children who existed one hundred years ago, if at all. I wonder sometimes if this condition is simply the result of poor schooling; I am more inclined to believe that it is the inevitable result of mass compulsory schooling and the fabrication of artificial environments by adults for children. Is it possible at all for adults to understand what children need and to change their institutions fast enough to keep up with changes in culture and experience? Is it possible for children to grow to their full size, to feel their full strength, if they are deprived of individual volition all along the line and forced to school? I don't know. I know only that during the Middle Ages they sometimes "created" jesters by putting young children in boxes and force-feeding them so that, as they grew, their bones would warp in unusual shapes. That is often how the schools seem to me. Students are trapped in the boxes of pedagogic ideas, and I am tempted to say to teachers again and again: more, much more, you must go further, create more space in the schools, you must go deeper in thought, create more resonance, a different feeling, a different and more human, more daring style.

Even the best teachers, with the best intentions, seem to diminish their students as they work through the public-school system. For that system is, at bottom, designed to produce what we sometimes call good citizens but what more often than not turn out to be good soldiers; it is through the schools of the state, after all, that we produce our armies. I remember how struck I was while teaching at a state college by the number of boys who wanted to oppose the draft but lacked the courage or strength to simply say no. They were trapped; they had always been taught, had always tried, to be "good." Now that they wanted to refuse to go, they could not, for they weren't sure they could bear the consequences they had been taught would follow such refusal: jail, social disgrace, loss of jobs, parental despair. They could not believe in institutions, but they could not trust themselves and their impulse and they were caught in their own impotence: depressed and resentful, filled with self-hatred and a sense of shame.

That is a condition bred in the schools. In one way or another our methods produce in the young a condition of pain that seems very close to a mass neurosis: a lack of faith in oneself, a vacuum of spirit into which authority or institutions can move, a dependency they feed on. Students are encouraged to relinquish their own wills, their freedom of volition; they are taught that value and culture reside outside oneself and must be acquired from the institution, and almost everything in their education is designed to discourage them from activity, from the wedding of idea and act. It is almost as if we hoped to discourage them from thought itself by making ideas so lifeless, so hopeless, that their despair would be enough to make them manipulable and obedient.

The system breeds obedience, frustration, dependence, and fear: a kind of gentle violence that is usually turned against oneself, one that is sorrowful and full of guilt, but a violence nonetheless, and one realizes that what is done in the schools to persons is deeply connected to what we did to the blacks or are doing now in Vietnam. That is: we don't teach hate in the schools, or murder, but we do isolate the individual; we empty him of life by ignoring or suppressing his impulse toward life; we breed in him a lack of respect for it, a loss of love—and thus we produce gently "good" but threatened men, men who will kill without passion, out of duty and obedience, men who have in themselves little sense of the vivid life being lost nor the moral strength to refuse.

From first to twelfth grade we acclimatize students to a fundamental deadness and teach them to restrain themselves for the sake of "order." The net result is a kind of pervasive cultural inversion in which they are asked to separate at the most profound levels their own experience from institutional reality, self from society, objective from subjective, energy from order—though these various polarities are precisely those which must be made coherent during adolescence.

I remember a talk I had with a college student.

"You know what I love to do," he said. "I love to go into the woods and run among the trees."

"Very nice," I said.

"But it worries me. We shouldn't do it."

"Why not?" I asked.

"Because we get excited. It isn't *orderly.*"

"Not orderly?"

"Not orderly."

"Do you run into the trees?" I asked.

"Of course not."

"Then it's orderly," I said.

In a small way this exchange indicates the kind of thinking we encourage in the schools: the mistaking of rigidity and stillness for order, of order as the absence of life. We try to create and preserve an order which depends upon the destruction of life both inside and out and which all life, when expressed, must necessarily threaten or weaken.

The natural process of learning seems to move naturally from experience through perception to abstraction in a fluid continuous process that cannot be clearly divided into stages. It is in that process that energy is somehow articulated in coherent and meaningful form as an act or thought or a made object. The end of learning is wisdom and wisdom to me, falling back as I do on a Jewish tradition, is, in its simplest sense, "intelligent activity" or, more completely, the suffusion of activity with knowledge, a wedding of the two. For the Hassidic Jews every gesture was potentially holy, a form of prayer, when it was made with a reverence for God. In the same way a gesture is always a form of wisdom—an act is wisdom—when it is suffused with knowledge, made with a reverence for the truth.

Does that sound rhetorical? I suppose it does. But I mean it. The end of education is intelligent activity, *wisdom*, and that demands a merging of opposites, a sense of process. Instead we produce the opposite: immobility, insecurity, an inablity to act without institutional blessing or direction, or, at the opposite pole, a headlong rush toward motion without balance or thought. We cut into the natural movement of learning and try to force upon the students the end product, abstraction, while eliminating experience and ignoring their perception. The beginning of thought is in the experience through one's self of a particular environment—school, community, culture. When this is ignored, as it is in schools, the natural relation of self and knowledge is broken, the parts of the process become polar opposites, antitheses, and the young are forced to choose between them: objectivity, order, and obedience as against subjectivity, chaos, and energy. It doesn't really matter which they choose; as long as the two sets seem irreconcilable their learning remains incomplete. Caught between the two, they suffer our intellectual schizophrenia until it occupies them, too. They wait. They sit. They listen. They learn to "behave" at the expense of themselves. Or else—and you can see it happening now—they turn against it with a vengeance and may shout, as they did at Columbia, "Kill all adults," for they have allied themselves with raw energy against reason and balance—our delicate, hard-won virtues—and we should not be surprised. We set up the choices ourselves, and it is simply that they have chosen what we hold to be the Devil's side.

If this is the case, what are the alternatives? I thought at one time that changes in schooling could be made, that the school itself could become at least a microcosm of the community outside, a kind of halfway house, a preparatory arena in which students, in semi-protective surroundings, would develop not only the skill but the character that would be needed in the world. But more and more, as I have said, it seems to me impossible to do that job in a setting as isolated and restrictive as our schools. Students don't need the artificiality of schools; they respond more fully and more intelligently when they make direct contact with the community and are allowed to choose roles that have some utility for the community and themselves. What is at stake here, I suppose, is the freedom of volition, for this is the basic condition with which people must learn to deal, and the sooner they achieve within that condition wit, daring, and responsibility the stronger they will be. It seems absurd to postpone the assumption of that condition as long as we do. In most other cultures, and even in our own past, young people have taken upon themselves the responsibility of adults and have dealt with it as successfully as most adults do now. The students I have seen can do that, too, when given the chance. What a strain it must be to have that capacity, to sense in one's self a talent for adventure or growth or meaning, and have that sense continually stifled or undercut by the role one is supposed to play.

Thus, it seems inescapably clear that our first obligation to the young is to create a place in the community for them to act with volition and freedom. They are ready for it, certainly, even if we aren't. Adolescents seem to need at least some sense of risk and gain "out there" in the world: an existential sense of themselves that is vivid to the extent that the dangers faced are "real." The students I have worked with at Pacific High School seem strongest and most alive when they are in the mountains of Mexico or the Oakland ghetto or out in the desert or simply hitchhiking or riding freights to see what's happening. They thrive on distance and motion—and the right to solitude when they want it. Many of them want jobs; they themselves arrange to be teachers in day-care centers, political canvassers, tutors, poolroom attendants, actors, governesses, gardeners. They returned from these experiences immeasurably brightened and more sure of themselves, more willing, in that new assurance, to learn many of the abstract ideas we had been straining to teach them. It was not simply the experience in itself that brought this about. It was also the feeling of freedom they had, the sense that they could come and go at will and make any choice they wanted—no matter how absurd—if they were willing to suffer what real consequences followed. Many wanted to work and travel and others did not; they wanted to sit and think or read or live alone or swim or, as one student scrawled on my office wall, "ball and goof." What they finally came to understand, of course, was that the school made no pretense at either limiting or judging their activities; we considered them free agents and limited our own activities to advice, to what "teaching" they requested, and to support when they needed it in facing community, parents, or law.

What we were after was a *feeling* to the place: a sense of intensity and space. We discarded the idea of the microcosm and replaced it with an increased openness and access to the larger community. The campus itself became a place to come back to for rest or discussion or thought; but we turned things inside out to the extent that we came to accept that learning took place more naturally elsewhere, in any of the activities that our students chose, and that the school was in actuality wherever they were, whatever they did. What students learned at the school was simply the feel of things; the sense of themselves as makers of value; the realization that the environment is at best an extension of men and that it can be transformed by them into what they vitally need.

What we tried to create was a flexible environment, what a designer I know has called permissive space. It was meant to be in a sense a model for the condition in which men find themselves, in which the responsibility of a man was to make connections, value, and sense. We eliminated from the school all preconceptions about what was proper, best, or useful; we gave up rules and penalties; we refused at all levels to resort to coercive force and students were free to come and go at will, to do anything. What we were after was a "guilt-free" environment, one in which the students might become or discover what they were without having to worry about preconceived ideas of what they had to be.

What we found was that our students seemed to need, most of all, relief from their own "childhood"—what was expected of them. Some of them needed merely to rest, to withdraw from the strange grid of adult expectation and demand for lengthy periods of introspection in which they appeared to grow mysteriously, almost like plants. But an even greater number seemed to need independent commerce with the world outside the school: new sorts of social existence. Nothing could replace that. The simple fact seemed to be that our students grew when they were allowed to move freely into and around the adult community; when they were not, they languished.

We came to see that learning is natural, yes, but it results naturally from most things adolescents do. By associating learning with one particular form of intellection and insisting upon that in school we make a grave error. When students shy away from that kind of intellection it doesn't mean they are turning away forever from learning or abstractions; it means simply that they are seeking another kind of learning momentarily more natural to themselves. That may be anything from physical adventure or experimental community work to withdrawn introspection and an exploration of their fantasies and dreams.

Indeed, it is hard for them to do anything without some kind of learning, but that may be what we secretly fear—that those other forms of learning will make them less manageable or less like ourselves. That, after all, may be one reason we use all those books. Levi-Strauss insists on the relation of increased literacy and the power of the state over the individual. It may well be that dependence on print and abstraction is one of the devices we use to make students manipulable, as if we meant to teach them that ideas exist in talk or on the page but rarely in activity. We tried to avoid that. When we permitted students the freedom of choice and gave them easy access to the community, we found that ideas acquired weight and value to the extent that students were allowed to try them out in action. It was in practical and social situations that their own strength increased, and the merging of the two—strengthened self and tested knowledge—moved them more quickly toward manhood than anything else I have seen.

One might make a formula of it: to the extent that students had freedom of volition and access to experience knowledge became important. But volition and access were of absolute value; they took precedence over books or parental anxiety; without them, nothing worked. So we had to trust the students to make their own choices, no matter what we thought of them. We learned to take their risks with them—and to survive. In that sense we became equals, and that equality may in the end be more educational for students than anything else. That, in fact, may be the most important thing we learned. New ways in seeing them were more effective than changes in curriculum, and without them nothing made much difference. But we must understand too that the old way of seeing things—the traditional idea of childhood— is in some way baked into the whole public-school system at almost every level and also hidden in most pedagogy.

In some ways it is compulsory schooling itself which is the problem, for without real choice students will remain locked in childhood and schools, away from whatever is vivid in life. But real choice, as we know, includes dominion over one's own time and energies, and the right to come and go on the basis of what has actual importance. And I wonder if we will ever get round, given all our fears, to granting that privilege to students.

One thing alone of all I have read has made recent sense to me concerning adolescents. That is the implicit suggestion in Erik Erikson's *Young Man Luther* that every sensitive man experiences in himself the conflicts and contradictions of his age. The great man, he suggests, is the man who articulates and resolves these conflicts in a way that has meaning for his time; that is, he is himself, as was Luther, a victim of his time and its vehicle and, finally, a kind of resolution. But all men, not only the great, have in some measure the capacity to experience in themselves what is happening in the culture around them. I am talking here about the fact that what is really shared among the members of a particular culture is a condition, a kind of internal "landscape," the psychic shape that a particular time and place assumes within a man as the extent and limit of his perceptions, dreams, and pleasure and pain.

If there is such a shared condition it seems to me a crucial point, for it means that there is never any real distance between a man and his culture, no real isolation or alienation from society. It means that adolescents are not in their untutored state cut off from culture nor outside it. It means instead that each adolescent is an arena in which the contradictions and currents sweeping through the culture must somehow be resolved, must be resolved by the person himself, and that those individual resolutions are, ideally, the means by which the culture advances itself.

Do you see where this leads? I am straining here to get past the idea of the adolescent as an isolate and deviant creature who must be joined—as if glued and clamped—to the culture. For we ordinarily think of schools, though not quite consciously, as the "culture" itself, little models of society. We try to fit the student into the model, believing that if he will adjust to it he will in some way have been "civilized." That approach is connected to the needs of the early century, when the schools were the means by which the children of immigrant parents were acculturated and moved from the European values of their parents toward more prevalent American ones. But all of that has changed now. The children in our schools, all of them, are little fragments of *this* culture; they no longer need to be "socialized" in the same ways. The specific experiences of every adolescent—his fears, his family crises, his dreams and hallucinations, his habits, his sexuality—all these are points at which the general culture reveals itself in some way. There is no longer any real question of getting the adolescent to "adjust" to things.

The problem is a different one: What kind of setting will enable him to discover and accept what is already within him; to articulate it and perceive the extent to which it is shared with others; and, finally, to learn to change it within and outside himself? For that is what I mean when I call the adolescent a "maker of value." He is a trustee, a trustee of a world that already exists in some form within himself—and we must both learn, the adolescent and his teachers, to respect it.

In a sense, then, I am calling for a reversal of most educational thought. The individual is central; the individual, in the deepest sense, *is* the culture, not the institution. His culture resides in him, in experience and memory, and what is needed is an education that has at its base the sanctity of the individual's experience and leaves it intact.

What keeps running though my mind is a line I read twelve years ago in a friend's first published story: *The Idea in that idea is: there is no one over you.* I like that line: *there is no one over you.* Perhaps that signifies the gap between these children and their parents. For the children it is true, they sense it: there is no one over them; believable authority has disappeared; it has been replaced by experience. As Thomas Altizer says, God is dead; he is experienced now not as someone above or omnipotent or omniscient or "outside," but inwardly, as conscience or vision or even the unconscious or Tillich's "ground of being." This is all too familiar to bother with here, but this particular generation is a collective dividing point. The parents of these children, the fathers, still believe in "someone" over them, insist upon it; in fact, demand it for and from their children. The children themselves cannot believe it; the idea means nothing to them. It is almost as if they are the first real Americans—suddenly free of Europe and somehow fatherless, confused, forced back on their own experience, their own sense of things, even though, at the same time, they are forced to defy their families and schools in order to keep it.

This is, then, a kind of Reformation. Arnold was wrong when he said that art would replace religion; education replaced it. Church became School, the principal vehicle for value, for "culture," and just as men once rebelled against the established Church as the mediator between God and man, students now rebel against the *public* school (and its version of things) as the intermediary between themselves and experience, between themselves and experience and the making of value. Students are expected to reach "reality" (whether of knowledge or society) through their teachers and school. No one, it is said, can participate in the culture effectively without having at one time passed through their hands, proven his allegiance to them, and been blessed. This is the authority exercised by priests or the Church. Just as men once moved to shorten the approach to God, they are moved now to do the same thing in relation to learning and to the community. For just as God was argued to appear within a man—unique, private, and yet shared—so culture is, in some way, grounded in the individual; it inhabits him. The schools, like the Church, must be the expression of that habitation, not its exclusive medium. This is the same reformative shift that occurred in religion, a shift from the institutional (the external) to the individual (the internal), and it demands, when it occurs, an agony, an apocalyptic frenzy, a destruction of the past itself. I believe it is happening now. One sees and feels it everywhere: a violent fissure, a kind of quake.

I remember one moment in the streets of Oakland during the draft demonstrations. The students had sealed off the street with overturned cars and there were no police; the gutters were empty and the students moved into them from the sidewalks, first walking, then running, and finally almost dancing in the street. You could almost see the idea coalesce on their faces: The street is ours! It was as if a weight had been lifted from them, a fog; there was not at that moment any fury in them, any vengefulness or even politics; rather, a lightness, delight, an exhilaration at the sudden inexplicable sense of being free. George Orwell describes something similar in *Homage to Catalonia:* that brief period in Barcelona when the anarchists had apparently succeeded and men shared what power there was. I don't know how to describe it, except to say that one's inexplicable sense of invisible authority had vanished: the oppressive father, who is not really there, was gone.

That sudden feeling is familiar to us all. We have all had it from time to time in our own lives, that sense of "being at home," that ease, that feeling of a Paradise which is neither behind us nor deferred but is around us, a natural household. It is the hint and beginning of Manhood: a promise, a clue. One's attention turns to the immediate landscape and to one's fellows: toward what is there, toward what can be felt as a part of oneself. I have seen the same thing as I watched Stokely Carmichael speaking to a black audience and telling them that they must stop begging the white man, like children, for their rights. They were, he said, neither children nor slaves, no, they were—and here they chanted, almost cried, in unison—a beautiful people: *yes our noses are broad and our lips are thick and our hair is kinky . . . but we are beautiful, we are beautiful, we are black and beautiful.* Watching, you could sense in that released joy an emergence, a surfacing of pride, a refusal to accept shame or the white man's dominance—and a turning to one another, to their own inherent value.

But there is a kind of pain in being white and watching that, for there is no one to say the same things to white children; no "fathers" or brothers to give them that sense of manhood or pride. The adolescents I have seen—white, middle-class—are a long way from those words *we are beautiful, we are beautiful.* I cannot imagine how they will reach them, deprived as they are of all individual strength. For the schools exist to deprive one of strength. That is why one's own worth must be proven again and again by the satisfaction of external requirements with no inherent value or importance; it is why one must satisfy a set of inexplicable demands; it is why there is a continual separation of self and worth and the intrusion of a kind of institutional guilt: failure not of God but of *the system,* the nameless "others," the authority that one can never quite see; and it explains the oppressive sense of some nameless transgression, almost a shame at Being itself.

It is this feeling that pervades both high schools and college, this Kafkaesque sense of faceless authority that drives one to rebellion or withdrawal, and we are all, for that reason, enchanted by the idea of the Trial, that ancient Socratic dream of confrontation and vindication or martyrdom. It is then, of course, that Authority shows its face. In the mid-fifties I once watched Jack Kerouac on a television show and when the interviewer asked him what he wanted he said: to see the face of God. How arrogant and childish and direct! And yet, I suppose, it is what we all want as children: to have the masks of authority, all its disguises, removed and to see it plain. That is what lies in large part behind the riots in the schools. Their specific grievances are incidental; their real purpose is to make God show his face, to have whatever pervasive and oppressive force makes us perpetual children reveal itself, declare itself, commit itself at last. It is Biblical; it is Freudian; it reminds me in some way of the initiation rites: the need to unmask the gods and assume their power, to become an equal—and to find in that the manhood one has been denied.

The schools seem to enforce the idea that there *is* someone over you; and the methods by which they do it are ritualized, pervasive. The intrusion of guilt, shame, alienation from oneself, dependence, insecurity—all these feelings are not the accidental results of schools; they are intentional, and they are used in an attempt to make children manipulable, obedient, "good citizens" we call it, and useful to the state. The schools are the means by which we deprive the young of manhood—that is what I mean to say—and we must not be surprised when they seek that manhood in ways that must of necessity be childish and violent.

But I must admit this troubles me, for there is little choice between mindless violence and mindless authority, and I am just enough of an academic, an intellectual, to want to preserve much of what will be lost in the kind of rebellion or apocalypse that is approaching. And yet, and yet . . . the rapidity of events leaves me with no clear idea, no solution, no sense of what will be an adequate change. It may be that all of this chaos is a way of breaking with the old world and that from it some kind of native American will emerge. There is no way of knowing, there no longer seems any way of estimating what is necessary or what will work. I know only that the problem now seems to be that our response to crisis is to move away or back rather than forward, and that we will surely, for the sake of some imagined order, increase in number and pressure the very approaches that have brought us to this confusion. I don't know. I believe that the young must have values, of course, be responsible, care, but I know too that most of the violence I have seen done to the young has been done in the name of value, and that the well-meaning people who have been so dead set on making things right have had a hand in bringing us to where we are now. The paradox is a deep and troubling one for me. I no longer know if change can be accomplished—for the young, for any of us, without the apocalyptic fury that seems almost upon us. The crisis of youth and education is symptomatic of some larger, deeper fault in our cities and minds, and perhaps nothing can be done consciously in those areas until the air itself is violently cleared one way or another.

So I have no easy conclusions, no startling synthesis with which to close. I have only a change in mood, a softening, a kind of sadness. It may be, given that, that the best thing is simply to close with an unfinished fragment in which I catch for myself the hint of an alternative:

. . . *I am trying to surround you, I see that, I am trying to make with these words a kind of city so natural, so familiar, that the other world, the one that appears to be, will look by comparison absurd and flat, limited, unnecessary. What I am after is liberation, not my own, which comes often enough these days in solitude or sex, but yours, and that is arrogant, isn't it, that is presumptuous, and yet that is the function of art: to set you free. It is that too which is the end of education: a liberation from childhood and what holds us there, a kind of midwifery, as if the nation itself were in labor and one wanted to save both the future and the past—for we* are *both, we are, we are the thin bridge swaying between them, and to tear one from the other means a tearing of ourselves, a partial death.*

*And yet it may be that death is inevitable, useful. It may be. Perhaps, as in the myth, Aphrodite can rise only where Cronos' testicles have fallen into the sea. It may be that way with us. The death of the Father who is in us, the death of the old authority which is part of us, the death of the past which is also our death; it may all be necessary: a rending and purgation. And yet one still seeks another way, something less (or is it more) apocalyptic, a way in which the past becomes the future in ourselves, in which we become the bridges between: makers of culture.*

*Unless from us the future takes place, we are Death only, said Lawrence, meaning what the Chassids do: that the world and time reside within, not outside, men; that there is no distance, no "alienation," only a perpetual wedding to the world. It is that—the presence in oneself of Time—that makes things interesting, is more gravid and interesting than guilt. I don't want to lose it, don't want to relinquish that sense in the body of another dimension, a distance, the depth of the body as it extends backward into the past and forward, as it contains and extends and transforms.*

What I am after is an alternative to separation and rage, some kind of connection to things to replace the system of dependence and submission—the loss of the self—that now holds sway, slanted toward violence. I am trying to articulate a way of seeing, of feeling, that will restore to the young a sense of manhood and potency without at the same time destroying the past. That same theme runs through whatever I write: the necessity for each man to experience himself as an extension and maker of culture, and to feel the whole force of the world within himself, not as an enemy—but as himself:

*. . . An act of learning is a meeting, and every meeting is simply the discovery in the world of a part of oneself that had previously been unacknowledged by the self. It is the recovery of the extent of one's being. It is the embrace of an eternal but elusive companion, the shadowy "other" in which one truly resides and which blazes, when embraced, like the sun.*

# If You're an Elephant Obviously You Need a Trunk, But That Doesn't Mean You Have to Be an Elephant

## BY EDGAR Z. FRIEDENBERG

Edgar Z. Friedenberg, professor of education and sociology at Dalhousie University (Nova Scotia), is the author of *Coming of Age in America, The Vanishing Adolescent,* and *The Dignity of Youth and Other Atavisms.*

WHAT DO schools really do? If you watched them, as a very, very intelligent Uganda native of the eighteenth century might watch a dynamo, would you say that they were in the society for the purpose of doing something you thought was desirable?

In the first place, under what circumstances do we have schools?

Look, for example, at the 1968 New York City teachers' strike. One of the most extraordinary aspects of that strike, it seems to me, is that fact that according to the press reports there was almost universal consensus among the people of New York City that some dreadful emergency had arisen because the schools were closed. Now as the teachers' strike continued, the garbage collectors also went out on strike, and that *is* an emergency: you don't notice the change very rapidly, but ultimately you can't get down the street any more and then you really do have to make other arrangements. The police were also on strike, and that is a situation that has, after all, the qualities of its defect. What people did was lump the strikes together, believing that the police, the

51

garbagemen and the schoolteachers ran institutions which had not only legitimate but also indispensable purposes. Thus for all the strikes there was great urgency to settle.

With the school strike, the urgency of settling became as great as it did because nobody thought to ask "Look, what do these schools do anyway besides baby-sit?" And if we can't get along without that for a while (which may be true in a society so organized that both parents have to go out to work to have a decent living), then you ought to look at that situation instead. However, instead of asking this question, the city went ahead and endorsed the teachers' assumption that education is something cumulative, that each day missed in school was a slice off the child's learning life. If you think back to the moments at which you learned relatively important things in your life, you'll find that the things that are, let us say, of grade B importance on the usual scale of 26 you learn in about a second. And the things that are of grade A importance, of course, you don't even know you know; you couldn't even say when you learned them. The notion of the cumulative effects of educational routine, however, is rooted deep: you should never miss a day.

The question immediately arises: why so much concern about the effects of cumulative education if the important things in life are known outside this process. What do the schools really do?

In the first place, let's remind ourselves that the school is a relatively new kind of institution. At least a school which is supposed to include any very large proportion of the population is a relatively new kind of institution; but I don't think I have to modify the first statement that much. In the U.S. in 1870—with the Kalamazoo decision—there wasn't any question of compulsory attendance at high school. The only question was whether you could pay for it out of public funds for the people who had the money and the marks to go. Obviously, there have been other social changes that make the high school a more . . . Here I hardly know what to say. I started to say a more useful institution, but if you're an elephant obviously you need a trunk, but that doesn't mean you have to be an elephant.

Let's say that social evolution has developed in such a way that the society certainly wouldn't work without widespread public compulsory education. There is no large industrial society, whether in the free world or in the Eastern world, using the conventional designations for these, that can get along without compulsory school attendance. They all seem to have agreed on a fairly similar number of years' limit on the age range.

The question is then, what do schools do that requires compulsory education, that requires cumulative education? What are their social functions?

## 1

The most important social function of the schools, it seems to me, is in defining *youth as a social role.* I would like you to consider what that may really mean. We generally think that youth is a natural category. There aren't any natural categories, however. There really are not *any.* I mean, if you are reasonably comprehensive in your survey of anthropology, you will find that even the living and the dead do not constitute for all societies, all cultures under all circumstances, two distinct categories or groups. In fact, with a different view of the supernatural there may well be little attention paid to the distinction. Obviously, a corpse presents certain practical problems, but they are not insuperable. The transition may be looked on as something having very little significance in the relationship of what we would call the survivors and the persona of what we would call the departed. The difference between men and women seems to be relatively more stable, but by no means always certain. The difference between races, however, is notoriously artificial. There are no Negroes in any part of Africa except Liberia and the Union of South Africa; for the rest of it there are black people who become Negroes if they fly to New York.

Youth is very much the same thing, and one reason that youth is youth is because (as with black people) it is subjected to certain specific, invidious, legally institutionalized distinctions, of which the school is the major source.

For example, since the War between the States it has not been unlawful simply to be anywhere because you are black. But this is obviously not true of young people either in Canada or the United States. It is an offense to be anywhere but in school during school hours. Since it is an offense you can be and will be apprehended, and you can be sent away to what we call a Juvenile Hall or Detention Home—the names vary. At any rate, there isn't any way you can hang loose. This isn't true of any other element of the population. It has even been elaborated in some jurisdiction in the states in ways that still astonish me. What compulsory school attendance does is to define young people as a subject category, and puts on both their movements and their perceptions certain kinds of restrictions which no one else is subject to at all. It does so, moreover, in a way which is remarkably total since even a veritable Samson has not the strength to grow out his hair within two hours between three and five in the afternoon when he may want to pursue some activity among his own peers, for which long hair is a desideratum.

The schools manage by virtue of manipulation of the authority invested in them by the education code. In other words they usurp or intrude upon their students' life space—not just his time in school—and this action they justify. In some ways America is getting a bit more liberal and the explanation of character building doesn't go down well in a society as heterogeneous as ours. It would have thirty or forty years ago, but there have been a few court decisions on the question, and American schools are not supposed to go around building your character without your consent. They have to say that long hair is so distracting that it interferes with the educational function of the school. The wife of one of the students who came with me to Buffalo from California and who is now teaching in the schools of a lower middle-class suburb of Buffalo, had the odd experience of having the principal come into her room a few days ago and ask her to search a young girl. The principal said he was being distracted beyond his capacity to perform his duties by the fact that somewhere on her person this girl had a bell. She knew she wasn't supposed to wear a bell at school, so she put it under a sweater or something; but he could still hear it tinkle. It was found and confiscated.

It is reasonably clear that the hegemony of the school situation is really a good deal grayer than it would be if it was only a place to which you go of your own choice because you want to learn something you are curious about or that is useful to you for purposes of your own. Once you put it in the context of your being the client (society supporting you in this definition of your own role), then it seems obvious that education takes on a totally different function than defining a social role for youth.

**2**

The second major function of the schools, one which is obviously related to the first, is the legitimization of a form of economic discrimination.

The main thing the school is supposed to do for children is to guide them in investing in their own future. Once you get people to agree to this, then you can avoid the question of having to pay students for what is, after all, a form of involuntary servitude. By assuming that what goes on in school prepares young people to earn more money and have higher social status in the future, you can get out of any implication that they ought to be paid for the labor of doing it: the school, the argument goes, is already contributing to what the students are laying aside, if you regard their higher income as a return on capital investment; and what else could a good North American regard a higher income as? This makes everything perfectly just and okay.

However, pieces begin falling off the above little model as soon as you begin turning it around so you can look at it closely.

Now all the books on the subject of income, status and schooling, even the relatively sophisticated ones, will say that one thing about schooling is that it does indeed assist you in getting a higher standard of living; it contributes to social mobility; it is necessary if you are going to get ahead in the world. The best of the books may be rather wry about that and say "Isn't it a shame that our traditional cultural faith in education seems to come to so little in comparison to the nitty-gritty issues of everyday life, and we wish people really were interested in ideas, but maybe we can't expect that . . ." Yet once you've shown a tight correlation between the number of years of schooling completed and the average income for the rest of your life and particularly, of course, for the highest level of income achieved, what have you really proved?

What you've proved, it seems to me, if you've proved anything, is the existence of a conspiracy. Because you are faced on the one hand with a very widespread agreement that you are not going to hire people who don't have the credentials, and on the other hand, if you don't hire people who don't have the credentials you'll never find out if they could have done the job or not, with no alternative ways of earning the credentials on the job. Increasingly we have no way outside the school system of legitimizing participation in the process of growing up, much less getting a license for a trade everyone agrees you need a license for.

What we need to justify educational participation is not the correlation of higher income to higher levels of schooling, but rather some direct indication of where or what the skills really are that enable a person to make it through life, and to what extent the school does in fact contribute to learning these skills. Further, if there are such skills, and there is no other place than school to get them, that still does not really prove that schools are the best method of passing on these skills. In fact, the argument that schools are the only channels for opportunity in American culture is a little bit like the argument that David would have made a suitable and pious husband to Bathsheba. There is still the question of his complicity in Uriah's fate and whether there would not have been something even better available except for what he did. In this case it isn't the schools themselves that provide the economic and social rewards, but then, in the biblical story, David isn't the murderer either. He's simply the influential administrative official.

If this were not enough to weaken the argument for schools as places for getting ahead, there is the fact that the statistics are interpreted in a kind of phoney way. In the first place, most of the arguments linking higher incomes and schooling are directed toward high school, concentrating on those who have or have not completed high school. The data for completing high school includes everybody who completed high school, which means people who go on and get university degrees. When you look at those who completed high school and didn't go on to college and those who didn't complete high school the difference in earning potential isn't very great. It averages out to something like an extra twenty dollars per month for those who completed high school—not enough probably to make up for the aggravation.

Of course, you can say "Yes, but we think everyone should go to college, and you can't do that unless you go to high school." But then you are faced with a couple of other things that a reasonably bright lawyer would raise in countering such an argument in a court of equity. You see, the financial value of a high school degree was great only at a time when the high school degree was relatively scarce and was a symbol of an elite position. So again we do not know that it was the high school education that caused the higher income. All we can say is that the people in the top 10 percent of the society, with the resources to not earn money and go to school, are likely to earn more money over the long run than those who didn't have the resources and didn't go to school. Further, when education becomes universal, everyone going to college, then it's possible that its fiscal utility will diminish; this seems, in fact, to be what does happen. You can't, I think, use any part of this argument to conclude anything with certainty except that the schools are a sentinel. They provide the check points along which you progress.

From the point of view of the corporations, however, the schools do perform a useful function: they instill or induce you to develop certain characteristics which are marketable, the kind of characteristics that allow you to work comfortably within the corporation. Of course, if you have a mind to, you can then argue that this means that the schools constitute a subsidy for so-called private enterprise provided by the taxpayers' dollars. So maybe students ought to get paid much earlier, and by the people who use them.

**3**

I think probably in order to understand the relationship between our corporate society, our schools, and our students in a general way—as to how schools do what they do—there is no better source than the sage of Toronto and two of his most familiar aphorisms.

In the schools, more than in most of the other mass media, it is indeed true that the medium is the message, which is one reason I haven't said a word about curriculum. What is taught isn't as important as learning how you have to act in society, how other people will treat you, how they will respond to you, what the limits of respect that will be accorded to you really are. What the schools teach is the experience of being a school child, and once you get used to that it's unlikely you will run amuck among the inhabitants of your community.

The other McLuhan point that seems to me to provide an even deeper source of insight is the observation that we don't know who discovered water, but we're pretty sure it wasn't the fish. What I mean by this is that the schools, by providing a continual social substrate—a kind which is, in effect, a caricature of the society—makes the society seem so natural that you don't notice the awful things that it does. In fact, even your ways of fighting the school are determined by what it teaches you to regard as propriety—or obscenity—whichever you happen to want to employ. In any case, it's essentially true that what the schools do is teach you how "it's spozed to be," particularly in a liberal democracy, where the schools embody the society's central contradictions.

In America, for example, we have a written Constitution to which the first ten amendments constitute the Bill of Rights. Most states have laws—laws made before the Supreme Court went over to the "Communists"—that compels you to teach the Constitution. However, if you learn the Constitution in the American public school system, you certainly are not going to go around thinking that the Bill of Rights applies to you. There has been a little research study, as a matter of fact, on what children really think the pledge of allegiance to the flag means, and there was a very wide divergence of opinion. A Master's degree student, who was more imaginative than most, simply went around and asked children to tell him what the pledge said, to repeat it for him. The nicest result, I think, was "One nation indivincable, with liberty and death for all." We have been trying to fulfill that promise all right, but when it comes to promises, say of freedom of speech in situations in which it creates real social disruptions, we've been less than careful in keeping our word. I don't want to put down the quite remarkable and creditable degree of freedom of speech in the United States in the sense that you are unlikely to be subjected to official sanctions for anything that you say. The point is that the function of the school is to teach you about the unofficial sanctions, to prepare you for the blacklist, to make sure you understand the implications of being labeled a "trouble-maker," which is the worst thing a school can call you.

The schools perform this kind of function, it seems to me, in a society that is lying about its traditions. A nicer way of putting it is to say the society still honors or likes to draw from components of its tradition that are nobler than it can in fact hope to institutionalize in everyday practice. But it still comes out lying.

One of the reasons this has happened is that we have included into the social process, with some degree of influence, people who would in an earlier, more conservative organization of society, have been déclassé and non-voting. Here, I think, we are at the heart of the matter. The schools have succeeded in becoming mass organizations, serving a much larger proportion of the population, and are as bad as they are because of their response to this process. The problem is not that they are serving people now who have less ability than before, but that they are serving people who in earlier days were treated by decision-makers as victims. When a society becomes more democratic and no longer feels comfortable about treating people as victims, yet still retains essentially the same exploitative social arrangements, then it has to create institutions that will induce people to choose to be victims. Choosing out of anxiety or out of a lack of sense of what their own resources might be or out of a realistic sense that they might not be smart enough to be rulers if they don't choose to be victims.

In the most general terms then the schools, like the society, hold in tension the contradictions of the liberal tradition as it grew out of British and, later, American society. They emphasize both the individual and the sanctity of getting rich, and so they obscure moral issues and at the same time tend to favor continual enlargement of the in-group.

There is real conflict, it seems to me, between provision through the school of increased economic opportunity and the support of cultural values that might treat all people more generously. The schools have been set up to avoid this conflict, although lately they don't seem to be having so much success. A serious polarization seems to be happening in America, for which I am glad, but then I'm not a liberal. The schools have tried to evade this polarization by defining the difference between the rich and the poor, not in terms of their relationships to the means of production and the consequent real conflicts of interest, but rather in terms of cultural deprivation. They take the sting out of this deprivation by making the authority of the things that really are associated with what is left of high culture so tenuous and so ridiculous that there wasn't much left but the implication that, of course, you must learn this culture just as you have to learn to put on a coat and a tie and comb your hair and have it short, because otherwise you won't get a job. Thus not having this culture doesn't have to mean you're inferior to anyone else. Now, it seems to me that a more valid human message would have been that you have the right to dress in a way you think becomes you, but no matter how you dress, it may indeed be true that you are inferior to other people. And this inferiority may be a consequence of experiences that happened so early and that were so intense that they will never be reversed. No school can be magical. There will be some things that you don't understand, that you will never understand, that certain kinds of schools could help certain other people understand if you would shut up. You have been permanently deprived of something that is of inestimable value.

The possibility of such deprivation we can't face up to. We are very suspicious of the cultivation of the kind of subtlety that builds only on antecedent association, very suspicious of going off with a few people to explore meanings that might be private, letting these people select themselves. You get everyone uptight if you form a self-selected group to talk about issues of importance to you. In American society this is a real violation. The whole thing is set up with the schools as a prime part of it, to keep anyone from fearing that there may indeed be a hidden treasure that they aren't going to find. As a result, it may have been destroyed, at least the one that came down through high culture.

The kids, on the other hand, aren't buying this loss and are rebuilding other modes of communication. Here we get into the best of folk-rock, the sound of groups that are communicating private experience. They are put down as hippies because the experience has to be private rather than political. Yet it is privacy that is being destroyed, not isolation. What we have increasingly lost is our social right to do our own thing with our own kind of people. Society's institutions are there to stamp it out. The result is that new forms of personal experience have to come in from areas that are not legitimized. If they were legitimate, they would be seized and democratized. It can only be done the other way—by working with materials which were assumed to be of no value until they are finally noticed, and one hopes that it will take years as it did in the case of the Beatles. With them it was finally noticed that there were enough people who shared their illicit longing for subjective communication to make someone rich. At that point the thing falls into the commercial pile and you have the Maharishi appearing, Brian Epstein committing suicide. In this way Western Civilization is carried on.

# *Educating* Contra Naturam

## BY THEODORE ROSZAK

Theodore Roszak, professor of history at California State College at Hayward, is the author of *The Making of the Counter Culture* and the editor of *The Dissenting Academy*.

SUPPOSE—INSTEAD of applauding, praising, but inwardly insisting that we know better—we heard and affirmed what the poet proclaims: that "heaven lies about us in our infancy"; that the child comes to us shaped by nature's hand a

> "Mighty prophet! Seer blest!
> On Whom those truths do rest
> Which we are toiling all our lives to find . . ."

Well then . . . what would education be but the fine art of watching and waiting, and in good time, of summoning forth from the child all that abides within: kingdoms, powers, glories . . . ? So the task of the teacher would be that of fireminder: keeper and feeder of the indwelling flame.

Yet if—believing this—we look about us at the world of men which is the result of our labor, what can we do but echo Wordsworth's lament?

> "Whither is fled the visionary gleam?
> Where is it now, the glory and the dream?"

Our pedagogy deals poorly with these visionary gleams, does it not? How many of us would recognize them if we saw them? In truth, did we ever really believe they were there—within ourselves, as much as in the young?

There is a drawing by William Blake: Age applying the scissors to the Wings of Youth. The image tells us what *our* education is all about, *must* be all about in schools financed by church or state and enforced upon the young by compulsion. Tolstoy put the point vividly more than a century ago when, throughout the West, compulsory public school systems were coming into fashion with the unqualified approval of all progressive opinion. He was among the few who saw through this pedagogical fad which was destined to become the iron social orthodoxy of every industrial and industrializing society. Tolstoy said:

> Education is a compulsory forcible action of one person upon another for the purpose for forming a man such as will appear to [society] to be good. . . . Education is the tendency toward moral despotism raised to a principle. . . . I am convinced that the educator undertakes with such zeal the education of the child because at the base of this tendency lies his envy of the child's purity, and his desire to make him like himself, that is, to spoil him.

A harsh judgment. I wince at it as much as you do. For it comes from one who was not only a supreme prophetic spirit but a gifted teacher of children. And like you I ask, *must* it be so? Is there no other possibility?

Of course there is. There is the possibility Tolstoy himself explored at his own voluntary school for peasant youngsters, Yasnaya Polyana, where, as he put it, "the criterion of pedagogics is only liberty."

"The people," said Tolstoy, "love and seek education, as they love and seek the air for breathing. . . . Some want to teach and others want to learn. Let them teach as much as they can, and let them learn as much as they will."

*That* is the other possibility: to teach in freedom, in complete freedom, in response to the native inclination of the student; to be a teacher only when and where and insofar as the student authorizes us to be.

But that libertarian possibility has nothing to do with our schools—our "free" public schools, where "free" refers not to an existential relationship between teacher and student but to a budgetary arrangement for the financing of a coercive institution.

"*Let* them learn," said Tolstoy. He did not say, "*Make* them learn," because he knew that true education satisfies a natural appetite. Why resort to force feeding?

And yet, how much of our educating proceeds from the assumption that the young must be *made* to learn? Made to learn . . . tricked into learning . . . charmed . . . inveigled . . . cajoled . . . bribed . . . as if in truth education were *contra naturam* and required clever strategies.

If we do not work from that assumption, then why is education ever anywhere a "problem"? A "problem" requiring mind, professional, specialized, full-time, and Herculean attention—and prodigious amounts of money?

If we do not work from that assumption, then why the compulsion? And I do not refer only to the legal compulsion of our lower grades, but to such forms of compulsion as military conscription, which has given us a male college population largely made up not of young scholars but of refugees seeking sanctuary in draft-deferrable occupations: the coercive process General Hershey once referred to as "choice under pressure." I speak too of the more subtle compulsions: the lure and the goad of jobs, status, licenses, and credentials.

Now it cannot be unknown to any informed person that in so-called primitive societies, as in many pre-modern civilizations, the whole of vast and profound cultures was easily and naturally transmitted from generation to generation without the intervention of an educational establishment. Rather, the burden of cultural continuity rested on what Paul Goodman has recently called "incidental education": learning in the home, on the job, especially at play, by way of observation and imitation, now and then, here and there, from whoever happens to know, as and when the spirit moves—above all, without fuss and bother.

The pedagogical theory of all this has been neatly summarized by George Dennison in his book *The Lives of Children:*

> These two things taken together—the natural authority of adults and the needs of children—are the great reservoir of organic structuring that comes into being when arbitrary rules of order are dispensed with.
>
> The child is always finding himself, moving toward himself, as it were, in the near distance. The adult is his ally, his model— and his obstacle (for there are natural conflicts, too, and they must be given their due).

"Incidental education"—how precarious this must sound to us. And yet each generation of Eskimos or Bushmen has stepped forth into life in full possession of the culture. This is not because the culture of primitives is "simpler" than our own: a preposterously ethnocentric assumption. What we mistake for the "complexity" of our culture (when we are not simply confessing to our own sad confusion) is really its technical and academic specialization—the correct measure of which is quantity, not complexity. Quantity is a blunt measure of disorganized amount; complexity measures the richness and integrity of the cultural whole within which all things known and valued should properly find coherence. In this respect—with reference to coherent moral, religious, aesthetic, mythological and ritual content—primitive cultures are often far more complex than the down-at-the-heels, *Reader's Digest* and Sunday-supplement version of Western civilization most of our fellow citizens are carrying about haphazardly in their heads. There is even a vast store of purely technical know-how every Eskimo and Bushman must learn—a much greater store than most of us need learn who undo the technical snags in our lives by looking in the Yellow Pages and dialing seven numbers.

I grant you, there have been primitive groups where harsh forms of indoctrination existed; but I call your attention to the others where little of this has been necessary because the culture, after its own fashion and style, gracefully gave expression to the many dimensions of human personality: the workaday practical, the metaphysical-speculative, the sexual, the communal, the creative, the visionary. Oddly enough, the single aspect of primitive culture many civilized people find least palatable are the often grueling rites of passage—especially those that transpire at puberty. But even these rituals have had at least a natural sanction: they have been the culture's way of dramatizing and illuminating an irrepressible constant in the nature of man—and so of integrating it into the personal and communal pattern of life.

How ironic and revealing it is that in our schools we permit children to be hurt, bullied and browbeaten if they display too much healthy animal energy in the classroom, or if they fail to revere what the school authorities pose as the social orthodoxies. These conformist demands that arise outside the child's experience may be severely enforced. But as for the biological imperative of puberty which arises mightily within the child—of this hardly a candid word may be whispered in many schools. Either teachers play dumb, assuming a comic and unbecoming chastity, or the so-called "problem" is treated by way of the most fastidiously anti-erotic sex instruction.

Our schools would be chagrined to graduate a student who did not know the ritualistic pledge of allegiance to the flag; but they feel no shame whatever to graduate adolescents who would be (for all their schools had taught them) sexual ignoramuses. And is this not in itself heavy evidence of how pathetically little our own culture knows of the nature of man: that we take a superficial national emblem to be more worthy of ritual elaboration than the deep demands of erotic experience?

Thus, even where primitive cultures have tended to be far more physically brutal than you or I would approve, they have by and large been true to Tolstoy's dictum: "Every instruction ought to be only an answer to the question put by life."

Water finds its level, the swallows fly south in winter, children learn. It is just that simple. That is what Tolstoy knew; that is what the primitives knew. And so they could say, "Let them learn." Societies that trust their culture can let nature take its course, knowing that in their own good time—and usually very promptly—the children will come round and learn what looks interesting and important to learn, that indeed their young lives, unless stunted or sidetracked, are nothing but the inquisitive unfolding of potentialities.

But when a society begins to fear that its culture is not interesting or important to the young—that indeed its culture violates nature—then it concludes that education must be *made* to happen: must be organized strenuously into existence and enforced by professionals. And then we have much heavy talk about methods, discipline, techniques, discipline, incentives, discipline, inducements, discipline, the "crisis in our schools"—and discipline. We also have blue-ribbon committees, top-level conferences, exhaustive surveys, bold reforms, daring experiments, courageous innovations—and the educational establishment grows and grows and grows.

Let us postulate a law: the less secure the culture, the larger the educational establishment. All of us readily recognize that a society in need of heavy policing must be in serious trouble—for the laws have surely lost their power to command respect. Similarly, a society that professionalizes and anxiously aggrandizes its educational establishment—its cultural cops—is also in serious trouble, for the culture has surely lost its capacity to command interest and involvement. The now chronic top-to-bottom state of emergency in our schools does not exist because the educational establishment is not good enough and needs repair. The crisis is that the culture is not good enough. The educational establishment, with all its compulsions, its disciplinary hang-ups, and—yes —even with its constabulary forces patrolling the corridors—all this exists in the first place only because of the insecurity of the culture.

Once we realize this, we can perhaps see that the feverish

efforts of even good-hearted educators to inspire and motivate their students are as pathetic as the belated efforts of our Special Forces in Vietnam to win the hearts and minds of the very people they have degraded and brutalized. Within the context of coercion all efforts to ingratiate are vitiated from scratch. As Tolstoy observed with respect to teachers who seek to achieve "greater freedom" in the schools:

> those gentlemen . . . resemble a man who, having brought up some young nightingales and concluding that they need freedom, lets them out of the cage and gives them freedom at the end of cords attached to their feet, and then wonders why the nightingales are not doing any better on the cord, but only break their legs and die.

Now if the law we have postulated is true, it leads us to an ironic conclusion about modern Western civilization. If there has ever been a civilization obsessed with what we call "free, public education," it is ours. We invented this quaint institution and we invest a special historical pride in it. We take it as an indisputable sign of social progress that we have built such colossal, affluent, and broadcast school systems. Until, at last, we begin to anticipate that education will soon become our largest "industry"—the major preoccupation of the society. Far from perceiving in this prospect the advanced cultural insecurity it betokens, we feel this is not only right but ideal. How better to use our wealth, our leisure, and our know-how than to train more teachers, build more schools, process more students?

Why does industrial society do this? Tolstoy's contemporary, Bismarck, knew why. "The nation that has the schools," Bismarck observed, "has the future."

Education as an adjunct of national power: a shrewd insight —one worthy of such a grim broker in blood and iron. But one did not have to be a Prussian autocrat and militarist to accept the hard-bitten logic of Bismarck's argument. William E. Forster, who led the good fight for compulsory public education in Great Britain, was a solidly bourgeois Quaker: an industrialist and a self-denying public servant. And here, very revealingly, is how Forster sized things up in 1870 in presenting his successful elementary-education bill to Parliament:

> Upon the speedy provision of elementary education depends our industrial prosperity. It is of no use trying to give technical teaching to our artizans without elementary education; uneducated labourers . . . are, for the most part, unskilled labourers, and if we leave our work-folk any longer unskilled, notwithstanding their strong sinews and determined energy, they will become over-matched in the competition of the world. . . . Civilized communities throughout the world are massing themselves together, each mass being measured by its force; and if we are to hold our position among men of our own race or among the nations of the world, we must make up the smallness of our numbers by increasing the intellectual force of the individual.

Note the telltale imagery of the argument: energy . . . force . . . power . . . mass. Education as mental steam engine; the school as brain-production factory. No doubt today the metaphors would draw upon computer technics or information theory. But the argument would nonetheless be the same. "Knowledge is power," said Francis Bacon more than three centuries ago at the dawn of the scientific revolution. And from Bismarck to Project Apollo, that fateful dictum has been the ensign of public policy throughout the developed and developing countries.

Tolstoy, whose healthy anarchist instincts were quick to sense which way the power-political winds of our time were tending, gauged the situation shrewdly. This time he speaks of higher education, but the criticism strikes at the same authoritarian-utilitarian vice which was for Tolstoy the curse of all state-supported education:

> No one has ever thought of establishing universities on the needs of the people. . . . The universities were founded to answer certain needs, partly of the government and partly of higher society, and for the universities was established all that preparatory lad-

der of educational institutions which has nothing in common with the needs of the people. The government needed officials, doctors, jurists, teachers, and the universities were founded in order to train these. . . . It is generally said that the defects of the universities are due to the defects in the lower institutions. I affirm the opposite: the defects of the popular . . . schools are mainly due to the false exigencies of the universities.

The words are as telling in the age of the multiversity as they were a century ago. Yet how easily we have come to accept the assumption—almost as if it were printed on every dollar our schools receive (for, in effect it is)—that education exists not to debate but to serve the preordained national priorities. How nicely it simplifies everything to define the good student as he who gets the grades that get the job—a deferential simplification that, incidentally, takes on no greater ethical complexity even if the pigmentation of the students who are pressed into service becomes as various as the rainbow.

In the dim and dismal past, there was indeed a time when aristocratic and feudal elites jealously defended a deep vested interest in the plain brute ignorance of peasant masses. Those days are gone forever. Industrial society requires not illiterate serfs and peons but trained workmen and trained consumers, bound together in the tight coordination of urban life. As rural routines break down before the thrust of modernization, the well-adjusted citizen must be capable of rapidly assimilating new stores of data: he must respond snappily to the myriad signals, commands, instructions of a changeful new world. The peasant guides his conduct by custom; the industrial worker by information. The peasant lives by tradition; the industrial worker by the news of the day. This is what accounts for industrial society's peculiar obsession with literacy: its facile and unexamined assumption that someone who cannot read is, of necessity, "backward," "underdeveloped."

In 1968, while I was in London, Granada Television produced a documentary film on the civil war that has been raging in

Portuguese Guinea for the past several years: an embryonic African Vietnam being contested by Portugal (armed by the United States via NATO) and the Guinean National Liberation Front. The report was presented wholly from the NLF side and it captured much of the idealism of these youthful rebels who are out to free themselves from the dead hand of the imperialist past and to usher their society into the modern world.

At one point we were shown an NLF jungle school where guerrilla teachers were drilling away at children from the bush—and at students considerably older too. One guerrilla, we were told, had learned to read only at the age of thirty—and this was now his proudest achievement. We saw the man poring laboriously over a sheet of paper, ponderously shaping out each word with his lips as his finger underlined it, and smiling broadly as each sentence of the text was conquered. It might have been an image out of our own American past: the familiar picture of the Polish or Italian immigrant learning his letters in night school, making the great leap forward into literacy and citizenship.

But what was it our night-school immigrants went on to read once the breakthrough had been made? Legend has it that they all went on to Shakespeare, de Tocqueville, and John Stuart Mill. Surely some did. But mostly they went on to the local Hearst press, the *Police Gazette*, Horatio Alger, the Sears catalog. And what was the text our proud Guinean guerrilla was draining of all its insight? Of course: a party bulletin—especially prepared for the feebly literate. It was all his formal education allowed him to cope with. And it was, in any case, about all the party was prepared to give him—though perhaps he will eventually graduate to the Thoughts of Chairman Mao.

Thus, for the peasant revolutionary as for the vast majority of our own more affluent youngsters, literacy is the royal road to propaganda. Why does industrial—or would-be industrial—society crusade so fanatically against illiteracy? It is hardly because illiterate people are necessarily stupid. They *may* be. But not necessarily so. Recall that high civilizations have been reared on this earth without the aid of the written word. It is hardly because literate people are necessarily smart. They *may* be. But not necessarily so. And to judge by what most of our almost universally literate citizenry patronizes in the way of newspapers, magazines, political oratory and television entertainment—to judge especially by its gullibility in the marketplace—literacy would seem to bear about as much relationship to intelligence in our society as a presidential convention bears to a town meeting. It is little wonder then that as of the year 1970 our political leaders come to the convenient conclusion that, in the arena of social controversy, the voice of the universally literate people is . . . a silent majority.

The simple truth is: industrial society has no use for unschooled people, because unschooled people are too difficult to organize. Lacking the sense of discipline and responsibility the schools provide, lacking the minimal literacy they purvey, people will not pay what they owe, buy what they ought, report for work on time, appear for induction when summoned, dial the right number, sign on the dotted line, fill out the form correctly. They will not know what the advertisement says, they will not know where to put their mark on the ballot, they will not know why the war is necessary, they will not know wherein lies the genius and honor of their leaders. Unless equipped with a good, practical education—"an education for life"—they may even revert to employing the sense they were born with, put two and two together, and *not* come up with a good solid official five.

Of course I know there are exceptions to the standard: exceptional teachers, exceptional students. But let us be honest about our history: the free public school system is a product of industrial necessity within the context of the nation-state. I am not unaware of the genuine idealism that has been and still is entrusted to this institution. Idealism is often planted in barren earth. Believe it or not, in the high days of the French Revolution, the conscripted citizen army—the *levée en masse*—was regarded as a shining expression of liberty, equality, fraternity. Ask our youth today what they think of this great democratic institution. Institutions have such a tragic way of devouring the ideals they exist to foster.

The function of the educational establishment in industrial society is to treat industrialism and all that it demands as "given": necessary, good, inexorably so—a veritable force of nature toward which one must be "practical," not "critical." The schools are built because they produce the skills that will turn the populace into interchangeable, socially serviceable units of a productive economy: at the least, reading, writing, ciphering—but also the sophisticated technical skills necessary for elaborating the industrial plant.

In addition, the schools enforce the virtues of what is called "citizenship": meaning, eager acquiescence in the national mystique, patriotic resolution, docility before official superiors, well-developed resignation before externally enforced discipline. In collectivized economies, the schools inculcate a deep and automatic appreciation of ideological inanity; in privatized economies, a profound piety for the privileges of property.

In brief, the elites of all industrial societies take their strength from technicians so narrowly proficient that there is no room in their busy consciousness for a single moral scruple, and from masses so minimally literate that nothing intellectually larger than a commercial advertisement or an official political stereotype can wedge itself into so abbreviated an attention span.

What, then, is the measure of the success of the educational establishment? Let me suggest two examples that vividly represent the excellence the establishment was in reality created to achieve. I could have chosen other examples, but I choose these two because they strike me as having required a superhuman effort in dealing with recalcitrant human material, and obviously because they give us much to ponder.

The first of these is the gargantuan Russo-American weapons system we call "the balance of terror." It is hardly a secret that, since the end of World War II, the building of this juggernaut has been public business number one for both the U.S. and the U.S.S.R. Nothing in either society—no matter of social justice or humanitarian need—has received more trained manpower or money than these weapons have. Yet there is no system of social ethics—excepting those of Tamerlane, Al Capone, and Joseph Goebbels—which offers a breath of support to this major international enterprise. Translated out of the official casuistry which covers their true character, these weapons represent an institutionalized commitment to the doing of genocide—perhaps on a global scale. They exist to kill children. Among others, to be sure. But I call attention to the children because we are teachers and perhaps this does the most to tear the heart. These weapons are aimed at children, not by accident or unavoidable necessity—but directly, specifically, intentionally, with painstaking malice aforethought, and without apology or guilt. That is what "terror" means. So they have been designed; and so they will be used— when the time comes. They are, as Thomas Merton has called them, "the original child bomb."

Now consider how efficient an educational establishment it requires to produce the scientists and technicians who will sell their necessary talents to such a project. Consider how carefully a curriculum must be designed to bring these specialists through sixteen, eighteen, twenty years of education without ever once unsettling their conscience. Consider how delicately their acquaintance with the religious and ethical traditions of their culture must have been arranged in order not to preclude their serviceability. Consider with what ingenious cunning they must have been maneuvered through the study of what we call "the humanities." Consider how diligently every inborn trace of moral inquisitiveness had to be surgically removed from their nature, along with every remnant of a sense of humanitarian service, pity, fellowship, or sheer existential disgust—until at last we had specialists whose only remaining ethical reflex would be "What they do to us, we do to them—worse!" And how many of these men, one wonders, have come from schools which have fiercely defended their right to have the words of Amos, Isaiah and Jesus read in class?

The second example I offer is an event now much on the public mind. I refer to what happened in the Vietnamese village of Songmy on March 16, 1968. What has followed from that event has led to a deal of controversy—though I learn from one public opinion poll, taken at Christmastime 1969, that 51 percent of those questioned refuse—like the Saigon government—to believe that anything untoward ever occurred in Songmy. But let us assume that the U.S. Army and its Commander in Chief know better and can be believed when they tell us that an atrocity there took place. In what grotesque sense of the word can that savage act be called a "success" of our educational establishment?

Once again, consider what a labor it must have been to produce the young Americans capable of such a deed. Such ordinary, such stolidly ordinary young men—a few years before they turned their guns on these women and children and shot them, they were perhaps going out for the high-school basketball team, planning heavy weekend dates, worrying about their grades in solid geometry. No moral degenerates, these: no more so than Adolph Eichmann was. But given the order to kill, they killed. Not because they were monsters but because they were good soldiers, good Americans, doing as they had been taught to do. Given the order to kill, they killed—the obviously innocent, obviously defenseless, crying out to them for pity.

Later, one of the men is reported to say that he has bad dreams about the deed. Did he ever learn in school that there are such dreams? Was he ever asked to decide for himself what his duty is to the state, to his own conscience, to his innocent fellow man? Did he ever hear of the Nuremburg Trials? Did he ever have a class dealing with the subject "orders one must consider *never* obeying"? Would any Board of Education, any PTA now demand that such a class be offered? Would the Department of

Health, Education and Welfare encourage it? Would the Department of Defense suggest it? Would the local Chamber of Commerce and American Legion permit it?

Well then: what respect has our culture for the moral nature of our young?

Again to quote Tolstoy, our school system "trains not such men as humanity needs, but such as corrupt society needs."

I have said that the great problem with education in our time is that the culture it exists to transmit—the culture of industrial society—is largely worthless and therefore without inherent interest to lively and unspoiled young minds. Worse still, much that industrial society requires degrades all natural humanity. It trespasses against reason, gentleness and freedom with a force that is plainly homicidal in intensity. This is why the schools—in their eagerness to advance the regimenting orthodoxies of state and corporation—property, power, productivity—have to distort education into indoctrination. That is why so much is incurably wrong with the schools—all the things keener critics than myself have raised to the level of common knowledge. I need not discuss here what writers like John Holt, Edgar Friedenberg, Jules Henry, Paul Goodman, Jonathan Kozol, James Herndon have so well analyzed: the compulsion of the system, the tyranny of "right answers," the surrealistic charade of lesson plans, methods, and learning resources, the obsession with discipline, above all the mercenary manipulation of competitive favors—grades, gold stars, good opinions, awards, jobs, status, power.

Nor do I have the time here to persuade those of you who do not already feel it in your bones like the plague that the West's 150-year experiment in industrialization is approaching a disastrously bad end. Our collective nightmares are available for all to consider: the bleak landscapes of the Brave New World and of 1984, hallucinations of thermonuclear extinction or total environmental collapse. If the bomb does not finish us, then the blight of our habitat very likely will. If not the atom's fire, then the poisoned air, water, earth: the very elements pronounce their sentence of death upon industrial society. Surely they will serve even for the least religious among us as the voice of God.

Whatever health remains in a corrupted culture gathers in the gift of prophecy or also perishes. And woe to the people who fail to recognize their prophets because they come in unlikely forms—for prophets are in the habit of so doing. The best and brightest of our young go barefoot and grow shaggier by the day; they scrap the social graces; they take despairingly to the streets to revile and cry doom; they abscond to the hinterlands in search of purity and simple dignities; they thrust themselves upon us in our public parks and on the stages of our theaters stripped naked and imploring us to "let the sunshine in." We can hardly be so plain ignorant of our own tradition that we do not recognize—for all the frequent zaniness and gaucherie—the gesture, the presence, the accusatory word that is here reborn before us. The prophet Micah, wild-eyed and wailing in the streets of Jerusalem:

> Arise and go, for this is no place to rest;
> because of uncleanness that destroys
>     with a grievous destruction. . . .
> Your rich men are full of violence;
>     your inhabitants speak lies. . . .
> Their hands are upon what is evil
>     to do it diligently;
> the prince and the judge ask for a bribe,
> and the great man utters the evil desire of his soul;
> thus they weave it together. . . .
> For this I will lament and wail;
>     I will go stripped and naked;
> I will make lamentation like the jackals,
>     and mourning like the ostriches.

In the finest moments of their outrage and anger, what the young are demanding is what every prophet has demanded of his people: that they too strip away the defiled garment of society, turn away and inward toward the first principles of the conduct of life. The great question is always the same. It was asked of King David, of Imperial Rome, and now of Imperial America, playing self-appointed policeman to the nations and conquering hero to the whole of nature. "What shall it profit a man if he gain the whole world and lose his soul?"

For those of us who teach, the return to first principles means a return to Tolstoy's critique of compulsory, public education: an honest admission that what our existing pedagogical machinery is programmed to produce is the man that industrial society in its benightedness thinks it needs; and what industrial society in its benightedness thinks it needs of us is but the shriveled portion of our full humanity—how small a portion one must almost weep to say.

But lest we despair, we must remember that for Tolstoy this bleak fact was only a minor blemish on the face of an abidingly beautiful truth: that the spontaneous splendors of the human personality return to us whole in every child and will struggle fiercely to be educated in accordance with their nature. Because he believed this, Tolstoy was prepared—indeed, compelled—to sweep away the state's claim to all educational authority, which could only be the authority to pollute the wellsprings of learning. There can be no more precise way to frame the matter than as he did in raising the question: *who has the right to educate?* His answer:

> There are no rights of education. I do not acknowledge such, nor have they been acknowledged nor will they ever be by the young generation under education. . . . *The right to educate is not vested in anybody.*

It was out of this clear perception that authentic education derives only from the need of the child, not from the right of the adult, that Tolstoy appealed for that which presently animates campus rebellion throughout the Western world—now in the colleges, but soon enough I suspect our high schools too will be ablaze (not only figuratively) with the demand: "freely formed institutions, having for their basis the freedom of the learning generation."

A steep demand. A demand that is bound to seem unthinkable to those who mistake a proper sense of adult responsibility for automatic submission unto the higher powers of the social order and to the bizarre necessities that come down to us from these obsessive profit- and power-mongers. Such resignation in the name of responsibility can only drive us to cling to the established way of things as if it were all the deck there is and everything beyond, the cruel, cold sea. Nothing to do then but clap the would-be mutineers in irons, rearrange the cargo, patch up the leaks, and continue the cruise to oblivion.

But the deck is afire, while the sea, if not benign, is yet filled with a multitude of inviting islands: the possibilities of culture on the far side of industrial necessity and nationalistic idolatry. The possibilities are there, though I think the diminished consciousness to which we are—most of us—beholden will see them only as mirages or not at all. That is why the expertise and technician-intelligence to which we habitually turn for solutions—as if with the reflex of duty well learned—are really no help to us: more statistics, more surveys, more professional shop talk and hair of the dog. As if there could be no knowledge of man that did not wear the official uniform of research.

But the poet Shelley tells us there are and have always been "unacknowledged legislators of mankind" whose age-old gift it is to "bring light and fire from those eternal regions where the owl-winged faculty of calculation dare not ever soar." A word from them does more than all our science and its dismal train of imitators to reclaim the wasted dimensions of our identity: the buried erotic powers, the truths of the imagination that yield meaning to song, dance, or ritual gesture, but which common literacy will never touch but to kill. Astonishments of the spirit . . . gods of the heights and of the depths . . . thrones and dominions that only the lamp of prophecy reveals . . . and all these inborn glories of our nature useless, useless for achieving what the nations would achieve. We deal here in vistas of experience in which the orthodox ambitions of our society shrivel to nonentity. Yet what else would we have the education of the young be but such an adventure in transcendence?

So the demand is for "freely formed institutions": education beneath the sway of the visionary gleam. From where we stand, a revolutionary demand. And I can hardly be sanguine that many of us here who belong to the establishment will prove to be effective revolutionaries.

Should I be asked, however, "What then are *we* to do?", perhaps for those having ears to hear, I can offer one minimal suggestion (since the maximum one can do is obvious enough): not a program, not a policy, not a method, nothing to be worked up into a research project or the grist of the conference mill—but only a silent commitment to be pondered in the heart and practiced with unabashed guile when opportunity permits. And it is this: might we not at least let go of our pretensions—and then simply let go of the students? *Let them go.* Help them to escape, those that need to escape. Find them cracks in the system's great walls and guide them through, cover their tracks, provide the alibis, mislead the posse—the anxious parents, the truant officers, the supervisors and superintendents and officious super-egos of the social order.

At least between ourselves and the young we might begin talking up the natural rights of truancy and the educative possibilities of hooky—which is after all only matriculating into the school without walls that the world itself has always normally been for the inquisitive young.

And who knows? Once we stop forcing *our* education on the children, perhaps they will invite a lucky few of us to participate in *theirs.*

# WHAT IT'S LIKE

Student alienation is often hard to understand for people not in school. "We made it through, why can't they?" is a common response. It's difficult to remember the boredom, rigidity, and sheer silliness of it all. Today's student, turned on by television and hardened by the Vietnam war, is not about to put up with it.

The best way to understand why students are resisting is to visit a school, attend the classes, walk in the hall, and eat in the cafeteria. This section provides that experience—through two extensive testimonies by individual students, a brilliant student position paper, sharp comments by others from the student press, memoirs of two teachers who stood with the students as long as they could, and reports of three outside observers. Together they convey the sense of what it's like to be in high school today.

# Diary

BY DANIEL HAUBEN

Danny Hauben wrote this remarkable diary of life in a New York City public school during the 1968–69 school year, when he was thirteen years old.

*September 30.*

Homeroom period. Extremely hot and muggy. Nobody talks. Not because they're not supposed to, but because the atmosphere calls for it. Drab. When I turn my head to look out the window, I get a kink in it. I try not to think of having a great time here but just getting it over with. Then I think: there are so many other days to go through. Well, no matter what class I go to now, I won't worry about what happens, but just look forward to the weeks and months ahead.

I find that I am looking at my watch about every five minutes without even realizing it. Schools are run by a time clock, so it makes my life run on a time schedule also. But why should I have to walk through the halls and get into the room in $1\frac{1}{2}$ minutes? Why couldn't it be 2 minutes or $1\frac{3}{4}$ minutes? I saw a school the other day with barbed wire on the top of the fence that surrounded the yard. Say, what are the schools turning into—prison camps?

I'm in the lunchroom now. Today, life is fine. For a day, or a week—but for fifteen years? Sick. Teachers yelling and taking advantage of us, as usual. I still haven't learned anything. We're going to have French this afternoon; it could be very interesting. We'll see! He teaches fairly well. But he says, like the rest of them: Test every day. You always know when you're going to have a test or a quiz. He talks like he knows what he's doing until he gets ready to tell us about a test and then his voice gets unsteady.

*October 3.*

Today, so far so good. Science was especially good. We did experiments to find out what some liquids were. Very enjoyable. In the other classes, little homework. Nothing bad happened.

Gym. Okay by my standards, but I didn't get any stronger or learn anything. We had four minutes of games and the rest of the time sat around in strict silence. The French teacher is hung up on keeping kids in after class. The shop teacher is a great guy. I feel really great in the shop room. He keeps the class in decent order. Today he talked to us for one hour about our futures—I learned a lot and felt great. This man knows what he's talking about. I think he enjoyed it more than we did. He talked a lot, maybe as much as we did. Kids would raise their hands and he'd let them talk for a while but pretty soon he'd cut in and continue himself. For the first time I saw the boys in my class smile.

*October 10.*

The assistant head of the lunchroom says everything is going great. The head of the lunchroom says: I think it's awful. Well, then the assistant says, yes it is awful, and they make us all stand up for five minutes. This week there were about five fist fights among the members of my class. I find the members of my class going through stages: first, they all say and do the same things and then they joke about everything—fighting, laughing and joking around. I wonder what'll come next. My back hurt in the 3rd period today, but when I went to lunch it felt great. Now, in the 5th period, my back hurts again. It must be psychological.

*October 11.*

Four Negro boys were walking up the staircase and so was my class. One Negro boy pressed his hand tightly on Peter's neck. (Peter is the boy who sits next to me.) When he let go, another one did the same thing to him. It wasn't a very pleasant experience. We had our first riot today in the lunchroom. Boy! The 7th grade is really *progressing!*

My math teacher, who said she came from a rough school herself, told us the only way to get the kids in order was by being tougher and louder than them. Now she yells all the time. Is that the way to handle kids? The assistant principal said today, "I am a rough man and a hard man, so you'll be treated roughly, and you'll have to be hard, too!" I really did it in math today. I just made one mistake because I misunderstood a number and she started taking me apart. She accused me of everything she could think of; she said I did everything wrong. This morning seemed like eternity. We were three seconds late because we stopped to talk in the auditorium. Teachers call anything outside school the "Outside World." But why should school be my life and everything else be extra? One of these days I'm not going to do anything and teach some other people that I can be mean too. It might be soon. I still haven't learned anything. When will I? We can't even open our mouths around here. What is this, a Communist country—the kids and teachers can't speak their piece. Can't stand one, single kid in this stupid, idiotic place. If I have to kill myself, I will get out of here.

*October 12.*

The school strike has gone on for a couple of weeks now, and there is no end in sight. Been doing all kinds of things, though not every day. Still, what I am doing, I'm doing on my own free will —and that feels great. Really set up the town. Went to three movies, downtown, to the zoo, miniature golfing, and Central Park. Did some educational things, too: listening to the radio, watching TV. Read the paper many times. I also got a chance to breed Shpritz with Softi. My time has been, all in all, very enjoyable, especially making my own decisions—saying no to some things, not going along with everything. When I think of going back to school I think of shop class, mostly; I really want to go back to that class. If all classes were like shop I would be willing to go to school.

*November 14.*

The strike is still on. Things are pretty good. I've certainly seen my family much more than I ever would have with school on. I visited Jay and spent lots of time with Phyllis. Visited Edward, too. It's very important to spend some time with people who aren't your own age, I think. It's important to see what they do, and how they think, and learn about their problems. When I was at Jay's house, I experienced living and being with people. They shared their lives with me. It was great getting up in the morning knowing I was a part of something, that I had an obligation to help, to change a light bulb, or clean the kitchen. Even though I didn't actually do much there it was the best thing in my life just living in a large house with a swing on the porch and people to talk to, people who think the way I do.

Now when I was with Edward, it was altogether different. It's a whole different environment being in the city. Ed has a lot of odd-ball friends who I got to talking with. And I did some drawing, a really neat one—weird! Evelyn and I went down to Canal Street and saw all the sights. She took me places I'd never seen before—stores that had things millions of years old and cost so little, and stores that only sold plexiglas items, all shapes and colors and sizes. Actually, just being there, in downtown Manhattan, was quite an experience.

I must say, I did so many things since the strike started. Went to three movies, the Planetarium and the Museum of Natural History. Went miniature golfing and to Jay's and Edward's. Went to the Bronx Zoo and the park, to Central Park and the zoo, hiked to Yonkers, visited the Allied Chemical Building on 42nd Street and went to the U.N. I taught classes; learned about the history of education at a class given at Harvard, took an art course at Cooper Union; went to a play and to the Sanctuary at M.I.T. And all this without the help of my fabulous teachers and school.

*November 19.*

School started again. Nothing different. The strike didn't change the ways of the kids or teachers. But I have another hope now—my parents. I talked them into at least thinking about my side and maybe to start contacting people about schools. When you go to school, if you don't have anything to look forward to you're dead.

*November 20.*

I think I lost my social studies book. This is a major crime, but it can happen so easily. Maybe I left it home. Any little thing that happens to you in school that's not right or any mistake you make is like one piece taken out of you by the teacher, and by the end of the year, you're virtually nothing.

*November 21.*

Started the day off great in the first period, art. Teacher gave me an "excellent" for my picture—first one I did. The science teacher has gone as far as *telling* us to write up an idea for her blackboard. The math teacher yells every time she gets a chance; makes you wonder whether she can do anything else. They're not all the same though. You go to another class and the teacher handles the same cases completely differently—no insulting the kids or yelling. Anyway, tomorrow I'll be at Jay's house, so I'll just glide through all my classes until shop and at shop I'll keep thinking about what I'm doing there and walk out of school happy.

*November 24.*

I think teachers shouldn't be able to stop kids in the hall, especially when they don't know them, and yell at them and make them late for class. This morning a teacher in the hall held me and two other kids back to let 200 kids pass by first. I didn't know they could do that and really, I don't see why that particular teacher had the right to hold me back for five minutes and make me late. But if he did have that right, he should at least know me and talk with me instead of yelling.

One kid didn't bring in his article for homework so the teacher didn't let him give his opinions even though he really had a few things to say. Just because it wasn't that article but a radio program he heard it on.

*November 25.*

I held the door for a bunch of people leaving the school, today. The last person had to come all the way down the hall, too. I started talking to her, a Negro girl in the ninth grade. She teased me, said she would tell Kurtz the principal how great I was, how polite I was to hold the door for everyone. It surprised her and she asked me why I did it. What's so surprising? Only in school are people amazed when a person is nice. I think students in my school want to be nice because everyone else is so mean and look for reasons to yell and scream. An old Hauben proverb: The teacher wants to give us the "test" not the "best."

*December 6.*

I'm back from being sick. Nothing happened while I was absent. Teachers don't even notice when you're out. It's as if I'd only been gone one day with a tiny, little cough, except, of course, I now have to do a whole week's worth of homework. Oh well, I still have hope in my parents. We'll see what happens. Some kids were coughing in French class so the teacher (the girls' gym teacher), who said she knew they were faking, kicked them out of the room. After that everyone had to hold their coughs.

*December 8.*

The English teacher asked each kid to give a good title to the paragraph we'd just read, and some of them came back with really great ones. We were having a good time thinking them up until he took all the pleasure out of it by answering it himself. No one had anything more to say.

A kid threw up in my class today. Every year at least one kid throws up. No one ever throws up in camp or any other place I've been to.

Boy, do I feel sick, I failed a test today. I feel as if it made a big dent in my life. My guidance teacher told me, "Now I don't want to make you feel bad, but you'll be dead if you don't get good marks on your tests from now on, and you won't make the EP standards either."

*December 9.*

This morning Mr. Simmons the assistant principal made the crass remark: "You kids could stand through your whole lunch period or eat during the period, it doesn't matter to me." Going over the math homework, the teacher told a kid, "Now I know why you asked me to explain—it was so I wouldn't notice you hadn't done your homework." "But I didn't understand it," the kid still insisted, "that's why I asked."

The first word most teachers write on the board is *Problem,* either Problem #1 or Problem in This or That. Why Problem? Why should it be a problem?

The English teacher had asked us to submit the name of a book we'd like to read for a report but then he turned every one down. Instead, he assigned the boys a book on sports or a biography and the girls *Little Women* or something like it. I did want to read *The Rest of the Robots* by Isaac Isamov.

My social science teacher is absent today; I hope she's sick!

*December 10.*

The boys in my class found a new pastime when the teacher's out: running around the room wrecking everything in sight. The girls watch and make bad comments. Actually, I don't even think they're really enjoying themselves but since it's so easy to do when the teacher isn't there, they just go ahead and do it.

*December 12.*

We had our second raid in the lunchroom today. Boy, these kids sure learn fast!

*December 13.*

I can't take it. (My math teacher in particular.) The word "similarly" was on the board. The teacher pronounced it "simerly" for a kid who had trouble reading it. When he repeated it just as she said it, the class broke up. Seven kids had to write "I am very sorry for disturbing the class." That's not so bad but they had to write the "very" 497 times.

*December 15.*

My math teacher showed a film on the commutative, distributive, and associative properties of multiplication. I'd never seen this before—it was pretty hard to understand—so when the teacher asked a couple of questions on it I tried to fake the answers, and they turned out wrong. Then she said, "Oh, I know you never pay attention—you're always talking! We're having a test next Monday, and I bet you get the worst mark in the class, and I'm not going to be a bit lenient with you!" With her attitude, who could learn anything in her class. In my opinion it would discourage any kid from trying to guess at the answers or even study on his own.

*December 16.*

My marks so far are 76, 73, 70, 70, 85, 84, 97 and 56 (78½ average) which is the worst thing that could happen at the beginning of the year. I've tried to do my best, but I guess it just isn't good enough. The teachers are going to start yelling, "You're such a bad student"—this is one of the reasons I have to get the hell out of here. I certainly won't make the EPs next year. My marks on my *reports* are excellent. Well, my hopes in my mother and father are dim now, but I have new hopes. On Saturday night, my friend David and I talked for four hours about school and we decided to tape the opinions of our whole class about life and experiences in school. Then we're going to mimeograph something like this:

ATTENTION ALL STUDENTS:
For those of you who disagree with certain things that go on in school and would like to do something about it, please come to a meeting which will be held by two of your fellow students. The meeting will be held—

Place:

Time:

Day:

The main topics we would like to look into, and bring up with our teachers or with the P.T.A., are the following:

1. the line in the middle of the hall
2. more shop periods
3. talking in homeroom
4. eating outside school
5. LESS tests, *more* learning

This meeting may lead to many others of its kind with topics such as an optional ninth period, less reports, etc.

*December 17.*

Mr. Morris said in the auditorium, "When you children talk, you are acting babyish and childish." Does that mean that adults don't talk? On the last math test the average grade was 62%—passing was 85% but the teacher changed it to 70%. The highest mark was 92% and the lowest 14%. I got 56%. Mrs. Kent, the math teacher, yelled when she saw books in the aisle. "Now I know you kids want to kill me." She began to scream her head off. It's funny how teachers handle things differently, because in social studies a kid left his stuff in the way and the teacher didn't yell at all. My math teacher acts like there is no other way but to yell at a kid and keep him in after school. Another teacher might just overlook the whole incident, or if not, he'd tell the kid what was wrong and how to fix it.

*December 21.*

Today was okay. The English teacher spent two years in Africa and showed us the slides he took. How different he seems now. I really saw a new person in that room. For a Christmas present the math teacher let us finish our test at home. That shows that in her own way she's giving in to us, and we haven't even realized it. My social studies teacher was absent—that was a pleasure. My guidance teacher was also absent. French went great; I like the teacher more and more every lesson. Science test, *probably failed.* My art teacher made me go on an errand because I finished all my work in class. I had to wrap a huge package in the girls' shop class. Meanwhile I overheard the teacher telling the girls how to make fried coconuts————. Blech!

*December 22.*

Today half the school was absent because of Christmas—it was optional to go. I came but spent three periods in Vivian's classroom putting up bulletin boards and things. I am now in social studies. The teacher wouldn't call on me when I knew the answers—I raised my hand for every question except one or two. She got me for the one I didn't know—just the time I didn't raise my hand. Now, for that one answer I didn't know, I'll get a bad mark.

When we walked into math class everyone said the room was cold but the teacher yelled, "It's not cold in here." How could she force it into us that it wasn't cold. It was freezing!

*January 3.*

My French teacher yelled at a boy today but he just sat there, not listening, not paying attention.

*January 7.*

Assembly. Kids gave their speeches for G. O. offices. Everyone promised the same things. They all said they would start by letting the girls wear slacks, and then they said they would change the lunchroom around and have meetings between teachers and students. They promised to do everything they could to improve the school but they didn't say what.

*MRS. KENT IS ABSENT!* That's my math teacher. She's had the fantastic record of never being absent in ten years. I guess we made her sick. Everyone's dancing around. The substitute is yelling, but what can you expect us to do when the most idiotic teacher in the world is absent for the first time.

Our science teacher said she would give us a test on atoms next Monday. We haven't talked much about atoms so we asked her what the test was going to be on. What we learn this week, she said. I think that's going a little too far—assigning a test even before we do the work.

*January 9.*

Today my English teacher said he was going to disregard school rules and make us stay in after 3:20 if we get to the classroom earlier than three minutes before the late bell rings. My class is always in before the late bell but now that my stupid English teacher made up this rule we are almost always going to be late! That's a narrow margin, three minutes. The teacher went on to say, "I don't like it any more than anyone of you do. But do it." That's what they all say! But if he doesn't like it, we don't like it, and the school has other rules, why should he give it to us? No other teacher does it.

*January 14.*

The hall was very crowded so a kid accidentally bumped a teacher and said, "Excuse me." Well, the teacher pushed him against the wall pretty hard and *he* said, "Excuse me." When the boy asked, "What?" the teacher yelled, "What did you bump into me for?" and pushed the kid out of the way.

*January 15.*

In social studies I raised my hand at least thirty times, and finally, when I didn't know the answer she called on me and made a fool out of me. She turned to the class and said, "What are we going to do with this kind of kid?"

Some girl stuck my boyfriend, Stacy, in the ass with a pin! He was bleeding, but he didn't want to show anybody. He told the teacher, but she wouldn't let him leave because he wouldn't show her.

*January 22.*

Today eight kids in my math class were absent. Mrs. Kent, the teacher, was still out. Yesterday, Mr. Cossa, my English teacher, was absent, and the day before my art teacher, Miss Roseman, was absent. Boy, everyone must love school. Nothing spectacular happened this week. I got a 92 on my English test. My overall average is 83%. Everyone acts as if his life depended on the mark he'll be getting on his report card next week. School is such a big part of everyone's life that every little thing that happens there is a big deal. It's hard to keep in mind that actually it doesn't mean much at all.

*January 24.*

All my teachers were absent today. We didn't do anything all week. If I'd stayed home I could have done twice as much and learned a lot more. But what can I do?

Two nights ago was Parents'-Teachers' Night. All my teachers said exactly the same thing—I was a bit quiet when the term began but I've adjusted very well. I think the teachers tell the same thing to every mother—one thing if their kid's been good and another if their kid's been bad.

*February 3.*

Mr. Lax is our so-called "permanent" English teacher. He is the fifteenth English teacher we've had this term. Frankly, I can't tell him apart from the other fourteen. After all, how's he different? So what makes a teacher? Someone who has gone to college and wants to get money. But they never know when they're hurting the kids—and they usually are. Last Friday, Mrs. Kent, my fabulous math teacher, told us very solemnly that it was her last day—Monday she was starting her sabbatical so she wouldn't be finishing out the school year with us. Well, today is Monday, and next period we have math.

For the first twenty minutes, Miss Caruso, our new math teacher, told us how strict she would be and she reeled off all the classroom rules and regulations she expected us to follow. She told us we'd have a test every week and homework every night. All this and other uninteresting babble scared the life out of the kids in my class. I didn't think it was possible, but this teacher is worse than Kent!!!!!

*February 4.*

Today the principal got rid of the late bell and the first buzzer for changing classes. In French class, we discussed songs and other things from France. It was great.

*February 7.*

Mr. Shen, our wood shop teacher, took a six-months leave of absence. He was one of the few halfway decent teachers we've had. Now we have a lady leathercrafts teacher and no shop room to work in, and besides, she is an old louse.

*February 14.*

Every Friday we have French 9th period with the girls' gym teacher, 900-year-old Mrs. Herman. Today we went over questions in first-aid. One was: if someone's arm is bleeding and the bone is sticking through the skin, what should you do.

*February 18.*

In English the teacher read my composition on how I think the class should behave. (Of course in this composition I said exactly what I thought.) He asked me to explain, so I said that when a kid comes into a classroom, he should know when he can talk and when he can't. This should be agreed on beforehand with the teacher. Students should be able to talk with each other whenever the teacher isn't actually teaching the class. After the class was over, Mr. Lax (who happens to look and act like my brother Larry) said he fully agreed with me. He also said that he believed that kids should have some freedom in school. That made me feel pretty good. He's okay. Mr. Lax does have a few bad points, too. For instance, he's got a list of the ten best kids in the class. Only ten, everyone else is left out.

*February 20.*

Yesterday I was absent because I was exhausted and had a slight cold. I accomplished building a pool-club area that is really beautiful and fits in every town. My town, I have not stated before, is for "wishniks." It has houses, streets, stores, cars, furniture —and everyone's got a real personality: a name, a job, and a house. Yesterday, when I called my friend to get the homework, he said nothing was done in class, lucky for me I didn't go. Today, nothing special happened either; we went to the library from English class.

I'm still very tired and can't absorb much of what's happening. It's the 5th period. I've gone to social science, science, English, lunch and art, and just think, yesterday at this time I was still sleeping. It is *12:15*.

*February 27.*

Our social studies teacher, Mrs. Kranin, said that what any student has to say privately to his friend is worth absolutely zero. She went on to say that when a kid is reciting, what he's saying is much more important than anything any one kid could possibly be saying to his or her friend.

*March 17.*

It's Monday afternoon, my uncle died last week. My whole family was in town for the funeral. I went to Boston yesterday and got back last night. When I came to school this morning I felt very depressed. After a few periods of classes I couldn't seem to think about school but yet I couldn't think about anything else either.

*March 18.*

I have just realized that the teachers disturb the class much more than they say the children do. A couple of words between students might bring about fifteen minutes of yelling from the teacher. I think if I could point this out to the teachers it might help to eliminate punishment for talking in class. In the social studies class, a girl dropped her book, and the teacher said to her, "It's not going to help you one bit to slam things around."

*March 20.*

Yesterday and today in social studies, the teacher, Mrs. Kranin, said we would have less than a week to do a report. Our class didn't like that idea at all so we decided to do everything she doesn't like. We crumpled paper and snapped open and close our loose-leaf binders. She is going crazy. So far not one kid raised his hand to answer a question and she doesn't know what to do! It is really great—getting the best of the teacher!

*March 21.*

Today, my math teacher, Mrs. Caruso, said that in June she would give each child a turn at being the teacher. This sounded like a fairly good idea, but then she said she'd tell us just what to do and say, and that we would have to test on it the next day.

*March 25.*

Today we had reading tests (city-wide) and this afternoon we are having a G. O. movie. The movie we picked was called too "mature" for us so instead we got a lousy movie called *A Man Called Adam.* This movie really stinks—and we can't eat, talk, move, or leave. If you talk, the teacher pulls you out of your seat and threatens you with no more films (which is okay with me) or he pulls you out of the auditorium so you miss the rest of the movie. If you're stuck and just have to sit and watch the movie, you can't do a thing because there's at least one or two teachers staring at you the whole time.

*March 26.*

Today we had three teachers absent. It was good and it was bad. Everyone yelled, screamed, etc. I really don't think they enjoyed it but they did it just to get back at all the times they couldn't do it.

*March 31.*

It is *Easter vacation.* I had a party on Saturday night and asked five girls and four boys from my class. They turned out to be completely different from what I had expected. It drew us together a lot. We all felt much closer.

*April 6.*

There was another party, a birthday party, last Saturday night. It was alright, and at least it was a first step to getting people together.

*April 7.*

The kids were talking during lunch, so Mr. Simmons, the seventh grade principal, said he wouldn't let us go outside after. That wasn't too bad, but then he had some kids close all the windows, and we sure were uncomfortable. It's like if we talk we are tortured until we don't talk anymore.

*April 22.*

We got two new rules from Mr. Simmons in assembly today. (1) We have to stand and say "Good morning, Mr. Simmons" after he says good morning to us. (2) While we are in the auditorium, we have to sit with our hands held quietly in our laps. This is idiotic! Little babies do that sort of thing.

We were walking into English class and this Negro kid called Mr. Lax a fucken white faggit! Well, Mr. Lax got up, took the kid by the neck and dragged him down the hall to the dean's office. When he came back, he thanked us for being quiet while he was out of the room. Then he told us everything that happened.

*April 23.*

Today we go back to our regular schedule: eight periods instead of nine. We had nine because of the school strike. I'm quite happy about this, but it's really not enough of a change. They should do more than just cutting off 40 minutes a day; they should do something about changing school itself.

Just to prove how rigid they are in this school: instead of eliminating a period because the teachers had to do an hour of clerical work this morning, they made the morning periods seven minutes each and we learned absolutely nothing! But it was fun anyhow.

*April 21.*

Mr. Lax, our English teacher, has been a good guy. He told us to bring in a written question—something that has been troubling us. Today he answered them and we got into good discussions.

Last period: math. We never have any discussions. With Miss Caruso, our beloved teacher, it's all just work—no special things on discussions, just plain ordinary math.

In guidance, Mr. Cassidy made the statement, "Teachers are human." I don't know if I can believe that! Almost everyone at that moment thought long about that statement and came to the same conclusion as I did.

*April 24.*

We just finished a science test. It just seems natural to cheat on something like this. I checked every answer with Mickey who sits next to me. I also had a couple of answers hidden in my desk, so how could I lose? Well, we'll see what mark I get. Now that I think of it, you have to be smarter to cheat in these ingenious ways than to take the test in the first place.

*April 25.*

I just asked four girls in my class if they wanted to go to the beach next month for my birthday. They all seemed shy and said they would have to ask their parents. In school I—and everyone else—find it very hard to communicate with girls, and vice versa. In another kind of situation where everyone is mutually involved, I'm sure everyone would quite naturally get to know and talk to everyone else. I just hope they will agree to go with me.

*April 29.*

We put on our French play for the seventh grade this morning. I had to learn three French songs which I didn't really like or even get to know too well. Once my brother and I learned some French songs. It wasn't in such a rush either. Actually, I know four now, and I do like to sing them. But these songs, I'm sick of hearing them because we practiced them every day and heard them over and over. Maybe we learned them quicker but it would be better if we enjoyed them, too.

*May 2.*

Today is ninth grade field day and our art and homeroom teachers are going to Bear Mountain. In homeroom we have our old Sherman tank, Mrs. Straus (the one who pushes kids over in the hall). Everyone knows her reputation for killing kids so they are quiet. Mr. Isaacson (French) is giving us a party for our good work on our play. Yesterday when we gave the play for the sixth grade we presented him with a tie and tie tack.

*May 8.*

Everyone in the class was talking, so the English teacher, Mr. Lax, ran out of the room—like a child—and didn't come back. After he left, my class, on its own, went on with the lesson. Actually it was even better than with the teacher but I don't know if the kids realized it. Nobody talked, we just went through the whole lesson. When Mr. Lax finally came back, he said he wouldn't talk to us and just sat at his desk. We all continued to do our own things, no one said a word. It was a good experience but I don't think it will help in the future because it doesn't seem important enough to the other kids. What I'm trying to say is that we found we had the ability to work on our own very well. But when not given that opportunity, we would just do whatever the teacher wants—merely be obedient.

*May 13.*

My mother left early this morning and woke me up as she was leaving. I set the alarm to ring in ten minutes but didn't get up until 9:30. So home I am. I remember when I used to stay home from school when I had a cold or something and I used to pretend I was getting the best part of the teachers—either by yelling at them or killing them or rebelling against them or something like that. I still think about doing that now but I think I am at the age now where I might be able to do these things for real. My brother's friend told me once he had this real nag for a teacher and one day he got so sick of her he just got up and told her off in front of the class. When I heard this story I really got inspired and I began to think about all the times I would have liked to do the same thing. Maybe some day I will.

About four weeks ago I stayed home because I had a cold and when I came back Mrs. Kranin (social studies teacher) said to me, "Daniel, you're absent so often, you better stop fooling around and get to work." From then on every time I see her I feel guilty. Today is a social studies test. I wonder what she will say to me when I get back tomorrow.

*May 26.*

On May 22, I went to have my Bar Mitzvah thing in a synagogue in my old neighborhood. I stayed home that day and did various things, including collecting money, etc. The next day was my birthday; it was a Jewish holiday, too, so I stayed home again. All my friends and relatives were at the house! Everything was hectic, but I was managing. Well, then my friend from school called and told me that Mrs. Kranin said I was doing lousy because I was absent so much and I could never make the work up. Then I started to worry. I shouldn't have because school marks are silly and unimportant. They are just an extra burden, and especially so when I am busy with my life which is hard enough.

On May 24, I had a beach party and asked the kids in my class, my friends, and some other people. I got to know everyone from my class so much better—I found out what they think about and like to do. It's funny—I'd been going to school with them for a full year yet hardly knew them at all.

Now I'm back in school after being home for four fabulous days. Yech!!

After school today my friends and I went to the park and waved to cars and gave them peace symbols. It was great; everyone waved back and honked their horns and blinked their lights. We also gave peace symbols to the Army convoy and they cursed us out and some gave us peace symbols back.

*June 16.*

There are 8½ more days of school. Things have eased off for the past few weeks. My brother Edward graduated from his fifth year of architecture at Cooper Union three weeks ago. I had my

Bar Mitzvah party for my aunts and uncles in Central Park three weeks ago.

This year for me has been very active, much has happened to change my life. A lot of important things went on. School confused me more than usual and added extra unnecessary burdens. Well, once school closes, I'll get a rest from its idiocies for the summer and then start the same old thing all over again next year. The thought makes me sick.

*June 17.*

*Last day.* Today we have only three periods, we'll just be cleaning all the rooms. Yesterday all our teachers who screamed at us all year said we'd been lovely students—we'd brightened up their lives. What bull! They hate us, just as we hate them, but now that school's over they're so happy they don't care what they're saying. They say things they don't really mean.

SCHOOL'S OVER!!!!!

# Wanted: A Humane Education

## BY THE MONTGOMERY COUNTY STUDENT ALLIANCE

The Student Alliance Report, *Wanted: A Humane Education*, was prepared by a group of students in Montgomery County, Maryland in the spring of 1969 and has become a key document in the movement for high-school reform. It is the best brief available on the deleterious effects of secondary schooling on its supposed beneficiaries.

FROM WHAT we know to be true as full-time students and researchers of the county school system (as well as from every attempt we know of to survey student attitudes in the county), it is quite safe to say that the public schools have critically negative and absolutely destructive effects on human beings and their curiosity, natural desire to learn, confidence, individuality, creativity, freedom of thought and self-respect.

More specifically, the county public schools have the following effects which are absolutely fundamental and crucial:

1. Fear—The school system is based upon fear. Students are taught from the outset that they should be afraid of having certain things happen to them: bad grades, punishment from authorities, humiliation, ostracism, "failure," antagonizing teachers and administrators are all things that terrify students as they enter first grade. These fears, which school officials use as a lever from elementary school through high school to establish and maintain order and obedience, have horribly destructive effects: they may be reflected in extreme nervousness, terror, paranoia, resentment, withdrawal, alienation; they may be visible, they may be sub-

merged, but in either case these effects should be of utmost concern to those who value the human mind and spirit.

2. Dishonesty—Schools compel students to be dishonest. In order to be "successful" (the school system loses no time in providing the definition), students must learn to suppress and deny feelings, emotions, thoughts that they get the idea will not be acceptable. In the place of these honest feelings, emotions and thoughts, students are taught that to "succeed" other exteriors—dishonest though they may be—have to be substituted. The clearly defined rewards and punishments of the school system have an instructional effect on an impressionable child, and the message is clear throughout elementary school, junior high school and senior high school: "unacceptable" honesty will be punished, whether with grades, disciplinary action or a bad "permanent record"; "acceptable" responses, however dishonest, are—in the eyes of the school system and therefore according to the values it instills—simply that: "acceptable."

3. Approach to problems—It is soon clear to students what types of responses are likely to be successful at playing the school game. And so, before too long a student's approach to questions and problems undergoes a basic change. It becomes quickly clear that approaching a question on a test by saying "What is my own response to this question?" is risky indeed, and totally unwise if one covets the highest grade possible (and the school system teaches the student that he should). Rather, the real question is clear to any student who knows anything about how schools work: "What is the answer the teacher wants me to give? What can I write that will please the teacher?"

4. Destruction of eagerness to learn—The school system takes young people who are interested in the things around them and destroys this natural joy in discovering and learning. Genuine, honest reasons for wanting to learn are quashed and replaced with an immediate set of rewards (which educators say are not ends in themselves but which nevertheless become just that). Real reasons for wanting to learn—the students' own reasons—are not

treated as though they were valid. As George Leonard points out in his book *Education and Ecstasy*, and as everyone who has gone through the public school system knows, our school systems smash the natural joy in learning and make what we know as an "education" into a painful, degrading experience.

5. Alienation—With its dishonesty and premium on dutiful obedience, the school system causes feelings of resentment and alienation, whether these feelings are expressed or (as is usually the case) hidden and submerged.

6. Premium on conformity, blind obedience to authority—The school system's values and priorities *as they are practiced* ultimately become those of its students. Students—keenly aware of the rewards and punishments that can affect them—are made aware of what the school system wants most from its students on an operational, day-by-day basis. The fact that the county school system as it presently operates puts a very large premium on conformity and "knee-jerk" obedience is, we feel, indisputable; students simply know this to be true as a fact of school survival life.

7. Stifling self-expression, honest reaction—The fact that students who "step out of line" are likely to be punished for it is not lost on students, and this provides students with a basic object lesson on how to "succeed" in the public school. Once again, this overpowering sense of rewards and punishments, which has been artificially created by the school system, has a very negative effect on the development of students.

8. Narrowing scope of ideas—The range of ideas students are exposed to by the school system is pitifully narrow, especially in the earlier grades; through use of textbooks which give only limited perspective, and through use of curriculum and teacher attitudes that are confining, students' minds are conditioned to accept what they are familiar with and reject what seems foreign.

9. Prejudice—By insisting that the schools remain pretty much isolated from ideas and cultures that do not blend in with those of the immediate community, school officials have the effect of solidifying and perpetuating local prejudices. Only with the

free exchange of ideas and life-styles can students gain a broad outlook.

10. Self-hate—Perhaps most tragic is what the school system does to the emotional and mental attitudes and subconscious of its students. The system, for instance, is willing to and does label students as "failures" at age eight, twelve or seventeen. In addition to the fact that this often acts as a self-fulfilling prophecy, this has a cruelly damaging and degrading effect on students, and is inexcusable. Further, tension has been shown to be an integral part of the school experience, with very damaging effects. The self-hate which results can be directed inward or at others, but whatever the case it is extremely unhealthy; a community which says it cares about human emotions and feelings should not permit this to go on.

The extent to which school officials appear unaware or unconcerned about how students feel and the effects of the schools is frightening and disturbing. Top county school administrators' discussion of the need for relevance, sensitivity of human needs and feelings, student rights and freedom of expression and exchange of ideas seems to have little connection with the policies and priorities the administrators and teachers at the individual schools are pursuing. As for many principals and teachers, they quite often are just not concerned; their concept of the school system is that its job is to mold the behavior and attitudes of its students, and those students who balk at being molded are viewed as undisciplined annoyances, to be dealt with accordingly. The feedback in the form of grades, scores and college admissions is apparently considered adequate to prove the merit of the system; all else, it seems, must take a back seat.

The Student Alliance plans to collect feedback in these neglected but crucial human areas. It is inexcusable that the Montgomery County School System has not made a real effort to seek this kind of feedback and enter it into the policy and organizational decision-making.

Perhaps most frustrating is the fact that leading Montgomery

County school officials have criticized the schools and their inability and/or unwillingness to view and treat students as individual human beings.

The grading system is a good example and extremely vital. Dr. James C. Craig, Assistant Superintendent for Instructional and Pupil Services, told a MCPS seminar on human relations in August, 1968: "Any school system which participates in or suffers to continue a system of grading which by its very nature is demeaning of the human spirit is cruel, inhumane—which approves and accepts the bright—which disapproves of and rejects those not so bright—such a school system is not worthy to be entrusted with any concerns involving differences among human beings. . . ." Yet no one has been willing to make the basic changes that would be necessary to stop this "demeaning, cruel, inhumane" system from continuing to take its toll on the minds and spirits of 120,000 Montgomery County public school students.

What it appears to come down to is a lack of a sense of urgency about these kinds of issues. If a school's heating system is found not to be working, it is quickly repaired. But say that the schools are destroying the minds and morale of its students and administrators—perhaps even agreeing theoretically—will give you a dozen reasons why corrective action cannot be taken.

If the county school system really believes what it says about its goals, then it must devote itself to bringing the actual situation in line with these aims. If the goal of allowing students to develop as free-thinking individuals is really basic to a desirable educational setup, then it is not enough to merely say, "It would be nice . . ." If only we could give the same priority to making the schools humane and relevant that we now give to keeping computerized attendance cross-check cards and catching and punishing students who skip classes.

It is important to realize what effect all this has had on students and what their resulting responses have been.

Just about every student in Montgomery County feels the oppressiveness of the school system. Their responses, however, differ widely.

Only a fraction of the students are oriented to organizing groups, developing analyses and recommendations and approaching school officials.

Some students drop out—for varying reasons, but increasingly because school is not relevant to what they are interested in doing. (A number of county high school students have dropped out of public school to attend a "New Educational Project" founded by unhappy students from Montgomery County along with several college graduates, including an Antioch intern who taught history at Montgomery Blair for the 1967–68 school year. Other students attend the school on a part-time basis.)

Other students cut classes or skip school entirely on a consistent basis—not an intellectualized reaction, but merely an immediate, logical response: despite the attempt at "sledgehammer" motivation through grades and threats of punishment, what is going on in the classrooms is simply not worth getting involved with. These students, thousands of them, are punished; they are providing feedback that the school system does not care for.

Even for students who are not able to maintain passing grades (or who are not interested in doing so)—and "fail" or even "flunk out," it is apparent that the schools are failing by being unable to meet a wide range of needs.

But for most students, the sad result is that they take it, in fact they learn to adapt to the system and do the best they can "to succeed"—they accept (though many of them will tell you they do so reluctantly) the idea of working for the goals that have been dreamed up for them by the school system—and they learn the most successful way to play the game. The goals—high test scores, high grades—have taken on an enormous importance. And, inevitably, in pursuing these goals, students learn the usefulness—indeed the necessity—of dishonesty, conformity and yesmanship.

But the system's impersonal and authoritarian way of dealing with these students has taken its toll; submerged though the effects may be, the system has caused resentment, lack of self-respect and self-confidence, extreme nervousness, and/or behavior to compensate for such serious anxieties.

It is becoming almost a cliché to say that the public schools are not relevant, yet very little positive action has been taken to do anything about it. Every student has things that interest him; but the sad fact is that the school system very rarely gives him an opportunity to explore these interests. In many cases the student is actually hindered by the pressures and restrictions of the school system. There is no provision for giving students the chance to explore different areas of interest and follow wherever this exploration may lead them.

Knowledge is very much interrelated—math, science, history, literature and psychology, for instance, all have a great deal to do with one another, and the ways in which they have interacted have been fundamental to the development of man. Yet the school system insists on compartmentalizing these topics and creates artificial boundaries around each area. This makes learning seem narrow and confining; there is no need for it to be anything of the kind.

By the time a student reaches high school, attending school often seems to be a dull, boring and irrational experience that is viewed as something that simply has to be tolerated. This state of affairs should not exist.

Very importantly, the individual student himself, what he feels, his concerns, are ignored. How does he fit into all this? What is important to him? What does this mean to him and his life? These questions do not fit into the school system's equation. Assisted by experience and efficiency, the county public school's operational equation seems simple; raw material (students) plus conditioning (classes, teachers, textbooks, discipline) equals products (graduates equipped to fill the necessary slots in society). The complexities of the individual, developing mind are passed over; the system is "successful," and, we are told, is among the best in the nation.

Instead of the system's being built around the needs of the students, the students are being built around the needs of the system.

## WHAT NEEDS TO BE DONE

1. Establishment of an ombudsman office, responsible directly to the Board of Education, to investigate and resolve complaints from students.

If the goals and realities of the school system are ever to be brought into line with one another, it is essential that a procedure be developed to deal with instances of questionable treatment of students. Every student in county schools should be informed of the existence and purpose of the ombudsman office, and they should be made to feel free to make use of it without any fear of retaliation. It is important that the ombudsman office not be in the position of having to be defensive about the actions of school administrators and teachers. Ombudsman officials, independent of any such pressures or biases, must take a stance of neutrality and work vigorously to correct the thousands of injustices which occur every year to students who presently have no way of seeking redress.

2. The school system must put an end to intimidation of students through abuse of college recommendations, grades, secret files and "permanent record files" by school officials.

These incidents are often hard to pin down, but students are definitely being blackmailed and intimidated—with varying degrees of subtlety—through use of these documents. Students must be given access to their own files and must have control over who can and cannot see them. The Board of Education should issue a firm memo to all teachers, administrators and counselors in the county schools emphasizing the Board's disapproval of intimidation and anything short of straightforward dealings with students in these areas. In addition, the ombudsman office for students should work to uncover and eliminate misuse of these files and documents.

3. Students must have an important role in the shaping and implementation of courses. They are also in an excellent position to provide meaningful feedback by providing continuous evaluation of the effectiveness, strengths and weaknesses of their classes.

The school system has "proclaimed" many policies and has made them stick. Teachers should be told that it is essential to have students discuss how courses and classes should be designed and operated. This continual re-evaluation will see to it that classes and courses of study are constantly improved and updated. County school officials determining courses of study must be willing to permit much more flexibility and originality than is presently allowed. Departmental faculty meetings, it should be made clear, are open to participation and input from students. On the individual class level, the successes and failures of the class can be continually evaluated by students and teachers working together and planning together.

4. Student input in teacher evaluations.

Being a good teacher involves many characteristics beyond the ability to keep accurate records, complete forms neatly, "control classes" and receive degrees from graduate school. Whether a teacher is stimulating, creates enthusiasm, is responsive to individual needs and problems of his students, can relate to students (and vice versa) and treats students with respect for their human dignity is all extremely important. Students are in the best position to provide very valuable information in these areas, and it would seem logical to construct a regular system for obtaining such feedback from students.

5. Tension and rigidity must be eliminated from the schools. Administrators must be made to stop constantly threatening students with arbitrary, almost whimsical disciplinary actions.

This implies a change in attitude; an elimination of the approach which says that to have students expressing themselves, verbally and through interaction, can pose a threat to the "authority" and "order" of the school system. Students are being pressured, threatened and suspended for skipping classes, being in the halls without passes or even possession and/or distribution of literature. A system which has an elaborate policing-system network for keeping students out of the halls and for catching students who chose not to attend classes is perpetuating tension which is absolutely unnecessary, damaging to morale and totally out of place in an institution which says it seeks to encourage learning and exploration.

6. Hiring of educators and researchers to deeply examine what effect the school system has on a student's self-concept, creativity, and desire to explore and learn.

Much of the evidence and research in this area, we feel, has already been developed (and is presently being ignored—no doubt because the findings are so very unpleasant). James Coleman's *Equality of Educational Opportunity* shows that self-concept and sense of control over one's own destiny is much more significant in the development of a child than the many other factors school administrators spend all their time worrying about. The forces which presently destroy a student's self-concept and feeling of control over his own fate must be eliminated immediately. We feel it is clear that this is going to have to mean elimination of the disciplinary threats and punishments prevailing throughout the school system, of the clockworklike class schedules and tension created by school administrators and teachers who have been encouraged to emphasize and flaunt their authority.

7. Elimination of letter grades.

This is extremely important. The use of letter grades as the basis upon which the school system is operated sets the tone and patterns of the public school experience. Its destructive effects have already been noted.

In elementary and junior high schools, grades should be abolished immediately and replaced with written evaluations by the teacher. In high school, students should simply receive credit or not receive credit for each course they have taken. In order for the students to get feedback as to how they are progressing, teachers should provide students with written and/or oral evaluations as often as necessary. Students should receive a copy of all written evaluations; a copy should be entered in students' files, but should not be released to colleges without student-parent consent.

Transition may seem rather difficult at first. But the benefits will be both immediate and increasingly apparent as students make the adjustment and begin to shake off the bad attitudes and effects of the old system. The natural joy in learning will re-emerge, and hopefully for those starting out in the system it would never be squashed in the first place.

If a complete change is made for all the schools in the county, colleges will have no choice but to consider each applicant from the county on his individual merits; they would be forced to do without grades and class rank in evaluating applicants (there are many other methods of evaluation), especially in view of the reputation Montgomery County enjoys nationally as a school system of unquestionable academic quality.

There are ways if there is the will.

8. Teachers must be encouraged and allowed to respond to the individual needs of their students. This will have to mean fewer regulatory restrictions, more flexibility.

9. Students must be given the ability to exercise control over what happens to them in school. Specifics: The right to transfer out of a course that is not satisfactory; the right to go on independent study at any time; the right to formulate their own goals and how they can best go about achieving them.

10. Rigid periods now being used in county secondary schools must be replaced with shorter and flexible modules.

Kennedy High School's use of modules—short blocks of time —make the school more flexible and open to different kinds of activities. There are now no provisions for spontaneous activities;

in fact, they are absolutely prohibited. Periods which last 50 minutes or an hour are confining and should be eliminated.

11. Students must have a right to print and distribute their own publications, and restrictions should not be set up to impose obstacles—as has been the case—but rather to provide students with an orderly means of distribution, such as tables in the halls, near doors or in the cafeteria. These requirements should apply equally to all student publications. (The fact that money is involved has been used as an argument against allowing "underground" or unsanctioned papers, but money is always also involved with sanctioned, official student newspapers.)

12. Students have the right to have the freedom to decide what they want to print in student newspapers, literary magazines and yearbooks. Censorship by sponsors or principals, whatever the degree of subtlety, must not be allowed.

13. Outside speakers must be given a chance to speak to students without favoritism or discrimination.

Military recruiters, for example, address assemblies at each county high school every year, but the same right has been refused to groups presenting different or opposing viewpoints. Students must make the decisions to invite speakers and arrange assemblies.

14. The providing of the names and addresses of senior boys to the armed forces must be ended.

The county school system makes a point of its desire to protect students from businesses who get hold of mailing lists of students, yet it provides the names and addresses of senior boys in county high schools to the military. Peace and pacifist groups have been refused the same privilege. The lists should either be available to groups which disagree with the military or should not be released at all.

15. Relevant courses must be developed to meet student interests.

Students should be surveyed as to what courses they would like to see offered and the results should play a determining role in the direction of course offerings. Racism, urban life, suburban life, drugs, human relations, foreign policy, police-youth relations and civil liberties are a few topics in great need of curriculum development.

16. Students should be free to arrange voluntary seminars to be held during the school day.

If schools are really to become relevant, students must be allowed—indeed encouraged—to set up discussions, hold workshops and seminars, hear speakers who are well informed about the subjects that interest students. The students should be free to invite speakers and outside authorities to come in and give their views, without the obstacles which presently exist. Schools must come alive. The concept behind the "Experiment in Free Form Education" being tried at Whitman for one week must be integrated into the everyday functioning of the schools. With school becoming much more individualized, students should be given the flexibility of attending seminars of interest during the school day.

17. Expansion of the range of resources.

Diversified paperback books giving different perspectives should play an important part in widening the scope of thought and exposure in the schools. Textbooks alone are just too limited in coverage and perspective.

18. Informing students of their rights.

The school system should take the responsibility of informing each student of his rights in dealing with administrators and teachers. If the School Board agrees that students do have rights, then it must be willing to make these rights directly known to each student.

19. Restrictions having to do with student dress must be eliminated throughout the county.

20. County seminars in human relations, racism and progressive teaching methods should be held for teachers.

An excellent week of seminars was held by the Montgomery County public schools last August for about 100 county administrators. It would be very good if the same sort of program could be set up for the county's teachers.

21. Material thoroughly exploring Negro history must be integrated into classes such as U.S. History and Problems of the 20th Century. Special training should be provided to teachers in order to make them qualified to deal with this very important aspect of American history and society.

22. The School Board should launch an investigation of illegal searches of lockers in secondary schools for drugs and the recruiting by school officials of students to become narcotics informers.

School officials have been known to actively seek and encourage students to become drug informers. The unhealthy atmosphere which such a situation creates should be a matter of concern. We feel the School Board would agree that it is not a desirable situation to have students promoted to act as spies on other students in school. Such activities have no place in an institution of learning.

23. School Board hearings for students.

It is important that school officials come into contact with the concerns of students. The Board could schedule hearings every two weeks at which time students would be invited to testify and voice complaints and suggestions.

24. Student voice on School Board.

The School Board would do well to include representation of students. Every semester the School Board could supervise the election of student representatives from among county high school students, printing a special bulletin for each high school student which would give the positions of each of the students who had volunteered to run for the positions.

# Andover: Even the Best Are Bad

BY THOMAS DOLAND

Thomas Doland (a pseudonym) was sixteen years old when he described his experiences at Andover.

I'M SIXTEEN years old. Most of my life I've lived in an apartment building in a good section of Philadelphia. My family is upper middle class. My father is an executive officer of a company, and he went to an Ivy League college and an Ivy League law school. My first eight years of school were spent in one of the richest and most exclusive private boys' schools in Philadelphia. I was overprotected there for eight years, so I had no fears about being kicked out for anything I did. My relationship with my teachers and deans was one in which I was their friend rather than merely their pupil. Thus from an early age I was allowed to voice my political feelings in the class, regardless of how immature they were, without being seriously reprimanded. I was put in the corner or maybe sent down for a nice little chat with the headmaster. But the school protected its own; and because it was a school of affluent children, it didn't want to get them into any trouble. And it wanted to preserve its image as a school that could get you into the boarding school of your choice when you graduated from eighth grade.

I went to Andover in ninth grade, or what they call there the junior year. My whole family comes from Andover and when it came time to choose a school, it was really between going to Andover and staying at home. I was attracted by the mystery of

122

Andover. I knew what it was like to go to a day school, but I didn't know what it was like living at boarding school.

Andover is a large, probably the largest, prep school in New England. It has 850 students and a large faculty of over 120. It differs from schools like Groton and St. Marks in that it accepts a large number of students from underdeveloped areas all over the world. Nevertheless it does maintain a very high tradition and a set of values which it tries to impose on all of its students. Andover's history goes back as far as 1778, from the early days of the Boston aristocracy. The Adams family, the Holmes', and George Washington all had connections with Andover, as have countless diplomats, generals, and financiers. The school still considers itself to be a training ground for America's leaders. An "Andover man" is expected to continue his education at one of the Ivy League or military schools, and eventually to carry another Andover banner into the respectable fields of law, business, or government. Returning to the school to prepare the next generation of Andover men is also acceptable of course; but it has generally been said, and I think quite truthfully, that Andover considers itself residence before Yale before Wall Street. The school's admissions policies are liberal—in that 40 percent of the students are on scholarship—but the educational policy (what Andover seeks to do with the Harlem, Park Avenue, and West Virginia students) is quite conservative. Andover tries to mold a diverse student body into its own image.

The first or second day I got there we had an assembly for all new boys to explain the extracurricular activities. Older students represented the different extracurricular activities at Andover, and were pushing all these activities and saying, "Join this, join that." When we went back to the dorm, the first thing the housemaster said was, "Don't join anything. You're here to work, and we don't want you to join anything." That was the first thing I was told: that I shouldn't join anything. They said you had to get involved with the school first. But I didn't pay much attention and ended up joining a political union, sort of like a congress. At the end of the year my housemaster wrote on my report that it was unwise for me to have joined any extracurricular activities, and especially that one. He said when I joined it that the political group was headed by "a bunch of radicals," and that was bad for me. I could tell then that they really didn't want you to be free at Andover. They wanted you to stay in your own class and not search for yourself. Let them search for you and make you what they wanted to make you. I saw the boys in my class fall exactly in the pattern of what the school wanted them to do. That wasn't what I wanted. I sort of knew what Andover stood for, and I didn't want to be molded. I had gone there for the experience of being away from home, and I also wanted to learn from going to the school. I didn't want the school to teach me.

Because I had done well in junior high school, I had gotten into some tenth-grade courses, though I was only in ninth grade. I was busy working hard in these, when after about a month or two I got mono and they put me in the infirmary for three weeks. While I was there, the school doctor urged me to drop out of the tenth-grade courses and to take only ninth-grade courses. He wanted me out of these courses because he thought I would be influenced by the older people in my classes. They had been there one or two years and knew what Andover was really like; and he was afraid they would turn me against it. When I got out of the infirmary I remained in the older classes. When I came out I didn't really know many of my classmates because I hadn't seen any of them for two or three weeks. That was a pretty long time since I had only been there a little more than a month. They were all formed into little cliques: all they talked about was what they had done in the dorm the night before, who had stayed up late, and what sports they were taking. I noticed that they were doing all the little things that I had envisioned as prep school life at its worst. They were all dressing in the same acceptable way—with tweed jackets and Weejun shoes—and they all seemed to drool with admiration over the housemaster's every word. The housemaster himself was a product of another New England prep school and then Harvard. His return to the prep school life without any interim experience on the outside, epitomized the limited background of most Andover headmasters. He was, as you might expect, quite narrow-minded, to the point where he would refer to the local citizens of Andover as "townies," different from "we up here on the hill." Though I considered him hardly worthy of respect, he had succeeded in winning the esteem of most of my dorm-mates. Uncritical respect for housemasters was also an expected Andover reaction.

The separation of the younger students from the older ones, which the doctor was aiming for with his advice, is done so the new boys will be more susceptible to Andover's indoctrination. It's easier to convince impressionable juniors (ninth graders) of something if there aren't any "cynical" upper classmen around to contradict. Physically, most of the junior dormitories are isolated from the upper-class dorms, and the juniors are separated in other ways as well. Juniors can only participate in sports with other juniors. Everybody else is eligible for the Varsity in every sport, but no matter how good they are, the juniors can only play on the junior teams. Sports is a big thing at Andover, and they want to get all the juniors together in this area so they can start shaping them. Start shaping them in the Andover way. The assistant headmaster actually came over to me once to say that he didn't want the juniors getting influenced by the people who know the school. He said that so far I hadn't fit into the Andover way and that our paths may soon part because I continued to hang around with older boys. Also all my friends had long hair and that made them somewhat short of ideal "Andover Men."

While I did object almost immediately to the way the school tried to mold me, my objections were kept silent, and consequently I had very little trouble with the rules at Andover. The first year, I got a demerit from my basketball coach for cutting a basketball game, but that was about it. However during my second year, I started getting bored with classes, and I began cutting them. Students are allowed sixteen cuts a year, five and a half for each of the three terms: I took eighty-one for the year. I worked this by switching courses several times during the term and confusing the records. I then could take a cut but miss having my named called from the class list for a cut. I was able to have only nine cuts credited to me for the whole year, while I had taken eighty-one. But it was always nip and tuck because I would end up taking one or two cuts too many: I would then have to go in and check with the excusing officer and work out some elaborate excuse so I wouldn't get Posted for overcutting. Fortunately I was lucky and was able to take many more term cuts than I should have and still survive. Rather than having to attend boring classes and athletics I wasn't interested in, I was able to spend my time in my room, reading and listening to music.

My second and more important involvement with the school rules had to do with smoking marijuana, which started out gradually in the fall and winter of my Upper year (eleventh grade). What first inspired me to take drugs was basically curiosity, and the fact that most of the other kids in my dorm were doing it. The first time I ever took drugs was at Andover, and the first drug I ever had was hashish. I smoked it in a pipe, and I liked it a lot. I took it with about six or seven other kids in a dorm room. One chick and five or six guys. I wandered into the room, and there was a pipe being passed around. I decided to join in just for the hell of it. That was in the beginning of the winter term. I smoked more as the winter term went on, but not very much. However, when spring came I decided to abandon all my studies and just try to pass them. That's just about what I did.

I spent most of my time taking drugs. A friend and I regularly went up to his room on the top floor of the dorm to smoke. We would smoke pot beginning at about eight o'clock, when study hours began. Sometimes we would smoke in the fireplace. We would lock the door, close the windows, and light up a pipe in the fireplace. Once, in a kind of a cruel way, we went down to the room of a kid who hadn't used dope before and asked him if we could use his fireplace. While we were smoking and rapping easily, the kid was really getting scared. He kept opening the door to see if the housemaster was coming, and telling us to keep quiet. He finally ended up having some dope himself, and he really enjoyed it. The other place where we used to smoke was in the attic. Getting to the attic involved boosting my friend up to a window enclosure in the ceiling right above the stairwell. He would fumble around in the dark, passing crates and mops, trying not to touch a thing. Then he would climb down a ladder in the janitor's closet, open it, and let me in. Getting back out was very dangerous. We would have looked pretty weird coming out of the janitor's closet at ten o'clock at night. But while we were up there we were in no danger of being caught. We could sit up on the rafters and smoke without worry.

We got into marijuana and hash very deeply. In fact at one point last spring we smoked up to forty or forty-five nights in a row. We disregarded our homework: did it in the afternoon if we did it at all. We'd go up into the attic to smoke, and then go back to my friend's room and listen to music. Music really sounds great on drugs. We usually ended up falling asleep exhausted at about one o'clock in the morning in a chair or on the floor. During the spring term I hardly ever slept in my own room. Both our studies went completely out the window, but we did enjoy ourselves. And we became experts on the different kinds of drugs around. We got so we could distinguish good Acapulco Gold from bad New Jersey stuff. We rapped a lot about it. In fact most of our conversation day and night was about drugs. Our housemaster knew that we were using drugs. It was obvious: the whole dorm used drugs, and we were going around stoned—laughing all the time and doing really strange things. Fortunately, however, the housemaster didn't do anything about it.

There are a hell of a lot of drugs pushed around Andover. Very few of the ninth graders take them, but the number increases by grade. There are several reasons for this rather extensive drug use. I think all adolescents want to get intoxicated, because it's a hard time to live in. You have all sorts of conflicts within yourself, and you can forget them for a while by taking drugs. People drink for the same reason, and there are still a lot of young drinkers around. Drugs are better though, because they don't depress you like alcohol does. They also don't make you sick.

The use of drugs has also gotten to be a status thing. The more you take, the more you can brag about it. People say, "Whoa, look at that!" There was one senior last year who won a good deal of respect in some circles because he set records for taking acid. He took more than anybody else. And one legendary senior a couple of years ago supposedly took a week-long STP trip. Drug use is very much a status symbol, just as drinking many cans of beer used to be.

The need for social acceptance and the desire for escape are the main reasons for drug-taking at Andover. Most fifteen- and sixteen-year-olds want to escape at one point or another, but at Andover the need is particularly acute. Andover is a very depressing place. In the middle of winter there are six feet of snow on the ground, and the paths are merely tunnels between the drifts. Anywhere you walk it's depressing. They only let you out of the place a couple of times a term. Many students experiment with drugs to help them escape: some people take whole semesters of classes stoned just to see what it's like. It's an escape to a different world. You get away from a depressing one.

It's impossible to talk about any boarding school and especially Andover without getting into sex. While sex really covers everything, it's the least talked-about subject in the entire school. There is for the freshman class a little sex lecture given by the medical department every year. Everyone snickers about intercourse, and that's about it as far as authorized sex education goes. Nevertheless, sex colors everything at Andover: the faculty, the students, and the administration. Andover is a closed, private, boys' boarding school, and there's very little sexual satisfaction for students or teachers there.

Poor sexual relationships obviously affect the faculty, because faculty members can't assert their masculinity at all unless they go out for athletics. Athletics at Andover has always been considered a good substitute for sex. It's on the gridiron that you're supposed to get rid of your physical desires, not in a bed somewhere. The sexual dissatisfaction of many faculty members affects their attitudes toward students. I sometimes get the feeling that I'm competing against the faculty members in everything: in athletics, in the classroom, and displaying wit before their wives at dorm parties. It's not the healthiest relationship to have between a teacher and his students.

In the past year, there has been a big move at Andover toward coordinate education. Abbot, which is the girls' school next to Andover, and has about 250 students, has now started to take courses with us. We also do lots of things like eat meals together, without sharing the same campus. The administration felt that the thing to do was to go slowly toward coordinate education. Everyone else is doing it, and if we don't do it we'll obviously become stifled and staid and we'll die out. So it was done. They started out with coed dining and some coed classes.

Sexual relationships between Abbot girls and Andover boys have actually grown over the past five or six years. Before that there were very few sexual relationships because most of the Andover boys who were respected were the athletes; and athletes had very little time for sex. They were too busy playing football and knocking their brains out. But now that drugs and new art concepts have come along, the long hairs and the artists are being respected. Drugs and art deal with sex, and the emergence of a new kind of Andover student has been a major reason for the better sex between Andover and Abbot.

Basically sexual relationships with Abbot girls run along two levels. First there's the level of going steady, which is kind of traditional in America. But going steady has faded out, because it's impossible to do anything with a chick up at Andover—at least legally. You can't take her into Boston. You can't take her around town, and there are very few opportunities to be alone together. Hence you can't have sex in any ideal setting. You can't go into a room where there's privacy. But this type of private relationship isn't big anyway. The type of sexual relationship which is now prominent between Andover and Abbot students is happening all over the country: communal relationships. A bunch of chicks and a bunch of guys will go off together in a group, on a kind of picnic. The group will go off to the Sanctuary, a large nature refuge on campus, and have a good time for the afternoon: smoke dope together, make love, and generally relate together as a group. The sex is not communal, but paired off. Being in a group removes the hardship of having to meet a chick, go out with her, and go through all the traditional rigamarole which you can't go through at Andover anyway because you can't take a girl out anywhere. You can't go through the talking and the other stages in the development of a normal relationship because you can't see a chick that much. So you have a rushed relationship, sort of like a sailor who has just gotten off a ship. You have all the fun you possibly can right away. In the last few years sexual relationships have become more and more rushed, especially because the younger Abbot chicks are sexually available and willing to go through any type of affair. So it's this type of communal sexual life that is growing at Andover. You do the most in the least amount of time without going through the bother of going steady.

The reason that sexual attitudes of Andover and Abbot students are changing is very simple. Free and abstract expressions of life—art and music—have become respectable and admirable to most of the student body. Any abstract, creative expressions in which you let yourself go—drugs, art, plays, communal things, and sexual freedom—fit into the model of the person who is admired at Andover, both by other boys and by girls at Abbot. Drug use is very rare at Abbot in comparison to Andover. I would say that only about fifteen girls at Abbot are deep into drugs at all—they may smoke dope once or twice a week. I also think that girls between the ages of thirteen and eighteen, even though they may be very intelligent, have a yearning to be dependent on the kind of creativity which an Andover student can develop. Because they don't have the ability or the facility around school to be particularly creative themselves, and because Abbot girls basically aren't into drugs and other liberating things, most of them have a very large sexual need which they transfer to the Andover student who is creative.

The Abbot girls are really good chicks. They're nice, and they have this built-in desire for sex, for freedom, and for just getting involved. After spending time with a guy in one of these communal experiences, they sometimes go way out to show their affection. I know of girls who spent the entire night in the Sanctuary with Andover guys. They'd stay out there, smoking dope and balling, all night. And it's not uncommon for them to come and stay in the senior dorms. I'd say it happened in about 20 cases last year. Girls at Abbot who had good relations with their house mistresses and didn't see them often would come up and sleep with guys in the dorms. They have unlimited weekends (although we only have from three to five a term, depending on the class) and sometimes go off with Andover guys. I knew one chick at Abbot who used to take a couple of guys up to a farm shed in New Hampshire every weekend last spring. The guys took off illegally after their allotted weekends were up. I guess it's sort of mutual assistance. They help us, and we help them, to survive at school. I don't know how we'd do it without them.

The need for creativity and self-expression on the part of students my age is, as I said before, one of the main reasons why sex and drugs are so important at Andover. I'm not exactly sure why my friends and I have this drive for creativity and self-fulfillment, but I do know that drugs and sex are among the few outlets possible at Andover. Sports used to be the main outlet and the main source of prestige for the boarding-school student. Sports provided a certain amount of controlled violence, group involvement, and organized educational structure; in other words, if you're a halfback you do this, if you're an end, you do that. Sports was the alternative which the school administration wanted because they didn't want an outlet in sex. Now, however, the students have discovered their own cultural and political outlets. Deep, intellectual people rather than strong, athletic people have become respectable as students. For what reason I don't know. I think a lot of it comes from the music and art of the late fifties. But whatever it comes from, the new outlet is definitely alienated from the Andover establishment.

Creativity is almost by definition an anti-Establishment thing at Andover. Teachers would try to refute that statement by claiming that they always encourage creativity in the classroom—in papers and on tests. That may very well be so, but classroom learning is a small function of the over-all Andover institution. The purpose of Andover is to process young men, turn them into "Andover Men," and channel them forward to a blandly orthodox life style and choice of professions. Andover tries to mold, groom, and refine its students; it cannot allow for true creativity which might be a threat to the school. Going to Yale and Wall Street is not creative; at least not if it's imposed on you by your school. You are strapped to an assembly line, unable to climb off. The sophisticated generation that is now at Andover is searching for creativity and identity, and dislikes being forced to do uncreative things. Playing football is not a creative thing. That's why other things than football are now respected at Andover. Art groups and musical groups are very popular among students. The new Art Center, which was built because our rival school Exeter had one, has become a gathering place for many of these anti-Establishment Andover students—and a worry to the administration.

There has developed over the last two years a group of about fifty people involved in the arts and together in outlook. There's a very strong bond between us, for which the school itself is responsible—primarily through one of the new interdepartmental courses it has instituted. In the last three years, Andover has managed to evolve a few interdepartmental courses that are experimental and quite free. The only reason they are approved was because everyone else was doing them—why shouldn't Andover make some token gesture to what is happening in education throughout the rest of the country in colleges and in some prep schools? So some art-English departmental courses have been started, a specific one being Contemporary Communications. This course is conducted entirely differently from any other course at Andover. The classroom is obsolete, and attendance requirements and grades are also obsolete. You get an automatic five at the end of the year unless you don't do anything at all. (A five at Andover is an honor grade.) The Contemporary Communications course has become a resting place for the alienated and artistic intellectuals who want to get together and work together. They have formed a very strong block.

Most of the people in the group are bright and independent and are opposed to the Andover kind of manipulation. I think this is the first time the school has felt threatened from within, and the administration is uptight about it. Dr. G——, who is the head of the infirmary, made a report to the administration saying that Con.-Comm. was an unhealthy course. He said it divided the community. It brought together one group of people, the creative people, and restricted jocks and other people from joining. Dr. G—— was admitting that Con.-Comm. was a focal point for alienated people at Andover to get together and organize. As a result, the administration has started to make it harder for these students to meet. When Contemporary Communications came up for renewal, plenty of people applied for the course. (You have to have only ten people apply for a course in order for it to hold, and there were thirty or thirty-five students interested in it.) But the administration announced that there were not enough people applying for the course, and Con.-Comm. was taken out of the interdepartmental category and turned into an art course. They decided not to eliminate it altogether because that would cause an uproar with the students; instead, they changed it so people would be discouraged from applying. Andover couldn't stand the subversive scrutiny that meetings of its students produced.

All the things I've mentioned so far—the use of drugs, the need to break rules in order to have sex, and the emphasis on creativity—have tended to alienate Andover students from the administration. This alienation, or general feeling of detachment, can't help becoming political. If a student takes drugs, whether he is a jock or an artist, he automatically becomes a lawbreaker and Andover becomes the enemy. Whether he is radical, liberal, or conservative doesn't matter, because once he becomes alienated from the school through drugs he becomes politically alienated as well. The same is true with creativity. When a person joins the artistic group at Andover, either because he wants prestige or because he wants to use his creative faculties, he automatically becomes part of a political opposition. There were artists last year who never had had any real political involvement in their lives, but who by the end of the year were getting deeply involved in demonstrations. They started off just being intellectually detached from the school, and ended up opposing certain concrete conditions and policies. When you join the artistic establishment, even though you may not have any political views at all, you become a member of the political opposition at Andover.

There are certain school issues that almost all the students at Andover agree upon. One is their desire to be given more freedom. At Andover we have to go to breakfast, we have to go to classes, we have to go to athletics. And up until last year we had to go to chapel twice a week—Wednesdays and Sundays. Many students objected to the forced chapel, for in addition to being another requirement, it was against free religion. We had heated arguments about it, and finally the administration made Wednesday chapel voluntary. All students are also in agreement on the tyrannical rules of the school. For example, disobedience to a faculty member is a major crime, and makes you liable to dismissal. In other words, if you just disagree with a faculty member you can get kicked out. The housemaster can have a little squabble with you when he's drunk, point to that rule, and have you kicked out. The rule really angers a lot of students. It angers me because so many things that the faculty do are wrong. And you can't tell them that they are wrong. These are the kinds of rules that aggravate both the moderate and the radical students at Andover.

There are about forty or fifty active radical students at Andover. And as I mentioned before, there are a lot of potential radicals. If things can go right, if things can be done anonymously, I think that about three-quarters of the student body can be counted on to support radical actions. An example was last year's election. Since 1789, every time the three upper classes elected presidents they were straight guys: football players and things like that. This year they elected three black students. In order for those three black students to be elected, they had to get at least 125 votes from each class. So you can figure that there are 400 to 450 students in the whole school who voted for what was basically a radical platform. They voted for avowed black militants against guys who had been presidents of their classes the year before. Then, in the Student-Faculty Co-operative elections, three white radicals were elected to the Executive Board. And both the black and white radicals had made their positions very clear. Over all, I would say that up to 500 Andover students (out of 840) could, if there were strong radical leadership, back a radical group, as they did in the Co-op. They would have to do it anonymously, but they would lend support to moves taken to change the school—moves whose means would be considered less important than their ends.

The Left at Andover embodies two different elements. There are those who are politically active on the Left and those who are artistically active. The artistically active students resist the administration by attacking its values and beliefs through their artistic expression. Through plays that they write, poems that they recite in chapel, and paintings that they hang in the Art Center, they disturb the administration just as much as someone who gets up in Co-op and talks. The artistic people aren't going to start a radical activity. They are the ones who will lend creativity and inventiveness to it after it's been initiated. Therefore the political and the artistic radicals both contribute toward the radical movement at Andover.

The radical students believe, and I agree, that you can sit around and change specific rules at Andover all day without doing any good. Liberalizing course requirements and offering more weekend privileges doesn't amount to much. You have to change the basic attitude and structure of the institution. It's that attitude which, while liberalizing the admissions policy and admitting more black students than most prep schools, still provides a fairly rigid educational experience—one in which a student enters, goes through a maze of courses and rules, and comes out an "Andover Man." It's that structure which gives the student a certain amount of freedom of choice to pursue different interests, but limits him to conventional, unradical opinions.

The radical student movement really started at Andover in the spring of 1968. At that time, the chairman of what was then the Student Congress put a few small proposals for rule changes to the faculty. All were turned down. He felt (and I think rightly) that he wasn't given enough chance to speak out on the issues and present his side. The faculty simply took his five or six small proposals and automatically turned them down. At that point, one student got really angry and planned a demonstration to support both the student views and the abolition of the Student Congress in favor of a more meaningful group. The administration was so incensed by the idea of a demonstration that they got out and stopped it and delayed response to the proposal. But the demonstration did force them to act, and at the beginning of the 1968 fall term a new student-faculty Co-operative was established. Anyone can come in and discuss any relevant issues with the Executive Board, which is made up of three students and three faculty members. The Co-op has improved faculty-student communications, but not to the degree that is necessary. The students still play a subordinate role, even on this purely consultative body: everybody can vote for the students on the Executive Board, but only the faculty can vote for the faculty. However, students can at least speak up now, and largely as a result of the spring demonstration.

In the fall term last year the Co-operative spent all its time discussing the religion issue. It was a bad first choice for an issue because it was very complex and abstract. But during this time the members of the Co-op became more and more alienated. Certain radical speakers began getting up and denouncing people like K——, the headmaster. Even though this did us no good, the fact that it was tolerated was a significant step. But there was vast disagreement on school changes, and nothing was done. So as winter term rolled around we started getting really frustrated.

A disciplinary incident that occurred about that time got more students fed up with the school. Jim L——, one of the radical and artistic leaders in the senior class, was turned in by a student for blowing his nose on a replica of the American flag. It was a scarf that he had worn in history class. But the faculty members on the discipline committee showed how narrow-minded and superficially patriotic they were by putting him on probation. There was a big faculty meeting about it, and four young teaching fellows—who had just gotten out of college and who sympathized with us—went into the faculty meeting wearing American-flag ties. They waged a fantastic fight for L——'s rights, and the campus was put in an uproar. The incident added a national issue, desecration of the flag, to local campus issues, and the students now were really agitated. Editorials in *The Phillipian* became more and more radical. The headmaster was criticized week after week. And there was great fear on the part of the administration. I remember talking to one of the deans in January. I was talking about the drug scene at Andover, and he was very scared that there was going to be violence.

In the spring there was a coat-and-tie demonstration. We have to wear coats and ties at Andover every day until April 30. In May and June we can take them off, but we don't want to wear them at any time. We organized a protest by circulating petitions, but it was a failure in terms of numbers. There were only about seventy or seventy-five students involved, and a lot of student skirmishes. But even small things like that really alarm the administration. They're not used to any kind of protest, and even a coat-and-tie demonstration drives them up the wall. One of the deans got very angry at *The Phillipian* for giving the demonstration front-page coverage, and he threatened to sanction the paper. He wouldn't be so stupid as to begin controlling the paper, but he could take away certain privileges—use of the press rooms and things like that—and make it very difficult for the paper to function. After this there was a violent protest which I was involved in. One night, some other students and I broke the windows in George Washington Hall, the administration building. And one student in the group broke some windows in Samuel Phillips Hall, the classroom building. We did it to dramatize student discontent and to show how serious we were about the issues.

There wasn't any cohesive philosophy behind all the student discontent but there was a cohesive movement. By the middle of spring term, there was an alliance created between the fifty radicals and the rest of the students. Coming from a depressing winter into the spring, when male sexuality demands freedom, the students were particularly irritated at the administration for clamping down on them so much. Consequently, by May there was a kind of union between the radicals and all the students who were discontented with the administration.

In May and June came the crowning blow, which convinced the students how rigidly conservative Andover was and how little regard was paid to their opinions. To give students the feeling that their ideas were valued, the administration called a special day on which classes were canceled and students met together to discuss changes in the school put forth by the Discipline Committee. The faculty got together in groups to hear what the students were saying, and then they held their own faculty meeting. They ignored almost every student suggestion. Things like unlimited senior cuts and hair and dress regulations were not approved. Even weekend privileges were slighted. And then the headmaster showed just how much he believed in school democracy and in listening to students. On the next to last Sunday at school, the headmaster got up and announced the final decision about the hair rule. He said that "long hair was destroying Andover's image." "From now on," he said, "I will decide whether or not a boy shall have long hair, sideburns, a beard, or mustache." The students now were really bitter, and they showed it in the question-and-answer period. First, there was booing and hissing, and no applause from anywhere. The headmaster's reasoning went like this: If a boy's record showed any honor grades, he could have a beard. If it showed him getting less than honor grades, he couldn't have a beard. Honor students could have beards and non-honor students could not. He said that right out in the open. He also said that students could not have hair styles in the extreme, and there were lots of sarcastic questions about that. One student asked him, "Well, does that mean that a guy who has shaved his head has to go around wearing a wig until his hair grows back?" K—— didn't like that question. He had just made an announcement denouncing blue jeans, saying, "We don't want any blue jeans around campus at all." One kid way in the back got up and said, "Everywhere I see gray jeans, I see green jeans, red jeans, orange jeans, and white jeans. I'd like to know what Andover has against the color blue." And of course, since blue is Andover's color—blue and white—this brought the house down; and it embarrassed K—— tremendously. By the end of the assembly people were really angry. A whole bunch of students got up and started singing "The Royal Blue," which is the Andover theme song, in a very sarcastic way. That was the note school ended on last spring.

I personally am fed up with Andover. I want to change this school even if I have to do violent things and take part in violent demonstrations. However, I can't afford to get kicked out. I really don't care what it will do to my status or future, but my father does pay for me to go there, and getting booted certainly would hurt my relationship with him and the rest of the family. While still working for change, I have decided to stay at Andover. I don't want to disappoint my parents by quitting or getting kicked out, but I'm also staying for other reasons. I came because of my ignorance of the place, and I've stayed because I feel that Andover is merely a reflection of this civilization and this society. There will be no better place. And there's the added incentive that the people at Andover are among the most remarkable I've ever encountered. They are from all walks of life, and some are really extraordinary. I have developed some very deep friendships, with other students and even with a few faculty members who are truly outstanding people. I know other students who feel the same way about the people at Andover, but they are generally disappointed with the school.

Most of the students at Andover, I'd say more than half, are dissatisfied. They feel that something's wrong with the school, that something isn't right. I don't know what the reasons are for all of them, but I think the basic character of the school has a lot to do with it. The regimentation and restrictions that students suffer, the lack of meaningful administrative responsibility given them, and the feeling of being groomed and manipulated to fit a preconceived mold, all contribute to an alienation from the school that can easily grow into hostility. The growing strength of the radical movement is a good indication of the degree of disenchantment. Last year the influence of the group of forty committed radicals grew as the year went by. The other disenchanted students were looking for a banner to get under, and they picked that of the black and white radicals. Thus by the end of the year the radical movement had quite a large power base, as seen both in the class elections and the demonstration against the headmaster at the assembly.

At Andover right now, the movement is just as good as it was last year. It still involves a continuation of effort by the small group of hard-core, self-avowed radicals. In the past, things usually faded back to normal soon after a demonstration. But with the election of radicals to the top six offices of the school, there's a good possibility that the pressure can still be kept on. And because the radicals have infiltrated the establishment organization, we don't need to form any new organization ourselves. In other words, we can use the establishment organization for our own purposes. We can turn it against itself.

Andover is not the only prep school that has dissatisfied, radical students. Students at Choate, Lawrenceville, Exeter, and other schools are similarly disappointed with the education they're receiving. Because of this, several organizations have developed to unite the different radical students and try to effect radical changes on all the prep-school campuses. One such organization is the National Prep School Union. Organized by former Andover students, the Union believes that secondary education should be redefined to provide the educational experience that certain progressive colleges and most graduate schools do today. These higher levels of education would be redefined accordingly to continue the specialization students need so desperately today.

The National Prep School Union has representative radical students at many different prep schools. Thirty some-odd prep schools, including Choate, Pomfret, and Lawrenceville, have been addressed by members of the Union, and some constructive results have already been produced. Some of the schools have instituted teacher-evaluation programs, and others have introduced off-campus studying projects.

The Black Prep School Students' Union is an organization for militant black prep-school students headed by a black at Mount Hermon. It is quite powerful, and has already brought about some radical changes at Choate. Like the National Prep School Union it seeks to rally students at the different campuses to the radical movement. Through the work of these two organizations, along with the efforts of unaffiliated radical prep-school students throughout the country, the basic character of American prep schools may change. Ideally, the schools will begin to treat students like mature young adults, and rather than process them uniformly toward traditional futures, begin to allow them—even encourage them—to develop as creative and independent men and women.

Most student educational criticism comes in the form of short articles in school or underground papers. Underground papers have proved a popular channel of student expression, and there are hundreds across the country. Some serve particular schools; others are citywide and reach kids throughout the system. In the following pieces from such papers, students have perceptive and important things to say about high-school education.

# The Classroom Maze

BY NORMAN SOLOMAN

THE PECULIAR maze known as an American public school education has steered students into a disturbingly practical and predictable approach to problems and questions which, based on past experiences, seems most likely to bring tangible rewards.

Not unlike test mice in a laboratory, students have learned through trial and error what responses are likely to bring them closer to their goal.

To a mouse in search of something to eat, proper reactions to situations—which are proper only because observation and firsthand experiences have shown that they work—are liable to net a piece of cheese.

In much the same way, the rewards to be won by a student are no less obvious. Good grades—the hallowed key to a high class rank, acceptance at a "good" college, and the all-American dream of financial and social success—lie waiting for those who are able to figure out what the teacher is looking for and give it to him.

The student who wants to get ahead learns to attentively swallow what the teacher has to say in class, accepting it without question, and obligingly spits it back on paper come test day.

Such an educational diet, students are able to see from experience, has proven on the whole to pay big dividends in terms of grades or impressing the teacher and rarely goes unrewarded.

## INDUSTRY PAYS OFF

I recall one instance when a teacher assigned students an essay expressing a strong point of view about anything the student wished. In giving the assignment, the teacher told the students what she would write if she had the assignment, and gave examples supporting her thesis.

When the essays were returned and some were read aloud to the class, students found that one industrious girl—no doubt bound for an Ivy League college and a brilliant future—had used the same theme and examples as the teacher had two weeks earlier.

The teacher, who may or may not have noticed the essay's strong similarity to her own dissertation, gave the paper an "A" and provided students with an object lesson on academic advancement.

On the other hand, taking issue with an instructor or his conclusions seldom is—or at least appears to be—advantageous, and can be hazardous; this too is not lost on students.

## RESULTS TO BE EXPECTED

Keeping all this in mind, the results are to be expected. In courses such as chemistry or trigonometry, the goal is obvious: one must arrive at the answer which appears in the teacher's answer book.

But in subjects such as English and history, there is no answer book. Nevertheless, the goal becomes equally apparent—try to arrive at the conclusion the teacher wants you to arrive at.

By the time students reach high school, they have unconsciously learned to approach a test asking themselves, "What is the answer that he [the teacher] is looking for?"

In this way, testing becomes a guessing game. Confronted

with an oral question or a written essay test, a student tries to figure out what answer the teacher is looking for, which—by definition—has become the "right" answer.

This adaptive process which students have developed is described in detail in a book by teacher John Holt, *How Children Learn.*

## "BEAT THE SYSTEM"

"Holt has noticed that children react by employing clever stratagems to beat the system and find that right answer," *Time* Magazine wrote in a review of the book.

"They detect the way a teacher unconsciously leans toward the correct answer of several on the blackboard; a student looks confused or stays silent, the teacher keeps asking leading questions and almost answers himself; other students mumble answers, aware that the teacher is attuned to the right answer, and will assume it was given. They fence-straddle, avoid commitment, live for the teacher's approving 'yes.' "

*Time* goes on:

"The 'tell-'em-and-test-'em' process, Holt claims, not only induces fear and discourages experimentation but leads to a concentration on answers rather than problems—and it is 'dishonest and the students know it.'

"In this 'temple of worship for right answers, the way to get ahead is to lay plenty of them on the altar.' The whole system, insists Holt, convinces most students that school is mainly a place where you follow meaningless procedures to get meaningless answers to meaningless questions."

Students are told that they are going to school in order to think and reason for themselves. Their experiences, however, do not bear out this concept.

### "IGNOBLE SATISFACTION"

"Holt considers much of present schooling a degrading experience for both teachers and students. Children are compelled to work for 'petty and contemptible rewards—gold stars, or papers marked 100, or A's on report cards—for the ignoble satisfaction of feeling that they are better than someone else.' They fear a teacher's displeasure, the scorn of their peers, the pain of being wrong."

While learning to cater to the whims and opinions of superiors may be good preparation for getting ahead in the outside business world, it is hardly conducive to the atmosphere of free thought and intellectual experimentation which our schools theoretically foster.

## Breaking In

BY ALICE DE RIVERA

BEFORE I went to John Jay High School I hadn't realized how bad the conditions were for students. One of the things which changed my outlook was being involved with the hostilities of the New York City teacher strikes in the fall of 1968. Students were trying to open the school and the teachers were preventing them.

It was then I found that students had no rights. We had no freedom of the press: many controversial articles were removed from the newspapers by the teacher editors. We were not allowed to distribute leaflets or newspapers inside our school building, so that press communication was taken away from us. We also had no freedom of speech. Many teachers would put us down in class for our political ideas and then would not let us answer their charges. If we tried to talk with other students during a free period about political issues, we were told to stop. The school was a prison—we were required by state law to be there, but when we were there we had no rights. . . .

I have been writing about the student's plight in general because it was my first encounter with oppression. It is such a familiar experience to me now that I think I can try to define it. Oppression, to me, is when people are not allowed to be themselves. I encountered this condition a second time when I realized *woman's* plight in the high schools.

The first time it really occurred to me that I was oppressed as a woman was when I began to think of what I was going to be when I was older. I realized I had no real plans for the future—college, maybe, and after that was a dark space in my mind. In talking and listening to other girls, I found that they had either the same blank spot in their mind or were planning on marriage. If not that, they figured on taking a job of some sort *until* they got married.

The boys that I knew all had at least some slight idea in their minds of what career or job they were preparing for. Some prepared for careers in science and math by going to a specialized school. Others prepared for their later jobs as mechanics, electricians, and other tradesmen in vocational schools. Some just did their thing in a regular zoned high school. It seemed to me that I should fill the blank spot in my mind as the boys were able to do, and I decided to study science (biology, in particular) much more intensively. It was then that I encountered one of the many blocks which stand in the woman student's way: discrimination against women in the specialized science and math high schools in the city.

Many years before women in New York State had won their right to vote (1917), a school was established for those high-school students who wished to specialize in science and math. Naturally it was not co-ed, for women were not regarded legally or psychologically as people. This school, Stuyvesant High School, was erected in 1903. . . .

There are only two other high schools in New York which specialize in science and math: Brooklyn Technical, a school geared toward engineering, and Bronx High School of Science. . . .

Out of these three schools I could try out for only one. This one, Bronx Science, is one and a half hours' travel time from my home. It presents very stiff competition because of the discriminatory policy which allows only a certain number of girls to enter, and also because all the girls who would otherwise be trying out for Stuyvesant or Brooklyn Tech have Bronx Science as their only alternative. I became disgusted with this, not only for my sake, but for all the girls who hadn't become scientists or engineers because they were a little less than brilliant or had been put down by nobody having challenged those little blank spots in their minds. After talking about it with my parents and friends, I decided to open up Stuyvesant and challenge the Board of Education's traditional policy.

The day on which we went to court was the day before the entrance exam was scheduled to be given. The Board of Education granted me the privilege of taking the test for Bronx Science (which is the same as the one given for Stuyvesant), and the judge recognized that the results of this test would be used in another court hearing to resolve whether or not I would be admitted. Five days after the other students had received their results, we found out that I had passed for entrance into both Stuyvesant and Bronx Science.

We went to court again a couple of months later, and on April 30th the New York City Board of Education voted to admit me to Stuyvesant High School in the fall.

There are a great many battles yet to be fought. Aside from being discouraged to study for a career, women are discouraged from preparing for jobs involving anything *but* secretarial work, beauty care, nursing, cooking, and the fashion industry. During my fight over Stuyvesant, I investigated the whole high-school scene and found that out of the twenty-seven vocational high schools in the city, only *seven* are coed. The boys' vocational schools teach trades in electronics, plumbing, carpentry, foods, printing (another example of Board of Education traditional policy—there is hardly any work for a hand typesetter today), etc. The girls are taught to be beauticians, secretaries, or health aides. This means that if a girl is seeking entrance to a vocational school, she is pressured to feel that certain jobs are masculine and others feminine. She is forced to conform to the Board of Education's image of her sex. . . .

In conclusion, there are three types of schools, twenty-nine in number, that the Board of Education has copped out on. These schools are composed of the specialized science and math school

Brooklyn Tech, twenty vocational schools which teach students their trade according to what sex they are, and the eight traditionally non-coed academic schools.

These eight academic schools are zoned schools which admit only boys or girls. The argument against these schools is that "separate but equal" is not equal (as established with regard to race in the Brown Decision). The psychological result of the school which is segregated by sex—only because of tradition—is to impress upon girls that they are only "flighty females" who would bother the boys' study habits (as a consequence of girls not being interested in anything but the male sex). This insinuates immaturity on the part of girls—and certainly produces it in both sexes. A boy who has never worked with a girl in the classroom is bound to think of her as his intellectual inferior, and will not treat her as if she had any capacity for understanding things other than child care and homemaking. Both sexes learn to deal with each other as non-people. It really messes up the growth of a person's mind. . . .

All girls have been brought up by this society never being able to be themselves—the school system has reinforced this. My desire at this time is to change the educational situation to benefit *all* the students. But I'm afraid changes *could* be made that benefited male students, leaving the status of females pretty much as it is. Female students share the general oppressive conditions forced upon everyone by the System's schools, plus a special psychological discrimination showed to women by the schools, the teachers, *and* their fellow students. So, since I don't want *my* issues to get swallowed up in the supposed "larger" issues, I'm going to make women's liberation the center of my fight.

# Why Did the Chicken Cross Broadway?

BY *TIME'S UP* STUDENT NEWSPAPER

TODAY, DURING lunch, as every day, escaping students were caught by the hundreds by that sly, watchful group of teachers whose sole purpose seems to be that of catching escapees as they cross the streets on the way to corner stores. At times it seems that the regulation prohibiting street crossing is perpetuated only so that these teachers will have something to keep themselves occupied. Looked at objectively, the street crossing rules seem rather foolish. Why should high school students be confined to the block during lunch? Many say that it is fear that the students will be "picked up" and never heard from again. Others say that "pushers" will be lurking in the shadows ready to pounce on pure and unsuspecting high school students and peddle their demonic poisons. These fears may or may not be justified but the main thing to consider is whether the street crossing rules remedy this problem. Is it any easier to pick someone up on one side of Broadway than it is on the other? Are there more demons hiding within the walls of the Public Library than there are within our own School Walls? Is one side of Ellery Street so much more dark and evil than the other? Any normally intelligent human being (which I hesitantly say includes the members of the School Department) realizes that crossing a street does not mean the difference between safety and danger, purity and baseness, or heaven and hell.

"What if," the school department matrons may ask, "a student does not just cross the street, but goes into some evil part of town," and then in a whispered voice, "like Harvard Square." All over the city grammar school students walk home for lunch and back without being mugged, slaughtered, robbed, or raped, but

153

High School students must "stay within the block for their own safety."

Maybe the teachers believe that once the students leave at lunch time, they will not return. It is possible that this is so, but how many of those same students are deterred from hooking because they aren't allowed to cross the street? Besides which, tracking down hookers would be much more exciting and stimulating for those quickwitted, ever watchful, guardians for school regulation who now have to be content with merely trapping escaping students.

# Grades, Bah Humbug!!

## BY *THE OPEN DOOR*, MILWAUKEE, WISCONSIN

GRADES OPERATE in a number of disguised ways. First they are the teacher's equivalent of the caveman's club. Since students need acceptable grades for desirable scholarships, jobs, and consequent social and economic prestige, the teacher's grading power is a penalty strong enough to give him the final voice in deciding the purpose, content and arrangement of instruction materials. Accordingly, to spend a number of years under the grading system is to be continuously conditioned to letting someone else decide which questions and data are important and almost unavoidably what answers are acceptable.

Teachers who favor this procedure of dictating usually state positively that it is a means of "transmitting a traditional body of knowledge." However, they fail to realize that a dictated selection of questions and information results in indoctrination in certain values. They come to think "these are the important questions to ask and this is the 'correct' way to answer them." When students are forced constantly to conform in their ideas to those of the system, they are conditioned into disinterested obedience, rather than responsible decision making, and they are prevented from becoming questioning, searching, resolving persons.

Second, this system seeks to measure in terms of grades those qualities which cannot be measured in these terms. By limiting educational material to what can be measured in grades, they eliminate from the classroom such goals as the development of ability to know one's self, to enter into serious, mindbending conversation, to think independently, to relate knowledge to obligation and so on—all of which are necessary for responsible decision making.

On the other hand, by pretending to measure the immeasurable (many teachers, for example, try to rate the value of student effort when they make out grades) teachers, through grades, can falsely reduce all experience to a search for facts.

Third, grades teach students to compete against each other. Anyone who may attempt to justify such competition may say that it motivates and prepares students for the big competitive outside world. If grades do motivate, then they reinforce a value system that makes equal the acceptability of self with performing better than others. Further it states the belief that private reward must and should come at the expense of the wellbeing of others. The logical outcome of such a value system is precisely the war mentality of the "big competitive world" with self-interest groups pitted rifle barrel to rifle barrel.

Furthermore, if one accepts at all the idea that education is primarily to create a society of emotionally stable and fulfilled persons, then competition is apparently nonsense. There are simply no grounds for comparing the development of myself with the development of yourself. Then not only is this competition nonsense but obstruction. For as psychologists like Abraham Maslow have pointed out, self-realization occurs primarily through human relationships based on trust and acceptance rather than on fear and power struggle.

Thus, since grades teach students to compete with each other for power, status and rewards, they obstruct self-realization. The grading structure, then, by encouraging competition, confirms operation for self-interest and for individual power over peers.

Fourth, students who have been passive for twelve years in the face of established authority will be superbly fitted for colleges that are based on submission to authority, research production and scholarly pecking-orders. They fit very well in an economic system based on submission to bureaucratic organization, mass production and cutthroat economic self-interest.

This argument against grades is by no means an argument against evaluation. Evaluation that is for, and largely by, the students. If students, their thought enriched by class discussion and reading, are enabled to arrive at standards of measurement personally meaningful to them. If they can avail themselves of the teacher's orally given insights about their personal progress in an area, if they are then in a position to choose what to pursue in light of their progress and interests, then evaluation educates rather than indoctrinates.

I have known teachers who declare that for social survival, students must be taught to obey, to compete, to focus on production. As totally as I disagree with their concepts about the possibilities of human beings, of human happiness, and of social organization, I grant them their honesty. For let us be clear: the current grading system precisely imposes the values of unquestioning acceptance of established authority, of unquestioning acceptance of the priority of products over persons, of unquestioning acceptance of organization. If one values in students independent, evaluatively critical thinking, if one values responsible decision-making, if one values cooperative behavior between persons based on trust and acceptance rather than competitive behavior based on fear and power-hunger, then one must judge grades as humanly degrading.

# Two Straight Kids

## BY JULES HENRY

Not all students fight back. The kids who accept the values taught in school, who knuckle under to the authority of teachers and administrators, who become "well rounded"—these are the expected products of the system and its true victims.

Jules Henry has taught at the University of Chicago and at Columbia University and is presently professor of anthropology at Washington University in St. Louis. He is best known for his book *Culture Against Man*.

IN OUR culture most of the features of adolescent life are a reverberation of adult life. It is impossible to understand why adolescents behave as they do in high school—their most important contact with the adult world, outside of their families—unless we know the shape of high school life. For the high school is not only a place where children spend five or more hours each day for three or four years, but it is an institution run by adults *for the entire community* and, because of this, expresses the demands of the community and the idiosyncrasies of the adults who run the high school.

When an institution is studied as a whole one can see the relationship among its parts. It stands to reason that the parts must somehow mesh, for otherwise the institution could not continue. Of course, there will be conflicts within it, but the conflicts will themselves be an expression of the interrelationship among the parts. A high school could not run at all if it did not meet major requirements of the students, and the students could not continue in the school if they did not meet the requirements of the school as conceived by the adults *and* by their peers. This is simple common sense. Thus if Rome High emphasizes athletics, it is because the community and the students want it so; and if the students like football, it is because if they do not they will not be able to endure the environment of Rome High. If Rome High encourages girls to dress in "high fashion" it is because this is what the community wants, and if the girls eschew high fashion they will be wallflowers. The same considerations apply to scholarship. Community, school, peer group thus become a self-reinforcing system.

Rome High is by no means entirely dedicated to athletics and fun; it is also an institution of learning. Yet fun looms large in life at Rome High. Let us spend a day there with Lila Greene, a fourteen-year-old freshman. We start at the researcher's meeting with Lila.

I pick Lila up at her house. When she asks her father for money he says, "What about the ten-dollar bill that so mysteriously disappeared?" She smiles, shrugs her shoulders, and says, "O.K., you win." On the way to school she tells me that it was really twenty, but if he's forgotten, "that's all right with me." Lila and her brother Bill are both interested in figuring the angles.

The first class we go to is gym. Lila introduces me to her girl friends—too many for me to catch the names of all of them—and to the gym teacher. Lila undresses and dresses in the shower stall in the girl's dressing room, saying that sometimes they throw girls in there to dunk them. They all like the gym teacher because they threw her in with her street clothes on and she didn't get mad.

The girls are all sharply dressed, except, of course, those who already have their gym suits on. There are mirrors everywhere and the girls are preening themselves in front of them. Lila says, "Most of the girls consist of padded bras and girdles, but they're clever artists; and besides, *what else can you do?*" Lila is not wearing a girdle.

Lila tells me about three girls in this class who dislike her and when I ask why, she says, "Jealous, probably. I make decent grades and have more physical ability and have fair success with boys. One of those girls, I guess, only goes out every three months. I didn't think that was possible. The senior boys were kidding around the other day about senior girls who have never been kissed. I didn't believe it at first." I say, "Oh, it's possible," and she says, "Never? Oh, my!" She asks about my dating habits and says she goes out at least four or five times a month, and was out until 2 A.M. at the backwards dance[1] Saturday. They went for pizza afterwards, and she paid her half of the bill because it was backwards. A couple of girls have asked her whether or not she paid.

Lila notices a boy circling the gym floor running, and says, "He's a nice guy, except he has beady eyes; you can always tell by their eyes." There are NO SMOKING signs everywhere. The boys and girls are separated and do not approach one another. Girls tend to clique up. Class seems to go from ultra-chic hair styles to long mops, with no middle ground. I see two bleached blondes. This gym class contains students from all years.

Gym class is over. Back to dressing room. There *is* a prevalence of padded bras and girdles here—and all of them so young! I ask, "Aren't the fellows disappointed?" and Lila says, "They don't know. Maybe some do, but most are fooled. I wear one once in a while." One girl, a junior, looks like a high-fashion model, bleached blonde.

French class. Mrs. Carling. Class is very crowded. The students get their exams back. Generally the class did well. Lila signals to me that she got A. Most girls wear expensive sweaters. If I had no job I'd have a hard job meeting this standard. I wonder how the less prosperous do. Boys in class all wear slacks but run-of-the-mill shirts. No outstanding marks of wealth among them and no bizarre haircuts.

One girl in the class is Danish. Lila asked her if she spoke Danish and the girl seemed disgusted at this oft-repeated question as she said, "of course." She was pale blond, wore heavy eye shadow, little lipstick. Class ring on chain around her neck, another on her hand. Apparently she has stripped her steady of all the tokens of love he possesses. He is hers!

[1] A dance where boy-girl etiquette is reversed.

The teacher is wearing a lavender wool dress, four-inch spikes, rope beads. She is stocky but not fat, has red hair, and wears glasses; not unattractive. Girls are segregated from boys.

The next class is Home Economics, where the room is a lovely pink with tan upholstered chairs, and is luxurious and roomy compared to other rooms in the school. One wall is covered with posters I imagine the girls made. They have to do with hair, skin, weight, posture, grooming. The teacher, Miss Clements, is probably about forty-five years old and is tall and big-boned. She is wearing a brown suit of good quality and glasses. Her brown hair is waved back and her lipstick is a little too bright for her age. Her rope beads may be a little frivolous but conform in general to the anticipated appearance of one in her circumstances.

Miss Clements announces that Mrs. Elphin, the special visiting speaker for today, will talk to us about wool. On the wall are posters from Helena Rubinstein cosmetics about skin care, Bobbie Brooks clothing ads, a poster on Facts About Perspiration, and in one corner there is a large, three-sided wardrobe mirror, in front of which a student, with the assistance of two friends, has been primping herself since class began. She is wearing a very elaborate oriental type hair style, piled intricately around her head, and with the help of her assistants she is combing the strays back in place. I am convinced she could not have constructed this by herself; or if she did, it must have taken her hours. She sits down before the speaker begins.

Miss Clements says notebooks are due today but she will understand if some are not handed in on time because today is Monday. Lila passes me a note saying that when the teacher talks, so do the students, and the teacher gets mad, shuts up, and so do the students. I say, "Can't win for losing," and Lila agrees. She thinks the situation is very funny.

Mrs. Elphin launches her lecture on wool with a history of British wool, the introduction of wool into our Southwest by the Spanish, the British law against sheep-raising in the Colonies, et cetera. "But to move on to *something more interesting,*" says Mrs. Elphin, "we're all interested in our personal affairs, 'How does this relate to me?' Now what sort of things interest us?" Hands wave, and one girl says, "Style." "Yes!" Mrs. Elphin explains that one example of adaptability of wool to style is the way it can be used in dolman sleeves (as in the wool jersey sweater she is wearing) without gathering or bulging. Another advantage is price: it cost a little more per yard, but it comes in extended widths—forty-five and fifty-four inches—so you're really *saving*.

Lila passes me a note: it says we have second lunch hour and that her stomach and backbone are one. Same here. I notice she is wearing a purple corduroy jumper and white blouse, both brand new. *This* is why she was wheedling daddy for money this morning, *she tells me*.

Mrs. Elphin drones on: "Now admit it, girls, most of us shop in the budget department, not among the higher priced dresses." I wonder! She gives advice on yard goods: "Don't buy a dress if you find the same pattern in the yard-goods department, because soon everyone else will have it and they'll be *dirty, untidy, cheap* people, and you'll be *so* unhappy! Then you'll have to keep wearing it to get the good out of it, and you'll be miserable. However, if you see high-priced dresses see if you can duplicate the materials in yard goods because that means it's coming into style."

I notice Lila is wearing a small silver band on her right hand. She says it is because she is one of four girls who go around together. I think we should look into clique symbols.

The lecturer says that wool is good even for summer because it is its own little air-conditioning unit; it keeps out both cold and warm air. One girl says, "I wear wool in summer but I was afraid to say so because I thought everyone would think I was queer or odd or something." If this is so, how did she ever venture into the street so attired? Might not her fellows see her and think her "queer or odd?"

Lila is interested in the lecturer's shoes. We saw a lady with turquoise spikes and Lila commented on them. In French class she was talking to another girl about three-inch heels that she wore to the dance. Mrs. Elphin advises us to remember not to *overload* the closet, otherwise our delicate woolens cannot breathe. You should always choose quality rather than quantity. Most girls could get along in school for a whole season with only two good wool skirts, though some girls think they need fifteen, and this is ridiculous. A girl says, "But you'd always look the same," and the lecturer says, "Not if you mix them with blouses and sweaters." The money you save on having fewer skirts can be spent on many sweaters.

The class is getting restless. Lila passes a note: "Next is English class with Mrs. Nasson. There's a tack epidemic, watch before you sit."

One Negro girl in the class is very well dressed and well groomed. She sits with the white girls. Her hairdo is very chic— probably a professional job. Three other Negro girls sit in a group by themselves. They are not as expensively dressed or as well-kempt, but certainly they are not messy. One is wearing a going-steady ring on a chain around her neck. She is more high-fashion than the others of her group.

I am introduced to Mrs. Nasson, the English teacher, who reads my credentials to the class. Since we are affiliated with the United States Department of Health, Education and Welfare she announces that I'm working for Kennedy's cabinet! Then she tells the class about their research project for this spring. She lectures them on the abuse of freedom, saying that stopping by the rest-room to smoke when you're on your way to the library is breaking two rules, because you have no intention of going to the library anyway. She says also that speeding is an abuse of the right to drive.

Lila tells me that when I was up front with Mrs. Nasson the boys in back were discussing whether or not to put a tack on my chair in order to teach me 4th-hour English culture. Lila says she rescued me in time by removing the tack. It could have been worse, she says, if she had left the tack there.

The research project is to be entitled "The obligation of freedom; its use and abuse." They are to write 500 words or less. The students think teacher is killing them with work. The essay is to be written either in ink or on the typewriter.

Mrs. Nasson then asks the class, "What if I'm a Communist and get up on a soap box and talk about how the capitalists are rich while I have nothing, and that therefore we should reapportion wealth through the medium of the state?" The class is horrified and seems eager to put her down. Apparently they are terrified of Communism. Then their anger gets lost in arguments about legal ways to silence the teacher (were she such a Communist). Mrs. Nasson talks about the fact that her husband and father have always felt free to criticize the government, and she and her family are certainly not Communists.

At this point Lila passes me a note: "That's Mildred talking. Mediocre person. The one in the corner is Carl Warren. He's in favor of tacks: one of the ring-leaders of the bunch."

The class gets into a discussion about Miss Pope, who, I think, is a teacher in Rome High. Miss Pope has made some comment about reckless teen-age drivers, and the girl next to me grumbles in great disgust, "They always blame it on us." The class, however, agrees that Miss Pope has the right to her own opinion. They decide also that the law must decide whether Mrs. Nasson can speak about Communism or not. Mrs. Nasson wants everybody to read the article "Erosion of individual liberties: current crisis could be decisive" by Marquis Childs, and use it as a reference for their theme. . . .

Lila remarks by note on other students. Eddie Strong is a tack-master. Nellie Burke is smart but not goody-goody. Rob is in the second stage of imbecilic ignorance; heaven knows how he passes! Tim Aupen is very smart, gets good grades, knows what's going on and how to be legally innocent.

Mrs. Nasson reads an outstanding essay from the previous assignment—it surprised her because the boy had been a gold-bricker and procrastinator. She mentions how Woodrow Wilson had died of a broken heart over the failure of the League of Nations and talks about Bernard Baruch, who is a Jewish man who was advisor to many Presidents: he used to sit around on park benches thinking. None of the students had heard of him. These are examples of topics not covered in the essay.

Lila passes a note about Tess Murray: very intelligent; scar on neck; Lila doesn't know how it got there. She is certain it's one of the reasons Tess "Just doesn't care. I wish she'd come out of it. I try to help her, but not much [can be done]; she's still the same."

There is a poster on the board by Eddie Strong:

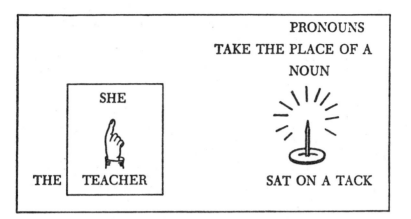

The students are upset because they get off Thursday and Friday and Mrs. Nasson expects them to prepare an outline for their paper during those two days. Poor imposed-upon kids!

Hour bell rings. Pauline comes up to Lila and says, "I heard about you going out and getting a drink after the dance on Saturday night. You silly kid—ordering a Tom Collins!" I ask Lila if she got it and she giggles and says yes. She mentions the place.

At lunch in the cafeteria the students are separated into cliques of boys and girls. The colored students sit apart from the white and they also are subdivided into all-boy and all-girl cliques. At our table I met the six girls Lila usually has lunch with. They are all rather plain except Pauline, whom I met in English. She is a very pretty blonde, with blue eyes. One girl gets the job of fetching and carrying the Cokes and candy bars for the others. I ask Lila why and she says it's because this girl is a minister's daughter and they tell her to be a good Samaritan and set them all a good example. When I look dubious Lila laughs. Lila tells me everyone cheats in math class *because* Mr. Snider only tells you how to do the problems *after* they're due, so you don't know how to do them. Also he doesn't give enough time to do them, so they copy from the more inventive students. All the girls wanted to know where Lila got served her Tom Collins. One girl says, "Where? I'll be there." A girl who says she has no desire to drink promptly gets cut out of the conversation. Lila won't tell where she got the drink. She says, "It wasn't something wild, *I just felt grown up,* so I thought I would: I didn't go out to get drunk." Liquor is available at the Greene house; her dad offered me some when I was there last time. Her brother Bill said he'd fix me a highball but wasn't sure how to go about it. I abstained.

Back in the girls' john: there is a large number of Negro girls, many of them sad-looking. Cigarette butts are all over the place. Several Negro girls are sitting against one wall. The white girls are competing for primping space at the mirrors. The john wall I get to investigate has scribbles of initials: JP plus MK, for example. Also "fuck" and lipstick smears; not as bad as some johns I've seen, by a long shot.

Now in algebra class. I've been mistaken before during the day for a sixteen-year-old, now I believe it: I've just been approached by a young playboy type called Charlie Nelson. I get to sit between him and Lila. A nice colored boy brings me a chair and I thank him; no one else thought of it! Heddie Celine is in here, all amazed to see me. Class chews gum like fiends. A beautiful brunette comes in and Lila introduces us. Lila says to me, aside, "In the hall she's okay, but just look at the insecurity all over her face when she comes in." Lila is very perceptive! She writes me a note asking if Charlie is making me nervous, and I say, "Get serious." She says, "*He* is," and I let the matter drop. But Charlie keeps looking over my shoulder. He asks me if I'd like to join the class, and I say, "Only for today."

The teacher, Mr. Snider, is a broad-shouldered, athletic, blond, crew-cut, rugged type. Married. Dominance in his whole voice and demeanor—a little bit of beer-gut, it seems.

A note has just been kicked in front of me in the most intricate manner. It gets kicked along the floor, like a piece of scrap paper, to its destination.

This algebra class contains all years. There are hoods and also innocent little freshman boys who seem less worldly than the girls of the same age. There are no levis in here but Elvis haircuts are showing up; there seems more attention to fashion on the part of the males. Revision: there is one pair of levis in here, belonging to Roger, a singularly unhandsome guy; tall. I ask Lila if he is a hood, and she says, "Um-m-m, I don't know. He goes out with girls for what he can get. I don't know him except by reputation." Teacher is now taking the class grades. Charlie Nelson is so busy trying to read over my shoulder he misses his turn and has to be called on it. He's also unhandsome. Chews gum viciously. Elvis haircut. In and out of his seat constantly. Lila tells me she will give me a story about him later that will make a "bunch of notes."

Mr. Snider is wearing a green, long-sleeved sport shirt, no tie, black wool slacks, tan belt. Looks more like a sport than a teacher.

Celine to the pencil sharpener. Looks sharp today: white blouse, very feminine, purple plaid full skirt, brushed wool. Nylons, black flats. Girls in here run about two-thirds for nylons, one-third for white bobby sox and bleached tennis shoes.

Sixth hour, Mr. Johnsberg's social studies class. A girl asks if it's true they're all going to Mr. Miller's class next semester. Johnsberg replies, "What does that have to do with what I'm saying?" Girl says, "Nothing—I just wanted to know." She's crestfallen. Johnsberg says, "Yes, it's true, but that doesn't make any difference." But a boy up in front says, "Yes, it does." The whole class is groaning. "We want *you,* Mr. Johnsberg." Johnsberg says gruffly, "Well, I'll miss you too. Now let's get on with it." Big bluffer, he's been touched by this. It is interesting to notice the boys are the loudest groaners in this show of affection.

Girls and boys seem to segregate themselves here as well as elsewhere. In here, a class of all freshmen, the boys fall back on the pattern of slacks, khakis, very ordinary shirts. There is no symbolic display of wealth among them. There seem to be even three or four girls in here who aren't competing in clothing, although they are well groomed and clean.

Lila and her friend Beatrice, who wears a clique band like Lila's, are giggling. Beatrice won't believe I'm a college senior. Lila tells me most kids have told her I look sixteen. The top estimate so far has been eighteen. I show Beatrice my driver's license.

Johnsberg is wearing a gray suit and bow tie, white shirt,

black shoes. He makes a very nice appearance before the class. Another teacher passes through the hall wearing a sport coat, tie, slacks. Johnsberg permits all the talk to continue without a word of admonishment. The students are cheating, trading answers to the study quiz right and left, but Johnsberg doesn't seem to care.

The last bell rings and there is a mad rush to lockers and exits. Boys and girls who haven't seemed to know each other all day leave the school hand in hand. No one loiters.

We have finished our day at Rome High with Lila Greene, and we have come to know her as a sharp fourteen-year-old, secure in her world. She has many friends, knows everybody, and is at ease in school: there seems to be complete complementarity between Lila and her environment. She has things sized up, and like so many of her fellows, she will get away with what she can. From the standpoint of *this* dimension of her existence, Rome High socializes Lila to the corrupt aspects of the adult world. Of course, this is not *all* of Rome High, but it is a significant part.

*Para-courtship and para-delinquency.* Lila is ingenious and thinks the world is to be handled; she seems comfortable in a world where one must "figure all the angles." In this the high school helps her, now in one way, through permissive teachers, now in another, through the students. Let us look at some of the ways in which the high school does its part. (1) Miss Clements tells the girls that "notebooks are due today" but that she will understand if some are not handed in on time because this is Monday. That is to say, recognizing that Friday through Sunday is largely spent in the *Midsummer Night's Dream,* where boy chases girl chases boy, one should not expect work to be accomplished. Actually this is the teacher's recognition that *ceremonial para-courtship* is so intense and so standardized, built in, and hallowed by the fleeting traditions of twentieth-century youth, that she really ought not intrude upon it with orthodox demands like industry and obligation. In the nineteen sixties, it has become so obvious that para-courtship is a necessary, rigid ceremonial which one must not offend that work and obligation become subordinated to it. How explain, otherwise, the students' complaints at the trifling homework assignments? In a broader context we might say that the development of the pattern of fun, of which para-courtship is but a part, has intruded so far into the orthodox procedures, obligations, and austerities of school, that it has received recognition by the school authorities.

(2) Since what stands out in the minds of many younger adolescents as the most important feature of the independent adult is the right to untrammeled impulse release, hard liquor is the veritable symbol of freedom to them. Everywhere the movement toward independence has its symbol. Alcohol, with its implied narcotizing of the Super Ego, is the liberating fluid for children seeking a taste of the intoxication of total freedom in the age of impulse release and fun. Lila, by drinking a Tom Collins on her date, has herself become the embodiment of adult liberty, and for this she receives suitable recognition and status from her age-mates. When one student dares to say she is not interested in liquor she is cut out of the conversation for contempt of the symbol of independence and "maturity." This incident and Lila's comment help us understand the importance of such *para-delinquencies* as projections and affirmations of group spirit and solidarity. "It wasn't something wild," says Lila, "I just felt grown up, so I thought I would. I didn't go out to get drunk." Thus Lila has done the thing that is right in the early adolescent world, where to get drunk is wild and bad, but where it's all right, thrilling, status-enhancing, and group-affirming to obtain an illegal drink occasionally *just to feel grown up*. A child's negation of adult *law* has thus become an affirmation of the condition of being adult. Extracted from the cultural complex by the sharp *Id logic* of adolescence is the generalization that it is adult for a child to violate adult laws in order to follow adult enjoyments.

(3) Everyone cheats in math, says Lila, because they don't like the way the teacher makes the assignments and because he does not give the students enough time. This is another of what

we may now call the *conventions of dishonesty* (*vide* the canons of pecuniary philosophy), the system of rationalizations by which one makes his frauds acceptable to his Self. The psychic function of these modes of thought is, of course, to defend the Self from inner aggression. Socialization to the adolescent culture thus involves an important inner gain: *adolescent culture provides its members with a system of defenses that protects the Self from attack by the voice of conscience.* Who has as much to offer them? Meanwhile we must bear in mind that these children, through being taught to lie to themselves, are learning how to pursue a life of decent chicanery in the adult world. Lila's assessment of Tim Aupen—that he "knows how to be legally innocent"—is culturally resonant. I do not, of course, give adolescent culture all the credit for the canons of dishonesty. What the adolescent group does is add certain thoughts of its own and lend a generalizing polish and group support to chicanery that makes it easier to absorb the finishing touches of later life. An honest adolescent life could be a crippling preliminary for many phases of contemporary culture.

In Mr. Johnsberg's class the cheating occurs right under his nose. Regardless of whether he approves of it or simply does not care, his students must surely learn that illegality of this kind is not a serious rupture of morals in the eyes of some adults. Given this postulate, we can trust their alert minds to generalize, simply by lopping off the words "in the eyes of some adults."

Consider now the fate and condition of a child who does not cheat either in Mr. Snider's or Mr. Johnsberg's class, who refuses to copy from other children and declines to let them copy from him. He would be more loathsome than the girl who was not interested in drinking. Who could stand against this tide?

Incidentally, Mr. Johnsberg and his wife, who teaches elementary school, are agreed that they "do not want books to interfere with their daughter's social life in high school!"

We have not yet exhausted the means of understanding Lila's surreptitious hand in her father's pocket. Look at the massive stimulation to raise her consumption level Lila encounters in

Rome High. Consider, first, the forthright talk of Mrs. Elphin on how to spend money and enhance status. Much of what she said is worth repeating. For example, after giving something of the history of wool she breaks off and says that in order "to move on to something *more interesting*" she will drop the history and discuss style. It is clear as the late sun streaming through the clouds after a dull morning that style is more interesting than history! On this whole day in Rome High, however, nobody except Mrs. Elphin said anything really close to the students. If Lila did not already know it, Mrs. Elphin, well dressed and the representative of a powerful industry, tells her that history is boring. There, in the comparative luxury of the Home Economics room, 'mid the posters on cosmetics, dresses, and perspiration, Lila learns how to raise social status, how to avoid being linked with "dirty, untidy, cheap people," and how to be happy in an ambient world of tidy, sweet-smelling people and expensive wool! This too is acquiring an identity! What is the prettiest room in the school? The Home Ec room, where Lila, a lower-middle-class girl, learns how to consume, to raise her living standard, and to move up in the social scale. This is the room that symbolizes the pressures on Lila to spend; this is where we begin to understand most clearly the compulsion to stick her hand in father's pocket when he's not looking. But it would be wrong to blame the sly hand entirely on the Home Ec class, when the students themselves provoke the drive to competitive display. Consider the following from the record:

1. The girls are all sharply dressed. . . . There are mirrors everywhere and the girls are preening themselves in front of them.
2. Class seems to go from ultra-chic hair styles to long mops, with no middle ground.
3. One girl, a junior, looks like a high-fashion model; bleached blonde.
4. Most girls wear expensive sweaters.
5. In one corner [of the Home Economics room] there is a large, three-sided wardrobe mirror in front of which a student, with

the assistance of two friends, has been primping herself since class began. She is wearing a very elaborate oriental type hair style, piled intricately around her head. . . .

6. One Negro girl in the class is very well dressed and well groomed. She sits with the white girls. . . . Three other Negro girls sit in a group by themselves. They are not as expensively dressed or as well-kempt. . . . One is wearing a going-steady ring on a chain around her neck. *She* is more high-fashion than the others of her group.

7. Girls in here run about two-thirds for nylons, one-third for white bobby sox and bleached tennis shoes.

8. There seem to be even three or four girls in here who aren't competing in clothing. . . .

The stimulation to spend money on clothes and grooming must be overwhelming for a normal fourteen-year-old lower-middle-class girl; and the school takes this preoccupation for granted. How could Rome High, in the center of a lower-middle-class neighborhood, be indifferent to its yearnings toward status and the high-rising living standard? How could Rome High block the glittering Id of progress? Can we expect Lila, hungering for the group, to sit against the john wall twiddling her thumbs while her peers, glorious in ultra-chic and high fashion, competitively display their cosmetic success? Those mirrors on the wall do not say who is most beautiful of all, but they do communicate to the children that the school supports their strivings toward standards of pecuniary loveliness. There is one girl who has outdistanced the field. She is the girl who, having achieved a coiffure so elaborate that she cannot manage it alone, has two others hovering around her like Nubian slaves, catching the wisps of hair, and shoring up the coils that have broken loose. She might well be Lila's goal, but such opulence is costly, and it is this sort of spectacle that helps to animate the hand that slips in and out of father's pocket in the darkness of his carelessness, fuzzy-mindedness, and nonobsessive attitude toward truth.

The Rome of which I speak is a lower-middle-class suburb. Its boys in football costume are *its* helmeted soldiers; there is a special dining room for them in the school cafeteria, special food for them, and all they want of it. In Rome High the athletes are the cultural maximizers, and it is the duty of Mr. Aurelius, the principal, to see that his teams win. Mr. Aurelius is not unique in this preoccupation with prowess and success in high school athletics but shares it with much of the Rome region, where high school principals, coaches, PTAs, and Fathers' Athletic Associations hover over the players, while scouts from distant universities offer scholarships to Rome's heroes. This does not mean that Mr. Aurelius has no concern for scholarship, but rather that the drive that is maximized in the high school spirit is the competitive sportive one. The most popular males are found in the athletic clique.

Next is a visit by a researcher to the home of Jim Evans, sixteen years old, a junior, and an outstanding athlete.

When I got to Jim's house he was not there, and his parents were very apologetic, explaining that the basketball coach had called a pop scrimmage, so he could not be there to receive me. They offered me a cup of coffee and a piece of chocolate cake, which I accepted. Their house was modest, I estimate lower middle class or working class. The living room was cluttered with newspapers, coffee cups, etc. Jim's mother was wearing a house dress and her husband wore slacks and a sweatshirt with *Meredith Co.* across the front and back—probably from a company baseball team.

Jim's father said that they've been going to basketball games for ages. Their oldest son is a freshman at ———— on an athletic scholarship, and he played first-string basketball all through high school. He has received offers of athletic scholarships from Northwestern, University of Missouri, Ohio State, and others. His mother, who was standing in the dining room ironing, said that it was "amazing how people cater to athletes." She said that when they took their son to ———— the coach met them at the parking lot, carried their suitcases, took them to lunch and on a tour of the university; installed their son in the dorm, et cetera, et cetera, "And all of this while the other kids were standing around not knowing what to do or where to go."

I asked if basketball took much of Jim's time nowadays, and they told me that he has practice every day after school for two and a half hours, games every Tuesday and Friday, and occasional pop scrimmages. But they did not seem to think that this was too much time.

Jim's mother said that the catering to athletes goes on in high school too, but she said also that a teacher told her that if Jim was good at basketball he would be assured of an education. She said that the athletes have a special lunchroom at Rome High, and that they get special food, as much of it as they want. The rest of the kids eat in the school cafeteria and get one serving of the regular fare. If the athlete's grades begin to fall he receives special tutoring from the teachers.

Mr. Evans is a manual worker of limited skill who has found a way to get his sons out of the little-initiative-and-little-education, low-living-standard rut. Sports readily became a way out for his sons because he himself is athletically inclined. He cannot know, of course, that what a boy on an athletic scholarship gets is a formal misrepresentation of an education.

Jim was not highly articulate in his interviews; we would hardly expect an American boy, tied up in athletics, to be very verbal. Still there is a great deal in his short, ungrammatical sentences.

The researcher reported the result of his first interview with Jim.

When I arrive at Jim's house, he, his father, and little brother are plastered to the TV set. Jim and I move into the dining room to talk. The TV is going rather loudly; there is a program on in which some guy is trying to get rid of a body— that of his former girl friend, whom he has just murdered. This makes it rather difficult to concentrate on the interview. It is a suspense-type movie, and I'm as anxious as the rest of the household to see if the murderer gets caught. I explain the project to Jim and we begin:

R: I'd like to talk about your friends—can you tell me if there is a bunch of guys you see a lot of?

J: Yeah. There's Burt Schneiderhof, Pickles Kovac, Dave Platmin, Tom Burke and Ed Laughlin.

R: Who would you say is your best friend?

J: Dave.

R: What do you do together?

J: We go to the show together and double date. We both drive. We double date about every three weeks or a month. We go to the show about once every two weeks. Sometimes I go out on a date alone, but not lately.[2]

R: Can you tell me something about Dave? What kind of a guy is he?

J: Well, he's president of the Student Council at Rome. He's ——.[3] He drives a car. He's got a real nice personality. He's a great guy. He's active in sports. As a matter of fact, we just came from a baseball game—Rome vs. Cliff Heights. We won.

R: What position do you play?

J: I play second base; Dave plays first base.

R: Your father told me you play basketball—did you have a good season?

J: Yeah.

R: He told me your brother plays too.

J: Yeah. He got a scholarship at ——.

R: How's he doing?

J: Real good. He's the best player they got. He helped me a lot with my game.[4]

R: What kind of a guy is he?

J: Oh, he's got a good personality. He goes out with girls a lot. Uh-h-h. We play basketball together and play games and cards at home. We have a lot of fun together.

R: What would you say gives a guy a good personality?

[2] Actually it took three questions to elicit these answers, but they have been left out in the interest of brevity.

[3] Nationality mentioned.

[4] Interviewer had to ask an extra question to get this information.

J: A sense of humor, and uh-h-h-h understanding—you know, when a guy can put himself in other peoples' shoes.

R: Do you think looks and clothes have anything to do with it?

J: Oh, yes. I think so. I don't know about clothes; I guess clothes do too—you know, if you dress too shabby or something.

R: What do you think is important about having a sense of humor?

J: 'Cause people like people who are happy-go-lucky and laugh a lot.

R: What do you think is important about understanding?

J: I guess because people like to be understood and like people who understand 'em.

R: Who would you say are your next best friends after Dave?

J: There's a couple: Laughlin and Kovac, I guess.

R: What are they like?

J: They're nice guys—they treat you nice. They're good guys.

R: Can you think of an example of a time when you got mad at Dave?

J: Well, like sometimes he wants to go home early Friday night or something and I don't want to go. But I don't get real mad.

R: Is there anything that you and he disagree about?

J: Uh-h-h, well, uh-h-h, we disagree about music. He likes jazz and I like popular music on the radio.

R: Let's see. Do you and Dave ever argue about music?

J: Yeah. We don't really argue, we just disagree and tell each other we're crazy. You know, friends are bound to disagree once in a while. We have lunch together every day; our gang all eat at the same table.

R: Are most of them active in sports?

J: All of 'em are.

R: Would you say it was a clique?

J: You could say that. There's pretty many of 'em. About sixteen or seventeen. You know, the more popular guys.

R: Are there other cliques around Rome [High]?

J: Uh huh.

R: Can you describe some of them to me?

J: Well, you know, the groups don't mix much. There's one group of guys that don't go out much on Friday or Saturday nights. You know, the brains. They're all pretty smart guys.

Our hero on the TV is smuggling the body out of a hotel wrapped in a rug. The desk clerk asks him where he's going and he replies that he is taking the rug out to be cleaned. It's about 2 A.M. Very tense situation.

J: Of course, there's girls' cliques.

R: What are the girls' cliques like?

J: Well, the most popular cliques are like the boys'. You know, they're sort of mediocre in grades. And the cutest girls are usually in the largest clique.

[Researcher then turns the conversation briefly to girls and elicits the fact that Jim went "steadily" for a while. The difference between going "steady" and going "steadily" is that the former is more binding than the latter.]

R: What did you do together?

J: We went to parties and to the show. I wasn't driving then, of course, so there wasn't much to it.

R: Did you notice many changes in your outlook on life when you started driving?

J: I guess you feel bigger; you know you can date more when you're driving. I think it's pretty important.

R: Did you make many new friends?

J: Yeah, I notice that anybody that learns to drive becomes more popular, especially with the kids that aren't driving yet— with the younger kids.

[The interviewer learns from Jim that he makes $7.50 a week working and that it goes for shows, dates and "things like that." He also elicits the fact that Jim helps Dave out occasionally by driving him to school or to the library.]

R: Is there anything else that you and Dave do for each other?

J: Not much.

R: How do you feel about sports?

J: I think it makes you enjoy school a whole lot more. I

think everybody should go out for at least one sport. It helps you to develop your body.

R: How do you think kids in general feel about sports?

J: Most of them like it pretty much. We have a pretty good attendance at all of our games. We have plenty of team spirit. And it helps to make you a lot more popular. Girls look up to you more and other guys envy you more.

It was nearly 9 P.M. and Jim was obviously getting bored, so I thought it time to conclude the session. As he walked me to the door he gave his little brother a healthy smack on the arm, and the little one said, "What are you, some kind of a nut?"

Athletics, popularity, and "mediocre" grades go together with inarticulateness and poor grammar. Standing as it does at the center of lower-middle-class Rome's need to *be* something, the athletic complex is the natural pivot of social life, school politics, and the competitive sexual ritual, where a girl measures her success by the athletes she dates. What is most important in attempting to grasp American social character, however, is that the athletic complex is a great machine for generating communal Selfhood. The teams are great hearts pumping Self-substance into the anemic Self of the community—students and school included. When you are on a team girls seek you out and boys envy you in Rome, because when the team wins the communal Self is replenished. In a sense one might say that Jim's poor grades and grammar are ransom for the community's Self. This must be understood in order to comprehend the American phenomenon of the athletic blockhead.

# Boredom, Utopia, and "Unprofessional Conduct"

## BY JOEL DENKER

Teaching can be a hazardous business for those committed to raising questions, not answering them, and to allowing kids to experiment and explore. Joel Denker found it impossible to be honest with himself and his students and yet remain in the public school system. He remained for one year, and then founded a new school, the New Education Project, which is prospering in Takoma Park, Maryland. Joel is a graduate of Yale University and the Antioch-Putney Graduate School of Education.

PUBLIC HIGH schools in suburbia are exploding; in the last two years boycotts, sit-ins, and other acts of rebellion have shattered these outwardly placid communities. But these are only the more visible signs of the disaffection which white middle-class kids feel. Many activist students burn themselves out trying to transform their schools. Others are too pessimistic about the possibility of bringing about any substantive change to even try. It is to these students that the idea of starting their own school, outside the system, has the greatest appeal. All over the country, small groups of students are beginning to band together in order to form free schools. They are doing this with the aid of discontented teachers, parents, and other friendly souls, but it is their own boldness, more than anything else, that supplies the real energy for these projects. Dropping out of school means not only overcoming the resistance of one's parents but also confronting the many regulations which the state has set up to hedge in the freedom of the young—the compulsory attendance, labor, antiloitering, and other

179

laws. Already a newsletter, *The New Schools Exchange*, has been started to serve as a clearinghouse of information for people who want to start schools, teachers who want to teach in them, kids who want to drop out. That many more kids are dropping out of school than ever before is important in itself. That they are dropping out in order to develop counter-communities that may in time further destroy the legitimacy of public schools in the eyes of parents and their children is even more significant.

I helped to create a free high school in Washington, D.C., and have been active in it for the past two years. In 1967–68, I was a teacher in a high school in suburban Maryland. I had just returned from a year of teaching in a refugee school in southern Africa. All my past teaching experience had been with black students in educational projects in the ghetto and in the South. Like many other activists my age, I felt that the black community was where the action was. When my graduate school placed me in a predominantly white high school, Montgomery Blair High School in Silver Spring, Maryland, I was very upset. I thought that the kids would be soft and complacent, that they would experience none of the anguish that is the common condition of black Americans.

After a few months of "cultural shock," I really began to enjoy my work. Not the classroom teaching but the relationships I was beginning to develop with the kids I was meeting in the building. Many were virtually suffocating from their routinized existence at Blair. Reciting Shakespeare or learning English vocabulary made little sense to them when they were experiencing acute personal tensions. A drug experience, a romance, a desire to free oneself from parental restrictions, an interest in the Poor People's Campaign—none of these concerns was a legitimate part of the curriculum. And they had little time during the school day to talk to their classmates about the things that were tearing up their guts. Attention had to be focused on the teacher, if they were to be ready for the next question. I would frequently meet kids who skipped their classes to walk out to the grove or wander the corridors just to seek out some social contact.

That fall, a number of students asked me to serve as a sponsor for an organization they wanted to start, to be called the Student Organizing Committee. They wanted it to be a discussion group that would deal with things that were banished from the school curriculum—the draft, race, rock music, experimental education, for example. But the school administration did not like the fact that the kids would be organizing independently of the official channels. The principal said that there was already a "critical issues" forum sponsored by the Student Council. He was also bothered by the role he expected me to play in the group. I was not going to mediate between the students and the school administration. Nor was I willing to be a moderate force in the group, to be there to introduce a note of caution whenever the kids got too self-reliant. And many of the faculty did not like the close, personal ties that were developing between me and the kids. They wanted to maintain their distance from the kids; their style was one of cool reserve. Later in the year, the principal told me that some members of the faculty had criticized me for "unprofessional conduct" because they had seen me sitting on the floor talking with students.

Our first conflict with the administration developed when one of the organizers of SOC placed a copy of Jerry Farber's article "Student As Nigger" on some of the school's bulletin boards. Beneath the article was an announcement that SOC (still not an official organization) would sponsor a discussion of that article at the end of the school day. Much to my surprise, the poster said that I would be leading the discussion. The fellow who had put it up had forgotten to tell me this. The administration panicked. They claimed that the article would inflame racial tensions at the school. We gave in too quickly on this issue. We didn't hold the discussion and we took down the posters.

For much of September and October we had what seemed an

endless round of discussions with the administration about the formation of SOC. The principal wanted to know whether we intended the group simply to be a discussion rather than an action organization. He was disturbed by the name we had given to our group and wanted us to change it. We stood fast. When we responded that it was impossible to separate critical thought and discussion from action, he was baffled. He was also concerned lest we present only one side of an issue. He maintained that the school's function was to make a balanced presentation of all social problems. I was learning how the rhetoric of "objectivity" could be used to conceal real biases and self-interest. For example, the Montgomery County school system, like most public systems, prohibited the circulation of leaflets and the posting of announcements without prior permission. They rarely gave permission to anyone who wanted to distribute controversial material—on the draft, on the war, on student rights. We were later to encounter tremendous resistance from the principal when we asked that the annual "military service" assembly (at which representatives from all the services spoke to the senior class) include a discussion of alternatives to the draft.

Both the school administration and its allies in the student council placed a number of procedural roadblocks in our way. We had to prepare a constitution and we were told on a number of occasions that we had made grievous errors in submitting it. They told us, for example, that we had given them an insufficient number of copies. One of our friends on the newspaper unearthed the fact that another student group, The Model Rocketry Club, had quickly been approved by the student government and recognized by the administration.

We finally were approved as an official school organization after much parliamentary and procedural hassling. We quickly organized a series of programs that enabled us to build a solid base of support among the students. Our first program brought the Nighthawk, a black disk jockey from the District, to Blair to expound on soul music. The gym was filled to capacity. Discussions on the "psychological hangups of teachers" (led by a local psychiatrist), on Buddhism, on the American right followed.

But kids in the group wanted to do more than talk. Some of them wanted to organize protests against the county regulations on leafleting and against the forthcoming military service assembly. Yet it would be misleading to describe SOC as an effective vehicle for political action. We talked much more than we acted. We never were able to attract enough student support to carry out a successful action and most of our plans fizzled. I suspect that we never quite believed that our actions would make the slightest dent in the way the administration ran the school. We had learned a lot from our experience organizing SOC about the resistance the administration would put up to even the most minor change in the status quo. Much of our energy was sapped in simply trying to survive from day to day in the school. A good number of the kids got stoned on grass just to get through the day. I myself returned home feeling physically exhausted from my struggles trying to cope with that absurd universe. We expended so much nervous energy simply trying to stay on our feet that we had little left over for practical organization.

The talking we did together and the close personal ties that began to develop between us were profoundly important. For more than anything else, SOC was a community. We were free to get to know each other without regulation from a classroom time-table. Kids who had once felt awfully alone, who had personalized their problems, met others who were in the same situation. The enthusiasm that many of the SOC kids expressed came from having acquired a new identity, an identity rooted in their involvement in a cohesive group. Free from many of the standardized roles and superficial forms of communication we had previously been locked into, we began to analyze the educational system that had been repressing us. We tried to figure out why schools were organized in the way they were. We tried to envision what learning would be like in a really free environment.

One night in February two students from Blair, a civil rights lawyer, Bill Higgs, and I were having dinner together at the home of another one of the kids, Norman Solomon. We were discussing the perennial topic of conversation, life at Blair, when Bill in a perfectly straightforward way asked us: "Why don't you guys start your own school?" Bill had a way of making the most outlandish experiments seem easy. At the suggestion of this idea, all of us became very excited. It was a perfectly outrageous idea that answered all our most immediate needs; that we hadn't thought of it ourselves was a measure of how constricted our vision had been. Blair was our universe; nothing else seemed quite real.

For the next several days and for several weeks thereafter, we talked in a visionary way about the idea and began to tell a number of our friends about it. We had to keep convincing each other that the idea could become real, that it just wouldn't stay in the fantasy stage. The compelling thing about creating our own school was that it would be something we would control and own. All our efforts to change conditions at the school had been going nowhere. We were becoming increasingly frustrated and had no answers for those who asked us what alternative we had for the present system. Here was an opportunity to begin living what we had been preaching, rather than waiting for utopia someday to come.

The kids at Blair who became involved in the project and I had one thing in common. We were all bored. No common ideology, no common view of what our school's purpose should be, bound us together. The atmosphere at Blair, we said to ourselves, was choking us to death; we wanted out. It was the atmosphere, more than any specific acts of repression directed against us, which made us leave; we were rebelling against a total environment.

Many people in the radical movement constantly talk about whether it is better to stay within the established institutions or to leave them and create alternative structures. But this issue didn't bother us at all at the time that we started organizing the school. It was an abstract consideration compared to the acutely personal impulses we then felt. We acted out of personal necessity; we had no other options. Neither the kids nor myself could survive another year in a public high school. One of the kids most active in the project has told me since that if the school hadn't come along he would have hit the road for California. It was only in the course of our day-to-day work in the school that we began to get a glimpse of the direction we might go in, the goals we might set for ourselves.

One movement organizer in the Washington area accused us of being utopian, as if this were a cardinal sin. She felt, and I think her point of view is shared by some segments of the left, that it was a cop-out for teachers and students to leave public schools. If students stayed locked in the jaws of Leviathan they would be radicalized, which was to be desired; teachers should also remain in the school to give political direction to the struggles their students would then undertake. This view makes suffering into a virtue and ignores the profoundly liberating effect of leaving the school system.

The center for organizing the school was Blair. I was teaching there and the kids most committed to the idea were students at the school. And through SOC we had met a large number of radical kids. But gaining new converts and keeping our own morale up was difficult. When we described a new school, we spun its outlines from our imagination. We had no building, no money, no definite curriculum—in short none of the things that most people associated with a school. If somebody was the slightest bit timid or conservative, he was not likely to stay with us for long. I remember asking myself what I would do if the school never got off the ground. Should I have another job waiting in case we failed, should I keep my options open? I plunged ahead into the unknown and threw my anxieties to the wind; in that sense the school helped me a great deal. The kids faced even greater risks. They were leaving the traditional route that led to college, career, and a secure life style, and they had to buck their parents, middle-class people, who never quite believed that we would pull off the project and feared the worst for their kids' futures. In some cases, we, the older people involved, were made the scapegoats for all the tensions that wracked the students' families.

When I look back on these anxious months, I wonder why we kept with it. Analyzing it later, I think I can say that we were all adventurous types; we had all done things before they had become fashionable. Some of the kids had been involved with drugs before they became a fad, had hitchhiked on their own, had already wrested a considerable amount of independence from their parents. One boy, Greg, had been very much influenced by the Beats, when he lived in California, had been moved by Camus and Sartre, had done a lot of acid, and had an intense interest in Eastern religion. I had helped to organize a freedom school in St. Augustine, Florida, during the summer of 1964. Bill Higgs was a white Mississippian who had defended James Meredith when he was trying to enter the University of Mississippi in 1961. I think we felt a need to prove to ourselves and to others that we could create something that no one else thought was possible.

We organized a series of meetings that lasted from mid-February through the summer. Interested high school students, teachers, and parents listened to us try to convince them that we had a serious project. Except for a hard core of eight to ten kids, plus myself, Bill Higgs, and two friends of mine who were teaching in black schools in the District, the faces changed from one session to the next. The fact that our constituency was constantly fluctuating scared us. When would we ever know, we asked ourselves, who was really with us? As it turned out, we would not definitely know until the first week of September, when we had rented a house, and the school had become something of a reality.

In the course of these meetings, at picnics, and at a retreat in the Shenandoah Mountains, we got to know each other very well. Roles of "teachers" and "students" that had previously obstructed communication began to break down in these informal settings. We talked a great deal about what we wanted our school to be—what kind of classes, if any, it should have, how we would finance it, how decisions would be made. These could scarcely be called "planning sessions." We envisioned few of the problems that we were later to face and our vision of the school we hoped to build was vague. One of the things we most often mentioned was that we wanted some kind of community that would break down barriers between teachers and students. One of the ways we planned to do this was by renting houses where those who wished could live together. These houses would also serve as the centers for many of the school's activities. We were also searching for a more "relevant" education than we had been getting. But these were still phrases whose content needed to be filled in. We knew much more what we didn't like about public school education than what we wanted to erect in its place.

These shared experiences were very important in helping to build a feeling of group unity and in fashioning a common educational philosophy, if only a vague and abstract one. We did not want a situation in which the older people would represent the interest of others in the group without their presence. Anyone could act as spokesman at meetings, could recruit new students, and carry out other necessary tasks. The older people at this point handled a lot more of the bureaucratic details (writing to colleges, checking out legal requirements, and the like) but this did not alter the feeling that we were all in this together, that we each had a say in determining the outlines of the school.

Before the school had formally begun, close ties of mutual trust and friendship bound us together. This was to help immeasurably in creating a more organic educational community. Had we simply bought a building, written up a curriculum, and then attracted students, the school would have been a much different place. We all learned as much (and probably more) from the painful struggle of creating our own school than we did from any of the formal classes that we later organized. And what's more each of us had a vital, personal stake in the project. Since we were building it together, there was no one to blame for our mistakes. In a public high school, we could always blame the school administration for all the problems we had; we were now making it impossible for any of us to cop out in this way.

The close relationships we had with each other were like those that developed between Northern college students and young Southern blacks in the freedom schools that the civil rights movement organized in the South during the summer of 1964. There too the process of creating a school from scratch was as important as any formal classes that were held, and the style of the classes was substantially different, much less abstract and impersonal, because of it. Staughton Lynd captures the spirit of the Mississippi freedom schools, the project he directed for SNCC in 1964: "There Northern white college students and Southern black teenagers had first to encounter one another as whole human beings, to establish trust. This happened in the process of finding a church basement together, deciding on a curriculum together, improvising materials together, that is in the context of common work; and it matured in that context too, as those who walked together in the morning registered voters together in the afternoon. . . . What we read together in the mornings was often James Joyce, what was talked about may have been French or algebra as well as Negro history. But I simply testify that the context of shared experience (which meant, too, that teachers characteristically boarded in their students' homes) made all the difference."

I worked in a freedom school in St. Augustine, Florida, in the summer of 1964 and carried back with me very much the same reactions to my experience that Staughton did. It seems strange that it was not until five years later that I became involved in organizing a free school in a white middle-class community. Like many other activists in the movement at that time, traveling South had been something of a vicarious experience for me. I was unhappy and bored by much of what I had studied at Yale and was alienated from many of the students who were preparing themselves for positions in the hierarchies of law, business, and government. It was easier for me to understand the plight of black teenagers than it was for me to understand how repressive my own education had been.

Once they had heard about the school, the Blair administration decided to make things as uncomfortable as possible for me. Some parents had apparently called the school because their children were threatening to drop out of high school and join us. Some of the teachers who taught "honors" classes felt threatened because some of the kids they regarded as their most creative students were talking about leaving. I remember one of my supervisors telling me that the teachers were concerned that we were manipulating kids, encouraging them to leave high school without giving them an honest picture of the risks involved.

Things came to a head when the principal called me into his office ostensibly to talk about my teaching experiences that year. One of the directors of my graduate program and my Blair supervisor were also present. Midway through the conversation they raised the question of whether the work I was doing to organize the school might represent "conflict of interest" with my duties as a teacher. In characteristic fashion, they simply hinted at this possibility. Leaving the question open, they probably felt, would scare me more than a definitive judgment on it. They said they would talk with the central office in Rockville to find out if I was in conflict with Board regulations. If they ever got a ruling from the central office, I never heard about it. But they succeeded in making my days as anxious, as suspense-filled as possible. I never knew from one day to the next whether I would be fired or not. The principal also cautioned me against using my classroom as a forum to proselytize for the school.

When we began to circulate a leaflet in the building announcing the creation of the school, the principal also tried to squelch that, but also unsuccessfully. (We had also gotten these leaflets to other high school students, had spread news of the school by word of mouth, and used the news media.) He again called me into his office and told me that it was customary to get prior approval before circulating leaflets in the school. I told him that this was a violation of free speech. He made no response and then said that since we had circulated a number of leaflets already there was little he could do about it. We did, however, circulate very few leaflets after this, at least not on a large scale, wide-open basis. We were reluctant to confront the anti-leafleting regulations head on. We had sufficient hassles resulting from organizing the school without adding any more. But as I look back on this experience now, I recognize how powerful a weapon the prohibition against free circulation of leaflets and other public notices can be. It enables the public school bureaucracy to define what acceptable speech and opinion is. Parents, teachers, and students who wish to see alternative schools become a reality for a majority of the students will have to overturn these regulations if they are to succeed.

Our announcement that we were going to start a school and the intense interest and enthusiasm this idea inspired in so many kids threatened the faculty and administration. It brought home to them the acute feelings of disaffection that many of the most creative kids in that school felt. And, most powerful effect of all, our school made a number of kids aware that they had an alternative to their daily routine. As long as students were incapable of imagining a life style radically different from the one they were accustomed to, they would tolerate it, no matter how boring it was. If we are ever to make an effective attack on compulsory public education, we must not rant and rave about how bad it is. We must make vivid to large numbers of people the existence of exciting alternatives to that system.

In the meantime, we were attending to the various details that had to be dealt with if we were to begin the school by the end of the summer. We had written to a group of colleges, mostly small progressive schools (Antioch, Goddard, Reed) but also to Yale, Wesleyan, and the University of Chicago asking them what their reaction would be to students graduating from an unaccredited school like ours. We wanted to assure kids and their parents that all their options would not be canceled by virtue of their going to the school. We did not want the school to be a college prep institution and we figured that many of the kids would ultimately decide not to go to college, at least not right away. But we felt that if the responses to our letters were positive, kids could make a more realistic decision about whether to join and about what they would do once they decided to leave the school. The responses we received to our letters were positive. This allayed the fears of the parents of some of the most committed students but others were still skeptical. They wanted a definite assurance from colleges that their kids would get in; or at least they used this as an excuse to hide more basic objections. I was amazed, though, how many people we talked to thought that going to college from a bizarre experiment like ours would be an impossibility. At least, we punctured that myth.

We spent a lot of time talking with the parents of the kids who wanted to go to the school. However, the real initiative on this score came from the kids themselves. Had they not convinced their parents that they were serious, that they had no intention of returning to public school, our arguments would have had little effect. Our presence certainly gave the project a legitimacy, an aura of adult respectability, in the eyes of the parents. At best, we provided reinforcement for decisions that were reached in a struggle between each parent and his son or daughter. With a few exceptions, no parent made any commitment or gave us any specific assurance until the last moment. This fact, of course, added to the general feeling of anxiety we then felt.

We had gone ahead from the beginning, blissfully ignorant of the laws and regulations that might affect our status as a school in the District of Columbia. Bill Higgs had assured us that we would have no difficulties, but we still did not know the hard facts. It was not until late June that two of us decided to sit down with Alex Rode, who had founded an early experimental school in D.C., to find out the legal difficulties we might encounter. Alex told us that since D.C. had no formal accreditation agency our real problems would come from the zoning board. No school, of course, could legally operate in a private residence of the kind we hoped to rent. A school had to be located in a specially zoned commercial area. Moreover, the late-nineteenth-century codes required a school building to have steel doors, fire escapes, stair wells, a parking space for each teacher regardless of whether he has a car. Since we had little or no money, we could not afford the renovating costs that an operation like this would demand. Alex's school had been closed down several times by the zoning people and he had once been taken to court. We decided that we would have most of our activities in the communal houses we planned to rent and that we would try to get a local church (which could pass zoning regulations) to be our official headquarters and mailing address. We hoped that this cover would protect us from harassment by the city. We also decided that we would register as a non-profit corporation and would try to get federal and District tax exemption.

One other important thing came out of these meetings. This was our decision to orient the school toward white middle-class kids. Any illusions we might have had about an integrated effort were dispelled when we spoke to some very savvy black kids from Eastern High School. They said they liked what we were doing but that it was irrelevant to the kind of "freedom school" they wanted. Their advice was that we complement and support each other, not try to duplicate each other's functions.

In late August of 1968 we found a house in an integrated, middle-class area off Sixteenth Street in Washington. Interest and enthusiasm soon began to pick up. Kids began to make the anxious decision to drop out of school, parents began to loosen their grip, and we began to pull our community together. There were twelve of us living in the house. Seven kids and five "teachers." We quickly realized that our project had greater political implications than we could ever have imagined. The landlord, an official from the Indian embassy who wanted U.S. citizenship, began to get uptight and put us on a month-to-month lease. The FBI began to make inquiries among our neighbors. The wife of a government official whose daughter goes to the school received a call over the White House line from an unidentified person saying that she should withdraw her daughter since our house was under surveillance. In the midst of all this, morale was high and our first "classes" got underway. This external threat had a way of helping us build solidarity when it was most crucial. We decided to move, to find a more comfortable landlord.

We now have thirty full-time students. The average age is seventeen. There are from ten to fifteen others who are involved in activities at the school, but who continue to go to their local high schools. There are five of us teaching full time—all except one former teachers in either D.C. or Maryland. We have managed to attract a number of other people—artists, a writer, public-school teachers, etc.—who are volunteering their services to the school.

We offer "classes" in a variety of areas ranging from creative writing and drama to utopian American radicalism. (We have a bulletin board where anyone who wants to get a course going puts up a time for a meeting; times of various local events—lectures, dances, films, government meetings, etc.—also appear.) These core courses, which meet once or twice a week, are intended to complement rather than serve as substitutes for the direct involvement that is central to the school. We aim to explode the classroom, to create the feeling that learning is more than a formal academic exercise, that to be worth anything it must be organically related to the person's most immediate needs and concerns. Students have done a variety of things this year: Several of the kids are working in apprenticeships with local artists—a metal sculptor and welder and a potter, for example. A trip to Baltimore to attend the trial of the Catonsville Nine got us involved in a demonstration protesting the mockery of justice in federal court and in picketing the courthouse. We went to the City Council to hear a friend protest against its avoidance of the police issue and heard the city fathers spend forty minutes discussing the question of civilian escorts for funeral processions. During the fall, classes frequently met in Rock Creek Park and most every weekend we camped out on some land in the Shenandoahs, the site of an old mission. A friend of ours has purchased land there so that we have access to it.

"Classes" in the school have been a very special experience for me after the formality of the public high school. I remember vividly a discussion a group of us had of Gide's *The Immoralist*. It started out with a discussion of our personal reactions to the novel. It soon became a dialogue in which we talked to each other about our own life styles, which ranged from social activism to a kind of religious mysticism. What impressed me was that we felt comfortable enough with each other to speak personally about our concerns—something which is frowned upon in the icy "objectivity" of the public-school classroom. After an hour of conversation, three kids said they felt terribly confused and went off for a long walk.

For myself, the ideal is to become a co-learner. The intimate relationships we have with each other in the community help to make this possible. For many of us the living situation—the communal living—and the learning experience cannot be separated. In fact, much of the richest discussion in and out of class centers on the quality of the relationships we are trying to build.

I have learned many things from my involvement in this project. I have realized how easy it is to bring authoritarian values into an otherwise free and experimental learning situation. The values we have absorbed from our families, our schools, etc., do not vanish just because we begin to organize for radical social change. *Unless we become capable of changing our own lives, of confronting these values, we will have changed nothing at all.* In our school, for example, some of the sharpest debate between the older people has revolved around the use of words like "teacher," "student," "staff," etc.—words which have more than a semantic function, which imply deeply rooted beliefs about the kinds of relationships people ought to have with each other. The younger kids have much better instincts than we do; they have been poisoned less.

We are all familiar with "liberation schools," "free universities," etc., which attempt to change the old curriculum—in the interests, say, of combatting racism or promoting socialism, goals which I heartily support—but which finally do not alter the human relationships which many kids are rebelling against in their homes and schools. It is these human relationships—the attempt, for example, by many teachers to hide their self-interest, their personal values and concerns behind a façade of objectivity —that frequently distort the learning process. By remaining unconscious of this problem, we change course content, but still relate to each other in the same authoritarian way.

The same criticism is applicable to many intentional communities. In our co-op a small group is seeking to institute a system of precisely defined roles and responsibilities, being too impatient to let them develop organically. If they were ever to succeed in doing this, our community would have the same hierarchical structure which a year ago our group got together to protest.

All of us have been so badly corrupted by our own education that it is hard to imagine, let alone share, in building a more humane learning and living environment. But this must be done, if we are not to reproduce the same kinds of institutions we so frequently criticize. Political organization and agitation within the schools is just not sufficient. *Contagious examples*—models of learning and living together—are also needed if the public schools are ever to change. This struggle is equally important for ourselves, for we have much to learn—I sometimes think I should say unlearn—if we are to change our own lives, if we are to build a new world together.

# Teaching in Springville

## BY JACK BLODGETT

Jack Blodgett also found it difficult to teach in the public schools. He was fired for advising a group of students about starting an underground paper and is now attending graduate school.

I'D BEEN teaching high-school English for several years in Springville—a little town settled in the hills south of Buffalo—pretending that changes in method, style, or curriculum were enough to free seeds from the closed pod of the public school and environs. I began the 1969–70 school year by deciding, despite the risk of losing tenure, to create just within what I believed to be the system's tolerance for various kinds of disruption a free environment using every liberative device I could think of. This proved suicidal.

Shortly after school began, several students who were becoming conscious of ways in which their lives were being regulated began talking with me and one other teacher in and outside of school. They had been critical at first of particular instances of their school environment: there was too much irrelevant work, the grading system was a whip, the student council was not concerned enough or had a lackey function, standards of dress and sex were myopic, the school newspaper was censored to meet the needs of public relations, etc. Gradually they decided that the regulations were front activities for the more profound campaign by administrators, teachers, parents, and acquiescing students to ignore, deny, or annihilate their private experiences. The students decided to publish an underground newspaper called *Trout Fishing in America.*

I got them in touch with a small cooperative press in Buffalo where they could learn to operate the equipment and print the paper themselves at cost of materials, and the first newspaper was distributed three weeks after school began. The charges which did most to attract the tornado which subsequently stormed through town were concerned with personal indignities. The outside lavatory doors had been taken off to facilitate catching smokers:

Now wouldn't it shake the establishment if every day during the "moment of silence" all the toilets in the school were flushed simultaneously. Or better yet, don't ever flush the toilets at all. Those who are left in their homerooms should sit down and refuse to pledge the flag, because it states, with liberty and justice for all. Where is our liberty? Where is our justice? Are we less than all?

Also, boys are required to swim nude in gym class, and one student urged that the double standard of dress be abolished— that is, unless our coaches here at G.I. aren't the great symbols of masculinity that we have been led to believe. I am sure (and desperately hope) that they have more healthful ways of enjoying themselves than to watch 60–80 naked boys splash around in the pool each period.

Many parents and students enjoyed treating the information in the paper as scandal and used it to attack the school in terms to which they were accustomed. But these people were ambiguously included in the majority belief that Communists were using Springville as a test site, that some "dissatisfied person lived there," that there were "outside agitators" involved (or as one old man asserted, "alligators," unwittingly giving the students a playful identity). A few parents and students became genuinely concerned and wanted to articulate feelings unexpressed for too long about educational practices. But the high priests of the school were already engaged in a more sophisticated mystification of what should have always been considered a natural phenomenon —free speech. In this case, *Trout Fishing in America* was a devil's work. The administration first attempted to control the paper by bringing it, with a list of apparently conciliatory rules, to a position within range of sanction, and then set out to find and castigate the instigator. There had to be one, given the disbelief that students can think on their own: if *we* do not control them, then who?

The students frequently had worked on the paper at the end of the day in my room and were now so confused and worried about the hostility their first issue met that they asked my advice about the style and content of the second issue. They had wanted to be taken seriously, but not to the extent of a general denial of the sense of humor. I helped them with the second issue, which then had to be distributed off school grounds. The New York Civil Liberties Union, incidentally, was standing by in sympathy, but was unable to act because the students would not supply a test case: when it came to it, parents would not give the needed support.

The day the paper appeared I talked with the superintendent and the principal. I wanted to clear things—the "responsibility" my department head felt for me, the misplaced accusations made against a friend, the issue of personal and political autonomy of the students, and my role as a teacher of potentially creative and joyful human beings. A replay may be helpful to others who will enter similar confrontations. The substance and style, omitting the silences, are as accurate as I can remember.

I was welcomed into the "carpet room" and, after the superintendent learned why I was there, was told that my classes would be covered for the rest of the day. I talked for a while, clearing my friend, etc. Then began the interrogation:

SUPERINTENDENT: If you knew about the newspaper you must have condoned the statements in it. Do you feel that you were acting as a responsible adviser?

ME: As I said, I knew little of the substance of the first issue, but beginning from its effect, I advise the students about improvements. On the other hand I didn't feel it was my right to censor material out of their paper. The students felt that they could follow or not follow my advice, as they wished.

SUPERINTENDENT: How are students acting responsibly when what they put in their paper can ruin a career, and they don't sign their names?

ME: I agree that the students should be able to take responsibility for what they write, but it is certainly understandable why they do not. Their paper is treated as something evil or something to be ashamed of instead of a creative effort to be applauded, despite initial flaws. They know because of the image their paper has been given that it will jeopardize their chances of further schooling—poor recommendations from school officials—and their parents would murder them at home. They've been well taught to worry about practical ill effects of acting on principles. How can you expect them to feel otherwise? If you treat the newspaper as a creative effort, perhaps they will take responsibility for it. There's just too much fear about this thing.

PRINCIPAL: I fear too. I fear for my life. . . . I feel my life has been threatened—"baptism of fire" [in content, obviously figurative]. Besides, what do these students have to lose? We have our careers at stake.

ME: Their lives feel just as important to them as your life and career feel to you.

SUPERINTENDENT: This word, "creativity," has come up several times and I personally feel that the word may be used as an excuse for doing anything an individual desires. Why does their creativity have to be so negative? Aren't there good things about the school that the students can write about? Didn't you encourage them to do that?

ME: You have to remember that most of the students involved are interested in change. With this in mind, their paper is bound to appear negative initially. And if attempts at change are frustrated, there's a likelihood that the style of the paper would take on an obsession which would *really* appear negative. Besides that, I feel that the process of creativity, whether it be in inventions of science or poetry, always initially involves a breaking down—a questioning—indeed a negating. But if you allow the paper to continue in good spirit, the paper, in your terms, would undoubtedly become more "positive." Also, I would allow students to make mistakes in their judgments so that they can learn from them.

SUPERINTENDENT: This would be a matter of some interest to me, Jack. I would like to compare this situation to the instance of a man driving his car down the street at a hundred miles an hour. What would your reaction be to this? Would you be willing to let this man function in this manner?

ME: You are referring to the distinction of responsible and irresponsible free speech. Does a man have the right to shout "Fire" in a crowded theater? I'd be willing to have students make any mistake which would not endanger their own or anyone else's life physically or psychically, or endanger anyone's career with false information. That is, I would try to restrain a person from making that kind of "mistake."

SUPERINTENDENT: Jack, I get the feeling that you are willing to set limits, but we have a disagreement about where those limits ought to be in view of your responsibilities as a member of our staff.

ME: The limits that I set should be obvious in the differences between the first and second issues of *Trout Fishing in America*. And by the way, as a further qualification or clarification of how I feel, the fact that the substance or style of a publication might lead to social discomfort is no criteria for limiting free speech. I know that an administrator's position may necessitate a special fascination for public relations. I realize that both of you are in the middle ground which may *be* the relationship between potentially opposing forces. You might decide on that basis that community pressure would make my role on the staff intolerable—too threatening to your position. The only thing to do then would be to get rid of me. If I were you, though, I'd choose the kids. The school must truly exist primarily for the students, and I think your decision should be based on a recognition of *their rights* as people. They have a right to publish their newspaper.

SUPERINTENDENT: Jack, I just want to say before we continue with this any further that I find your attitudes very disturbing. I see this whole matter as extremely unfortunate. I think that you've been unfair to myself and the principal. I think you've been unfair to the community; I think you've been unfair to your colleagues on the staff, and, furthermore, I think you've been unfair to the students. I'm not sure what action we will take on this as yet. We'll have to make *some* decision. . . .

ME: How is it that you think everything I've done is unfair, when the Supreme Court of the U.S. would undoubtedly call it "fair" on the basis of First Amendment rights? In other words, if this matter would lead to legal proceedings, I feel that I would win.

SUPERINTENDENT: That sounds a little like a threat. . . .

ME: No, I don't mean it that way at all. I merely mentioned it for the principle involved. I have no interest right now in court action. There's another matter that may be relevant to your decision, too. I've honestly tried to improve the students' paper. The initial conception of the paper included obscenities scrawled all over the cover page. If you decide to get rid of me, you might consider what the paper could possibly become with no adviser. If you're concerned with public relations . . .

SUPERINTENDENT: That sounds a little like blackmail. . . .

ME: It's just a consideration based on some information I've given you.

PRINCIPAL: If we allow the paper to be distributed freely, aren't we opening the door to outsiders to distribute any form of material to our students—including out-and-out pornography?

ME: There's probably a difference between interschool communications and communications coming from outside the school community. In any case, though, I think you have a right to see any material first—only to see to it that such material would not imminently threaten the operation of the school.

SUPERINTENDENT: Jack, there are two things which I try to stress in my family. The first is to refrain from the use of any obscene or lewd language, and the second is to avoid what I refer to as "curses." Now in the second issue of the paper I happened to see a certain four-letter word [shit]. And even though the word was within a quotation I feel the effect was the same. Don't I have a right to object, as a parent, to the access my son has to such language through the student publication? Don't I have the right to remove that language from his access?

ME: I don't believe you have the right to do the latter. I would react by discussing the matter with my son to find out how we each felt about it.

SUPERINTENDENT: Didn't you feel a responsibility, as a member of our staff, to encourage the students to use the established channels for voicing dissatisfaction? If you'd encouraged the students in that direction instead of the other, I feel that the result would have been more satisfactory.

ME: I did encourage the students to get involved in Student Council, but you have to remember that many students, silently and vocally, have already lost faith in the established channels. They feel that the activities of Student Council resemble a puppet show. The students are no longer interested in going through motions which cannot bring real change in the educational structure. The students are *looking* for involvement, participation in decisions which affect their lives. When this desire is frustrated, they will turn to other means.

SUPERINTENDENT: Were you ever turned down, cut off, or ignored by the administration in anything that you've suggested as an innovation here in school?

ME: I've been turned down, but I've never been cut off or ignored. There's an insinuation here that I have been frustrated by school bureaucracy and have therefore turned to other means. I want to emphasize that the students have initiated the newspaper, and I am supporting them—defending their right to publish, and helping them when they come for help. I also encourage them to operate within established channels to voice their concerns.

PRINCIPAL: Why is it that the really good students, the high IQs, and really sharp students aren't all involved in the newspaper if the changes some students are after are so important or desirable? There's only a small number of students involved, and those involved all have a somewhat unfortunate family situation. . . .

ME: Many of the "good" students may be ignoring or accepting the injustices done to them in school.

PRINCIPAL: Do you mean that many of these students are only paying me lip service?

ME: This, unfortunately, is what they've been trained to do—please the teacher.

Before we finished, much of the above conversation was repeated in various forms and degrees of intensity.

Four days after the session, the superintendent called a special meeting of the school board and asked the members to support his recommendation that I be fired. He gave no reason; they supported him and agreed not to discuss the matter with anyone. I was summarily fired at the end of the next day, a Friday. Some of the phone calls I made over the weekend asking why I was fired were remarkable.

I told the president of the school board that I thought I had a right to know why I was fired. He said that he could not tell me any reason—that he was sworn to that position. Proceeding Socratically, then, I asked him if there *were* a reason. He said no, there was no stated reason. This led me to some interesting observations: the board voted to fire me and doesn't know why; there is no reason why I was fired; etc. His only further comment was that "their reason was that they had no reason," and he hoped that I didn't think he was "using double-talk."

Next, I called the superintendent. In reply to my question all he could say was that my "probationary appointment has been terminated." He sounded slightly annoyed when I referred to the proceedings illustrated in the conversation with the school board president as irrational. "Are you calling me irrational, Jack?"

The next conversation with a member of the school board lasted two hours. The only relevant comments fall into an odd juxtaposition:

1. He was, he said, the only "intelligent" and "objective" member of the board, and was therefore the only man who had looked at this whole matter "intelligently" and "objectively."

2. He had "personally investigated" my teaching methods and had concluded that he didn't like them. The kind of self-conscious approach to group interaction that I tried to foster, in hopes of better understanding among students and the subsequent improvement of communications, resembled the "Catholic confessional," he felt—something to which he was entirely opposed.

3. When I asked the reason for my dismissal, he confirmed my suspicion that the board did not know the superintendent's reason, and merely voted on his recommendation. He said that the superintendent's reason for no reason was "veiled in his opening remarks," which concerned a threat to his career.

The following Monday morning I was surprised to hear that about 25 percent of the school's nine hundred students staged a sit-in and 150 were suspended. The incident drew substantial media coverage, and the students soon found themselves in a special light in the western New York area. This had been the first demonstration of any kind for most of the kids involved, and it was a shock for many schools, where activism was already more entrenched under the skin, to see such a movement bloom in a happy country school.

Springville was, of course, more shocked. Springville "children," even the "good" students, were now "rabble-rousers," "radicals," "hippies"—but generally lemmings. And who was responsible for blinding the children and leading them off before TV cameras? There were two explanations. One included subversion, indoctrination, disruption of the established school program in almost total disregard of the academic objectives of the students (I had been "teaching the children to communicate like apes"), and the flower of rumored lechery, narcotics dealing, and abortion. The other largely established a case for denial of the above charges. But, however more enlightened the latter position was toward the ambiguities involved in the charges, it remained trapped within the context of public school structure and morality. "We saw a student's notebook, and it appeared that he *was* preparing the students for the Regents." "He didn't give a test on Vietnam in his English class. It was a student's independent project." "There was nothing really indecent about the student newspaper." "He was a highly innovative teacher."

Being "innovative," as an identity formed out of the fabric of public education, I found to be as interesting as a loose thread in a drab blanket. Invention by default.

My supporters, for example, were quiet about a more positive challenge to the system. On the first day of school, I wrote my name on the board, Jack Blodgett. There were murmurs around the class, and I was a bit sorry I had revealed so much so fast. In some classes I was made to feel as though I'd walked in with my fly open. Gradually, several students came to ask what I would like to be called. Some students were already calling me Jack, and giggling or squinting or smirking. Others were calling me Mr. Blodgett and feeling "un-hip." I told them that they should call me what they wanted to. It may even be that they would call me Jack one day, Mr. Blodgett the next, according to how they felt about what was happening in class. This seemed to make a lot of sense to them. Around the time I was fired, many students seemed to feel comfortable calling me Jack. The supporting group of parents chose to overlook this phenomenon as a possibility for defense. It was perhaps not an improvement of the rules but a contradiction of the game itself.

The parents of the paper's co-editor had their diner burned beyond repair and were further terrorized with phone calls. Both editors and others more or less involved with the newspaper have been forced, literally or figuratively, out of school with only limited opportunity to go off to a free school. A friend was identified with the various dimensions and directions of the tornado, threatening his job. Rumored phone taps destroyed much of the trust needed for any sort of communication to take place between opposing people in town. Much of the broken acquiescence of students in the sit-in has or will be healed over into a callus of disillusionment. The supporting parent group, which calls itself the Listening Post, still lives but perhaps only as a mushroom feeding on decay.

Dennis Hopper says that if Billy, in *Easy Rider,* had not given the finger to the duck hunter, the hunter may not have been driven, in his existential crisis, to pull the trigger. The fact is, in a strong sense, I really don't feel justified in my dealings with death: let the monster die of its own, become extinct through a process of natural selection. If there were an independent school down in Zoar Valley, and another one over in Gypsy Flats, and another in Ashford Hollow, I wonder how long our public school could hide the wrinkles of the last dying. Once robbed of what is now the remnant or semblance of the energy and devotion of the young, it would not be necessary to infest the school with an infection which hurts the innocent as well as the guilty. This, of course, may be naïve. I speak naturally from a sense of only my own particulars.

Only as a record of what these particulars have brought me to, as an ex-public school teacher, trying to reconcile the space he knew with the space he knows, do I include part of a going-away letter to Springville. It may help to illuminate a *paralysis* accomplished not through the arrogance of confrontation this time, as undoubtedly felt in the previous conversation between the administration and myself, but through a humility of understanding and acceptance:

Let's not permit a fascination for objects or methods of teaching or school board policies in question to obscure our vision of what we are really concerned about. We could all talk on into the night, a bunch of foolish Brer Rabbits punching tar babies till even the dawn has been blackened through lost sight of why we wanted the other to say Howdy in the first place. We want a community. In times when there are very few things we can feel certain about, we need a community where we can trust, where we are in touch with the integrity of others, where we are not afraid that an undercutting dishonesty will rob us of even more of what we need to survive in an uncertain world. I believe that the intense and sometimes violent reactions to recent incidents, whichever side of the briar patch people have scrambled to, come from a fear that the needed trust and integrity have been threatened. And in a sense, we've all made our dreams come true in a nightmare of alarm, suspicion, and even hate. And so we have to begin again. We have to awake to see each other again before we are so covered with tar, some of us with tar and feathers, that the dawn will disappear forever with the reason for saying Howdy.

Despite mistakes or misjudgments which have been made, please consider that most of us want about the same thing; a community of people open to growth in every sense and to the critical appraisal of present conditions which makes growth possible. Please trust me that this is true. Let's listen to each other. There's a young language to try to understand, but however new, it is trying to touch in the same way that an older language is trying to touch the young. The old and young have much to create together. Let's hope it's not a war which one or the other must subsequently lose.

I'm sorry I can't begin with you where I started. As you know, I no longer teach. Now I can act as a human being rather than as a teacher. This unfortunate opposition has the one benefit of giving me the new freedom to write to you now and to live hopefully out of the deepest and most honest intention—something which teachers generally find very difficult to do if they are concerned about honesty at all. Thank you for listening, but after all, we owe each other at least that.

# Schools for Scandal

## BY IRA GLASSER

Because school is compulsory, administrative edicts acquire the force of law. Too often these regulations are arbitrary and designed to deny students the civil liberties other citizens enjoy. Students learn more about the relationship of the individual to authority through these regulations and the hierarchial structure which enforces them than through any course in civics. This is one of the tragedies of school, because the lessons learned are that arbitrary authority must be obeyed and that privacy, dignity, and civil rights are not to be respected. Increasingly, students are revolting against these regulations—hence the frequent outbursts about hair length, dress style, free speech. Insurrection also teaches important lessons about the costs and rewards of resisting authority.

Ira Glasser is Associate Director of the New York Civil Liberties Union and one of the nation's leading authorities on student rights.

THERE ARE only two public institutions in the United States which steadfastly deny that the Bill of Rights applies to them. One is the military and the other is the public schools. Both are compulsory. Taken together, they are the chief socializing institutions of our society. Everyone goes through our schools. What they learn—not from what they are formally taught but from the way the institution is organized to treat them—is that authority is more important than freedom, order more precious than liberty, and discipline a higher value than individual expression. That is a lesson which is inappropriate to a free society—and certainly inappropriate to its schools.

208

## I. PROCEDURAL RIGHTS

Walter Crump is a slim, eighteen-year-old, esthetic-looking Negro college student. On first impression he is talented, articulate, and gentle, and further meetings do not alter that impression. Until May 4, 1969, he attended the High School of Music and Art, a special academic school in New York City, compiling a satisfactory academic and disciplinary record. With graduation only a few weeks away Walter Crump was looking ahead to college in the fall and from there to a career in the theater. On May 4 all that very nearly came to an end.

Early in the day, Mr. Crump was involved in a minor verbal altercation with a teacher. The facts of the disagreement are unimportant; the incident at worst appears to have involved an undetermined amount of rudeness and discourtesy on both sides. No violence or threat of violence occurred. It was the kind of a verbal flare-up that occurs daily in almost every imaginable setting, and which usually passes without damage to either party.

Later that afternoon, however, Mr. Crump was summarily suspended and told to go home until further notice. (That procedure was unambiguously in violation of the New York City Board of Education's own rules, which require that a suspended student be kept in school until a parent is informed prior to sending the student out of the school.)

Further notice did not come until twelve days later, at which time Mr. Crump's foster mother was told to come with Walter to a hearing—the board called it a "guidance conference"—eight days later on May 22, at the office of an assistant superintendent of schools. (That procedure also was in violation of the board's own rules. The maximum period that a principal may suspend a child is five days, and a "guidance conference" with prior notification to the parent by certified mail must occur within that period.)

Mr. Crump was unable to persuade his foster mother to attend the hearing, so he went himself. When he arrived, approximately forty-five minutes late, he discovered that the hearing had been held without him. Before the hearing began, two separate requests were made by parents of two fellow students at the High School of Music and Art to attend the hearing in support of Mr. Crump. Both requests were denied, despite the fact that a state law had been passed and signed by Governor Rockefeller that very month granting the right of students to be represented—even by a lawyer if they wished—at hearings arising out of suspensions of more than five days. The denial of these requests, therefore, was in violation of state law.

At the "hearing," Mr. Crump was summarily "convicted" (of what, nobody knows) and, just a few weeks short of graduation, dismissed from the school. On May 23, Mr. Crump's foster mother received a letter from the assistant superintendent curtly informing her that a "guidance conference" had been held in absentia and that Walter had been discharged from school, effective immediately.

The expulsion of Mr. Crump from full-time public education was totally lacking in even the minimal rudiments of due process of law. He never received a meaningful hearing; he was never informed of his right to be represented by counsel; he was never informed of the charges against him; and his supporters were not permitted to speak in his behalf.

But that was not the end of it. A few days later, Mr. Crump's foster mother received another letter, this time from the Bureau of Child Welfare. The letter informed her that since Mr. Crump was over eighteen and now out of school (the Board of Education had been thoughtful enough to allow a bureau caseworker to attend the "guidance conference" and to send his supervisor a copy of the dismissal letter), board payments to his foster parents would soon end.

At that point, one of the High School of Music and Art parents who had been refused admission to the guidance conference arranged an appointment for Mr. Crump with an attorney from the New York Civil Liberties Union. NYCLU immediately informed the Bureau of Child Welfare that the dismissal from school was being contested, that in their judgment the dismissal was illegal, and that a federal suit was being prepared that very afternoon. To no avail: The Bureau cut off board payments the next day, also without a hearing and without even the courtesy of a reply.

Mr. Crump's attorney subsequently filed suit in federal court, obtained a new hearing (which he was allowed to attend), and, not surprisingly, Walter Crump was reinstated, more than a month after the initial suspension. He was graduated without incident three weeks later.

If what happened to Walter Crump had been an isolated instance, it would be no less outrageous; but at least one could not easily draw inferences about an entire school system. In fact, however, the procedures which governed Walter Crump's case govern other cases as well. The frightening thing about the procedures followed by school officials in the Crump case is precisely that they were *routine*. The independent experiences of several respected agencies in New York—the NAACP Legal Defense and Education Fund, Citizens Committee for Children, the New York Civil Liberties Union, the Metropolitan Applied Research Center, Mobilization for Youth, and several parents associations—suggest that what happened to Mr. Crump happens regularly and widely to anyone facing suspension. Two things may be said about the procedures governing student suspensions in New York (and there is no reason to believe that New York is unique; although some other cities may enjoy better procedures, cases raising the same issues have arisen all over the United States):

1. The procedures represent a gross denial of the constitutional right to due process, including the right to a fair hearing.

2. Even those inadequate procedures are regularly violated by school officials.[1]

---

[1] A startling fact in the Crump case was the extent to which school authorities broke even their own rules and regulations.

If Mr. Crump had not had a friend knowledgeable enough and aggressive enough to seek legal help, it is difficult to say where he would be today. Certainly he wouldn't be in college. Other students, perhaps I should say other *children,* have not been so fortunate.

Even when legal redress is possible to obtain, it may not be possible to undo the damage inflicted in the meantime. Nothing illustrates that better than the mass expulsions that occurred at Franklin K. Lane High School in New York.

On January 27, 1969, 670 students, most of them black or Puerto Rican, were summarily expelled from Lane. They received no notice of, nor any opportunity to contest, the action taken against them. Letters were sent out on January 24 informing parents that they had a week to contest the expulsions, but only three days later all 670 were expelled and informed that there was no chance at all to reverse the decision. Moreover, January 24 turns out to have been a Friday and January 27 the following Monday, so actually parents received no notice whatsoever.

The alleged reason for the expulsion was to relieve overcrowded conditions at Lane by eliminating multiple sessions and by putting the school on a single session. Yet two-thirds of the sixty-one academic high schools in New York City were more overcrowded than Lane, some of them substantially so, and only one operated on a single session. The truth is that what happened at Lane was the result of severe pressures arising out of the bitter teachers' strike during the fall; those pressures finally resulted in an agreement by the powerful—teachers, administrators, and politicians—against the powerless—students and their parents. It is precisely to protect the powerless against the excesses of the powerful that the Bill of Rights was invented. Yet here that protection did not exist. It is ironic indeed that a city which was capable of being whipped into a frenzy over the issue of due process during the strike was conspicuously silent during what was surely the single most stunning denial of due process ever to have occurred in the New York City school system.

Once the decision was made to expel the students, a mechanical rule was devised: All students who were absent thirty days or more during the fall semester and who had maintained an unsatisfactory academic record in the fall semester were to be expelled.

The decision to expel based on student attendance records and academic achievement during the 1968 fall semester seemed peculiar indeed. After all, it was during that semester that Lane was struck for thirty-six days as part of the city-wide teachers' strike. In addition, there were several brief boycotts by students and parents over dissatisfaction with the strike settlement. Finally, there was a severe flu epidemic in New York that fall, causing widespread absenteeism among both students and teachers. Hardly a typical semester by which to measure either attendance or achievement!

Although we hear much these days about procedures which supposedly protect the guilty, it is ultimately out of a concern for the innocent that fair procedures were developed. Consider what happened to a few of those caught in Franklin K. Lane's net:

1. *Arthur Knight.* Mr. Knight was expelled on January 27 as he attempted to re-register for the spring, 1969, semester. Prior to the fall, 1968, semester, Knight had maintained a satisfactory academic record. He was legitimately absent for the entire fall semester due to a serious kidney ailment. On his first day back he was expelled.

Later by more than a month, during which he was out of school entirely, he was directed to report to a special annex to continue his "education." (Inexplicably, some of the expelled students were ultimately assigned to this annex instead of being expelled completely.) But the "annex" offered no grades, no examinations, and no homework. There were few if any books, and only three teachers. The entire annex was only open from 9 A.M. to 12 noon. It was clearly a custodial institution, not an educational one.

What had Arthur Knight done to deserve such punishment? Why wasn't he allowed to contest the punishment at a hearing?

2. *Oscar Gonzalus.* Mr. Gonzalus was notified of his expulsion

by mail. He had no chance to challenge it. Yet the criteria by which students were expelled did not apply to him, because he had been absent less than thirty days during the fall, 1968, semester. Furthermore, most of those absences were due to an attack of the flu. Finally, Gonzalus had maintained a satisfactory academic record before the fall semester. All these facts could have been proven at a fair hearing *before* expulsion. But no fair hearing was allowed.

3. *Marcine Chestnut.* Miss Chestnut was expelled because of an allegedly deficient attendance record. Yet despite her poor attendance, partly due to a severe case of the flu, she maintained a satisfactory academic record during the fall, 1968, semester, as she had during previous semesters. Like the others, however, she had no chance.

More than two months later, a complaint was filed in federal court in behalf of all 670 students. In late April, 1969, almost three months to the day after the initial expulsion, Federal Judge Jack B. Weinstein reinstated all 670 students and ordered the school to provide remedial work to make up for the lost time. Judge Weinstein found that the action against the 670 had denied them their constitutional right to due process.

Beyond the legal question, of course, is the larger morality of what happened at Lane. Though many students were innocently caught up in the action, and all were denied due process, many others were indeed absent for more than thirty days and did have failing academic records. For these students, the penalties were even greater, for these were students in grave trouble. For such students, the legal victory was meaningless because the educational damage was irremediable. It says a great deal about a school system whose response to students hanging on by the slimmest thread is to cut that thread for reasons of administrative convenience.

## II. FIRST AMENDMENT RIGHTS

Procedural rights are not the only rights denied to students by public schools. Attitudes toward individual rights are indivisible; institutions that do not protect the right to a fair hearing are not likely to protect free speech either. The schools are no exception.

Indeed, the most publicized conflicts between school authorities and students involve First Amendment rights: free speech, freedom of the press, freedom of assembly. All across the country, from New York to Mississippi, from Iowa to Texas, from California to Alabama, courts are being asked, for the first time in many cases, to consider the demands of students for freedoms normally guaranteed to adults but traditionally denied to students. Like soldiers in the military, students are suggesting that the Bill of Rights applies to them.

In 1965, a group of black students in Mississippi were suspended for wearing buttons saying "Freedom Now." The suspension was challenged in federal court and eventually resulted in a landmark decision by the U.S. Court of Appeals for the Fifth Circuit. The court reinstated the students on the ground that no significant disruption of the educational process had taken place as a result of the wearing of the buttons, and that therefore there was no legal basis for suspending the students.

It is instructive to note that on the same day the same court decided a similar case *against* another group of suspended students. In that case, school officials were upheld because there was clear evidence that the students wearing the buttons harassed students who did not wear them and created a variety of other substantial disturbances.

Thus the court sought to limit the power of school officials to prevent the free expression of views, but nonetheless upheld the power of school officials to regulate disruptive conduct. In effect, the court constructed a factual standard which requires school officials to provide conclusive evidence of substantial interference with the educational functioning of the school before they may prevent political expression by students. In the absence of such a factual determination one way or the other, implied the court, we are simply granting public school officials a blank check to suppress political speech arbitrarily, a right no other civilian public official has.

Despite this decision, students all over the country have been regularly denied the right to peaceful political expression during the past few years, whether or not such expression involved substantial disruption. In 1967, John Tinker, then a fifteen-year-old high school student in Des Moines, Iowa; his sister Mary Beth, thirteen; and a friend, Christopher Eckhardt, sixteen, decided to publicize their opposition to the war in Vietnam by wearing black armbands to school. The form of expression seemed to fall well within the standard enunciated in the Mississippi case: What could be a more passive, less disruptive form of expression than the wearing of armbands!

The principals of the Des Moines schools responded by first banning the wearing of armbands and then suspending the Tinkers and their friend. Parents of the students filed suit in federal court, and the case eventually reached the U.S. Court of Appeals for the Eighth Circuit, which upheld the principals' action. That decision was in clear conflict with the earlier decision by the Fifth Circuit Court of Appeals in the Mississippi case, and no one could resolve the conflict except the U.S. Supreme Court, which agreed to hear the case.

On February 24, 1969, the Supreme Court reversed the lower court's decision and upheld the students' right to wear the armbands. The court made the following points:

1. The wearing of an armband for the purpose of expressing views is clearly within the protection of the First Amendment.

2. Both students and teachers are entitled to the protections of the First Amendment. "It can hardly be argued," said the court,

"that either students or teachers shed their constitutional rights to freedom of speech or expression at the schoolhouse gate. This has been the unmistakable holding of this court for almost 50 years."

3. While actual disturbance which intrudes upon the work of the school or the rights of other students may be banned, the mere *fear* that such a disturbance might occur is not sufficient. As the court said, ". . . in our system, undifferentiated fear or apprehension of disturbance is not enough to overcome the right to freedom of expression. Any departure from absolute regimentation may cause trouble. Any variation from the majority's opinion may inspire fear. Any word spoken, in class, in the lunchroom, or on the campus, that deviates from the views of another person may start an argument or cause a disturbance. But our Constitution says we must take this risk; and our history says that it is this sort of hazardous freedom—this kind of openness—that is the basis of our national strength. . . ."

4. The standard of the Mississippi button case was upheld; that is, before an expression of views may be prohibited, school officials must show that the exercise of the forbidden right would "materially and substantially interfere with the requirements of appropriate discipline in the operation of the school."

5. Students are constitutionally entitled to freedom of expression not only in the classroom but also elsewhere in the school hours. Freedom of expression, said the court, "is not confined to the supervised and ordained discussion which takes place in the classroom. . . . A student's rights . . . do not embrace merely the classroom hours. When he is in the cafeteria, or on the playing field, or on the campus during the authorized hours, he may express his opinions. . . ."

While the *Tinker* case appears to settle the problem of wearing buttons, armbands, or other symbols in school, other First Amendment rights are still in dispute, and some are currently in court. These chiefly involve the right of students to distribute political leaflets and other material such as unauthorized newspapers in the school. In one case in Jamaica High School in New York

City, Jeffrey Schwartz, a senior, was suspended for *mere posses-sion* of an unauthorized newspaper which in previous issues had been harshly critical of that school's principal, particularly with respect to students' rights.

When the suspension was challenged by the student's parents and their lawyer, the school decided to waive Jeffrey's remaining requirements and graduate him about six months ahead of time. When his parents went into court to contest the action, the Board of Education lawyers argued that the case was moot because the boy was graduated; his diploma was available to him anytime, they insisted. But after making that argument for six months, the principal refused to grant him his diploma in June on the grounds that he had not fulfilled the requirements which the principal had waived months before! Subsequently, after being out of school for an entire semester, Mr. Schwartz had to attend summer school in order to be able to get into college in the fall. Along the way, the principal caused a New York State scholarship, won by Mr. Schwartz in a competitive examination, to be revoked for failing to graduate on time in June.

The issues raised in the *Schwartz* case are typical of those being raised in high schools all over the country.

It is particularly difficult for students to reconcile what they learn in their social studies classes about James Madison and free speech and John Peter Zenger and freedom of the press with what they confront when they try to exercise those rights in school. It is even more difficult to reconcile what they learn about fair trials with what they are subjected to at "guidance conferences." In the end, students learn less about American values from formal class-room instruction than from the way the school is organized to treat them. Unfortunately, what they do learn is that where indi-vidual rights collide with discipline and authority, individual rights inevitably recede. That such lessons are taught by our pub-lic schools is an educational scandal of major dimensions.

## III. PERSONAL RIGHTS

No discussion of students' rights is complete without mentioning the widespread attempt by school officials to regulate the dress and personal appearance of students. Nothing illustrates the repressiveness of public schools more. All across the United States, thousands of students have been suspended or otherwise excluded from classes for the style of their dress or the length of their hair. In almost all cases, questions of offensiveness, health, or safety were not present. Such cases have arisen practically everywhere and have been decided differently in different places. In New York, the Commissioner of Education has clearly upheld the right of students to wear their hair or their clothes as they please within limits of safety. In Texas, the U.S. Court of Appeals has upheld the power of school officials to regulate the length of a student's hair, and similar rulings have occurred in Connecticut. In Wisconsin a federal court recently declared such actions by school officials to be unconstitutional. And in Massachusetts federal judge Charles Wyzanski has written and eloquent opinion in support of a student's right "to look like himself." The U.S. Supreme Court has so far considered the issue too trivial to deserve its attention.

Beyond the legal questions, however, consider the social significance of the attempt by school authorities to regulate personal appearance so closely. Consider the institutions of our society which insist on regulating dress: prisons, mental hospitals, convents, and the military. All these institutions depend for their existence on maintenance of a rigid system of authority and discipline. The slightest expression of individualism represents a threat to the structure of authority. These institutions recognize that the strict regulation of personal appearance is an important social mechanism to maintain control by creating a climate in which unquestioning obedience to authority will flourish. Whatever justification for such a practice may exist in prisons or in the military—or for that matter in political dictatorships whose first official acts usually involve the rounding up of "hippies"—what possible justification is there for such repression in the schools of a free society? In fact, the denial of personal rights must be seen as part of a pattern which includes the denial of First Amendment rights and procedural rights as well.

It is not the students who are radical. They seek completely traditional American rights, rights which are guaranteed in the Constitution but denied to them. Rather, I think, it is the principals who violate students' rights who are the radicals. They are the ones who deny the traditional protections of the Bill of Rights to students, and they are the ones who are subverting the traditional balance between freedom and authority by perpetuating rules which sacrifice individual rights at almost every opportunity.

As the U.S. Supreme Court said in the case of *West Virginia v. Barnette:*

> The Fourteenth Amendment, as now applied to the states, protects the citizen against the state itself and all of its creatures —boards of education not excepted. These are, of course, important, delicate, and highly discretionary functions, but none that they may not perform within the limits of the Bill of Rights. That they are educating the young for citizenship is reason for scrupulous protection of constitutional freedoms of the individuals, if we are not to strangle the free mind at its source and teach youths to discount important principles of our government as mere platitudes.

That was twenty-six years ago.

# Dangerous Saintly Tragic Brave Subversive*

BY JONATHAN KOZOL

High School is not an isolated phenomenon but the culmination of many years of schooling. This next piece shows how the attitudes and methods of the lower schools inevitably affect high-school education.

Jonathan Kozol, author of *Death at an Early Age*, is director of the Storefront Learning Center in Boston.

IT IS the custom among those who speak most freely on the subject of the student revolution to refer to the recent developments in questioning tones of clinical condescension. We speak of the rebellion of young people as if we were physicians looking into the window of a home for troubled children or as if we were psychiatrists looking over the walls of an asylum.

I do not believe that clinical observations of this sort are accurate or useful. It is not young people who are in most serious need of swift examination. It is not they who stand in chains before the world: it is their teachers.

Two hundred years from now, if anthropologists should wish to examine the nature of servitude and acquiescence in the face of mediocrity during the late years of the 1960s, I am afraid that they cannot do better than to study with great care an extraordinary document which goes under the name of the *Teacher's Guide* to the *Scott Foresman Basal Reader*.

This is a document created to lead a teacher through a year

* This is the text of a lecture delivered before the National Association of Independent Schools, November, 1969.

221

of intellectual experience with scarcely a moment of independent choice or a single instant of volition. As such, I think, it is an ideal case study in what the publishing industry thinks of classroom teachers.

It is not all bad poetry. And, in any case, it isn't the quality of the work that troubles me—it is the arbitrary nature of the guidebook. It tells you exactly what the children will think, and it tells you *how* to make them think it. If it doesn't work, if the class does not respond, then either you did it wrong or else the class is stupid. . . .

The teacher goes home each day and spends the evening writing out her lessons: or maybe she does it all on Sunday afternoon. She writes her careful lesson-plan, according to the directions which she has been given. Next morning she goes into the class and tries to sell it to the children.

What happens if a child won't buy it?

The teacher is talking. "Who can tell Miss Sullivan," says she, "the reason for the special loveliness and beauty of the metaphor in stanza six, line three?"

A little child says: "I think it stinks!"

What do you do?

You send her off to the adjustment counselor. The child's in trouble; and so, of course, are you. She ruined the lesson, rendered all your hard work useless, wasted your Sunday afternoon. You'll never get back on the old road now. You might just as well have spent Sunday morning lying in the meadow for all the good your lesson-plan will do. What went wrong? The unimaginable happened. Someone had the unspeakable audacity to interrupt the literary education of her classmates by saying something she *believed!* And, in so doing, one honest voice destroyed the lesson. Trouble-maker: send her to the adjustment counselor. She's dangerous now, but she's only in the fifth grade. If she doesn't drop out, or blow up the school, we've still got seven more years in which to teach her how to adjust to mediocrity.

I think that this is a pitiable story, and one repeated every day through America. Saddest, of course, is that the teacher is not wicked, or calculating, or unkind. She does not mean to deceive the young in front of her. She things that what she offers them is "culture," but what they see instead are tedium and fear. She fights to defend the prison that she lives in, and she cannot afford to be reminded, even by one child, that she is not free. It isn't just the textbook industry that robs her of autonomy. It's in her whole life training. She never knew what culture might have been (a thought of her own making, a feeling coined in her own soul, a piece of her own deep passion placed on paper), and so she was willing forever to accept the borrowed words of other people; and now she intends to pass the same thing on to children.

I remember a curious and rather sad example. It is one to which I made reference in my book, but which I do not think I ever understood. On the wall at the back of the room in which I taught in Boston was a list of words that I had noticed many times but never carefully examined. It was a list of adjectives intended to be used by children when they wrote their book reports; the point, judging by the nature of the list, was to upgrade the children's vocabulary, along with the level of their cultural pretensions, by teaching them some rather fancy adjectives. The problem was that all the words were laudatory; there was not a single pejorative among them. I remember reading up and down the list with some surprise: INTERESTING, COMICAL, HUMOROUS, COLORFUL, MARVELOUS, ADVENTUROUS, FASCINATING. Every word was favorable; there was not one syllable of criticism.

I thought about this list for a long while and wondered what would be its consequence. Children clearly, in writing book reports and, we might assume, in reading books as well, were being asked to make only a rather narrow area of decision: not *whether* the book was good, but only *why*. The fact that it was good must not be doubted. The school had bought it, the company printed it, the writer written it, the teacher ordered it. And the child would *read* it and *love* it and *enjoy* it. He would have his choice only of the way in which he *chooses* to enjoy it. He might find it MAR-

VELOUS, or else perhaps he would strike out on a bold road and find it COLORFUL or FASCINATING. He would not, however, decide the book was BORING. BORING was not an authorized adjective; it was not included on the list. The child, in fact, would do well *not* to find the story boring.

In such a way as this does the child learn what is expected of him if he intends to keep ahead and not get into trouble. In this, the adjective list, as in the old Scott Foresman reader, the character instruction lessons, the pledge of allegiance every morning, are admirable preparation for the lives the children are expected to live in later years within America. The range of adjectives available to the option of the child as he writes his book report is excellent preparation for the range of options available to the adult voter. The child chooses between alternatives of equal meaning and so, precisely, do his mother and his father as they go into the polling place to cast their vote for President. Shall it be Humphrey (MARVELOUS) or Nixon (COMICAL, ADVENTUROUS, FASCINATING)? Certainly it will not be McCarthy (ENIGMATIC), Bobby Kennedy (BRAVE), Dr. King (TRAGIC), Gandhi (SAINTLY), Thoreau (DANGEROUS), Jesus (SUBVERSIVE) . . . No, we have our choice between COMICAL and MARVELOUS and leave the saints to history. The children have their choice of adjectives.

Often I wondered what influence this list of adjectives might have had on younger children, and one day I had an opportunity to find out. I was working with a group of young boys in remedial reading. This was fourth grade, and we were working on a book entitled *Wide Doors Open*. It was a small group, about six or seven children, and I was doing all that seemed to be within my power to try to convince them, along with myself, that the story was worth reading. It was about Rapunzel, the woman with long hair, and, if you ask why we should have been reading a story of that sort, the answer is that Rapunzel was "the story for the day" and "taught the concept" stated in the fourth-grade lesson-plan.

So there I was, a man of twenty-seven with a group of boys around the age of eight or nine, doing my best to get them interested in the story of Rapunzel. "Let's all turn the page and see what's going to happen." And, of course, they'd already turned the page and peeked ahead of me; and they didn't care—they *knew* it would be boring. They were wiggling and twisting and turning all around and shooting little spitballs at each other, and no one was paying any attention to the story. I closed the book and asked them how they liked it.

"Well, what did you think?"

There was a long moment's pause during which they looked with a searching gaze at my expression, as if the answer by some miracle would be written on my forehead. Then, one by one, like light bulbs brightening, the hands went up before me: "INTEREST-ING?", "COMICAL?", "HUMOROUS?", "COLORFUL?", "MARVELOUS?", "ADVENTUROUS?", "FASCINATING?" They did not even make their hypocritical guesses with conviction; it was not even a declarative statement; it was all in the interrogative: "INTERESTING?", "COM-ICAL?", and so on. They were asking for a single answer, as if I surely knew it, as if there were a *right* word someplace and all they had to do was find it out and guess it.

I marveled at the thought that there could be a single answer; and wondered, if there were, then who would know it? But the children assume that somebody does: that someone, someplace, knows it—the author, maybe—I suppose he'd be the only one. . . .

I recall, on that occasion, losing my temper finally and asking the children how they could tell me all those things when they had been squirming and fooling around and not paying any attention while we read the story. One boy just raised his hand with a slight smile and said to me softly, with a ring of candor that I have not yet quite forgotten: "Mr. Kozol, it was boring."

The story of the adjective list seems comical to many people; I know that manipulation and denial can seem funny to us sometimes. But humor slips away very quickly when we recognize the cruelty and bitterness at stake in a manner of evasion and manipulation that effectively destroy not only a teacher's self-respect but also her capacity for anything like open, warm emotion. A child speaks of devastation in his home, or grief at school, or on the street outside the building. The teacher hears, compassions, condescends, but does not weep or grieve. When something silly happens—bizarre, unexpected, comical, absurd—the teacher chuckles cautiously, with reservation, but she does not laugh with glee. And does she cry and can she weep? the children wonder. Her concept of professional behavior is devoid of most intensities; she does not easily yield to indignation, weep for passion, rage at grief. Grief and sorrow are not in her lesson-plan; they do not teach a major concept or convey a basic skill. All that we love in drama, all that we find of joy in films, all that is tragic, comic, intense, extreme, remarkable, is filtered from her manner. If film and drama were restricted to the range of feelings present in this lady's classroom, the theaters would quickly empty and the people would pour out on the streets.

As the teacher has charted out her teaching by Scott Foresman, so has she charted out her life by careful lessons. Control and prediction are its guidelines: stylized banality, compulsory moderation, avoidance of ecstasy, avoidance of grief. Imagine this woman now, assigned to work within a ghetto classroom. She lives, in all likelihood, out in a segregated suburb, one which is neither elegant nor sordid but rather something halfway in between. She drives each morning on a soulless superhighway in her compact car, right into the heart of the black ghetto. She comes with a manner of decency and a style of well-meant protestation. She *cares* about the children, as she tells herself, and she offers her energies to bring them what she feels she has to give. When she takes her own pulse, the message she receives contains most of the right signals: she does not dislike black children, nor does she feel aware of any reservations about their capability of learning. She tells herself that they can learn "as well as anybody" and that it is her role and mandate to do all within her power to enable them to be successful. Despite her best efforts, they do not learn; nor in fact, do they particularly seem to like her.

Each morning she looks out at them with a mixture of longing and compassion. She places her hand across her heart and turns her head to face the flag above the window. Looking up with an expression of dedication practiced over decades, she incants, quite without thinking, the words of that old pledge that has been her faith and credo, as it seems, forever.

The children, if they are still young enough to be obedient, follow her words with childish emulation. Yet something of the meaning of the syllables begins to creep in gradually as a child grows older. By fourth grade there are a few kids in the class who begin to hear the words they are reciting. INDIVISIBLE is a difficult word; young children stumble on it frequently. Perhaps, in stumbling, they have a better chance than otherwise to stop and think about its meaning. LIBERTY and JUSTICE are not difficult words. But they are cruel words, when they mock reality in front of you. By sixth grade, children begin to know enough reality to know what mockery means.

There stands the teacher. There, above the window, hangs the flag. Beneath the flag is a wall of peeling paint, cracked glass panes, nailed-down desks, and broken tables. Books appropriate to other days and other ages fill the cupboards. Stale air and thankless yellow light are, as it seems, unmoving, fixed forever in the doorway. At the back of the room, a portrait of Abe Lincoln looks down upon this class of segregated children, segregated still one hundred years after his assassination, sixteen years since the highest court in all the nation rectified the first proclamation with a second no better meant and no less deviously applied than the original.

So the teacher smiles: "Let's sing 'God Bless America!' " Lincoln's dark eyes meet her own for a brief moment. If they speak at all, they tell her that it is she who is in bondage. Because she pretends to herself that she lives in a just and decent nation, because she passes on this pretense to the children, because she covers with platitude and banality the cynical hoax which is reality, because she believes that she is the bearer of good tidings while representing and purveying so much evil, because of these things which she cannot see and does not wish to know, she lives in bondage. She thinks of her school as a fortress built of culture. It is not that; it is a prison of dismay. She thinks that she is the keeper of the castle. She is not that; she is its only life-term prisoner. The children come in, cellmates for a season; alone, the teacher sees the seasons pass and fade away, without reprieve. She pledges her flag, she washes her board, she spends her Sundays writing out the lessons. When decency comes her way, like a bird accidentally flying in the window, she treats it with affection, but finds it rather scary. Nor does she go out of her way to ascertain its whereabouts.

This teacher is not evil or exceptional. She is not strange or sinister or special. She is the ideal product of American education, and, as such, burdened with the curse which all of us received.

There are many ways in which we seek to pass this heritage on to younger people, some of which we know and some we do not see. In certain respects, what are billed as "modern methods" —new styles of supposedly open-ended class discussion—are even more dangerous than the honest and unconcealed manipulation of the earlier days. Earlier we used to tell the children what to think, handing them, as it were, the bottle and the spoon. Now we lead them, by the pretense of free inquiry, to ask for it themselves. I am thinking, for example, of methods devised to create a semblance of honest argument and of open disputation but which in fact are quite as meticulously predetermined as the reading lesson or the list of adjectives posted on the wall. There is a way of dealing with a controversial problem in the classroom, in a manner that seems conscientious, honest, openminded, and leaves one with a sense of having "faced the issue"—and yet in which the odds were really fixed before we started and the purpose all along was not to meet the issue but only, as it were, to tell ourselves we had. This is the way in which almost all dangerous ideas are now defused in public classrooms. Teachers pretend to open up a dangerous issue when in fact they close it more emphatically than it has ever been closed before. The teacher who encourages this false sense of confrontation with a painful issue is denying more to a pupil than a teacher who avoids the issue altogether; for the latter, whether she knows it or not, has at least left the possibility that the pupil, in rebellion, will search out the forbidden area at a later time and find something in it to enrich or challenge him. But the pupil who has had the false sense of meeting the issue in a classroom stacked against it has seen the issue sterilized forever.

How many of us remember classes on the problems of democracy—classes in which all questions have been respectfully included except the only ones that really matter?: "Do we have a democracy?" "Do we want one?" "Could our economy survive it?"

"Lead children, by free and open discussion, to discover the five major reasons for the failure of state socialism in Red China. Allow them latitude in pinning down these reasons. . . ."

The children—still worse, the teacher—go away with the curious idea that they have just looked into the jaws of ideological temptation and emerged victorious.

I have spoken of the way in which we attempt to defuse or domesticate a serious issue in the classroom. It is apparent that we attempt to do the same with well-known people to whom we feel obliged to pay lip service but whose ideals we do not wish the young to follow. What we do, essentially, is introduce the name and the face into our classroom and maybe, as well, a certain cautious selection of his stated views, but all in a manner that dilutes and undercuts his deepest meanings, and all in a way that renders him undangerous and sterile. Dr. King, in this manner, becomes a kindly Negro preacher "who went to college in order to improve himself and help his people, believed in God, believed in his fellow man, and won, as a reward for his moderate position and nonviolent views, the respect of his fellow Americans, both white and black, and the Nobel Prize for Peace."

We do not remind our students, if we can conceivably manage to avoid it, that Dr. King also encouraged his followers to break the laws of this society and openly to obstruct the execution of its policies, so long as those policies appeared to conflict with good conscience.

We do the same, if it is at all possible, with the creative work of most provocative people. The intensity of a man's conscience, the ferocity of his thought, are allowed into the classroom only after having been subjected to a process of intellectual castration. I do not think it is a surprise that schools attempt to do this. It is not dissimilar to the national manner of either emasculating or else assassinating heroes.

In neither case do we wish to pay much honor to these men until they are well on their way to burial. We honor brave men after they die, cowards and executives while they are living. I am thinking of Thoreau, to whom Americans today pay nervous tribute. Nervous, I suppose, lest he should suddenly reappear. For fifty years after his death he was forgotten. In his own day he was no more beloved than his inheritors in S.D.S. are loved today. He spoke of freedom and offended nearly everyone who was then living in the state of Massachusetts.

> How does it become a man to behave toward his American government today? I answer that he cannot without disgrace be associated with it. . . . When a sixth of the population of a nation which has undertaken to be the refuge of liberty are slaves, and a whole country is unjustly overrun and conquered by a foreign army and subjected to military law, I think that it is not too soon for honest men to rebel and revolutionize. As for adopting the ways which the State has provided for dealing with the evil, I know not of such ways. They take too long and a man's life will be gone. . . . What is the price current of an honest man . . . today? They hesitate, and they regret, and sometimes they petition; but they do nothing . . . with effect. They will wait, well disposed, for others to remedy the evil, that they may no longer have it to regret. At most they give a Cheap Vote . . . and Godspeed to the right as it goes past them. There are 999 patrons of virtue to one virtuous man. . . .
>
> The greater part of what my neighbors call good, I believe in my soul to be bad, and if I repent of anything, it is very likely

to be my good behavior. What demon possessed me that I behaved so well? You may say the wisest thing you can, old man . . . you who have lived 70 years, not without honor of a kind. I hear an irresistible voice which invites me away from all that. . . .

Those are the words of Thoreau in *Walden* and the *Essay on the Duty of Civil Disobedience.* I think it is important for us to understand quite clearly that many of our students have taken the books we gave them seriously. I think we hoped that what we offered them was something like inoculation. I think we hoped that what we could do was render the message of a great man sterile and innocuous, providing our students with only a careful, measured dose. Obviously, for reasons complex and numerous, our expectations foundered. A great many students, as it now appears, have learned a better lesson than the one we thought to teach. In a great many cases, Thoreau was introduced to children in the high schools as a "nature writer." Perhaps, in such a manner, schools or teachers thought to render him undangerous, and for a long while such an expectation seemed well founded. Today, however, a great many students have found, in the books we gave them, meanings which we did not intend and which we had perhaps, too many times, forgotten. The consequence of this, and of a good many other factors too, is a student upheaval, growing rapidly into the dimensions of an ethical revolt. Almost all ideas which we have accepted without question are now being held up to a new light and being tested by new questions. Patriotism itself, as a final and unquestioned value, is now being viewed in a far less easy manner than at any time before. Chauvinism and the automatic reflex of obedience, as we knew them, are dead letters.

This observation is somewhat distant and removed from the fourth-grade lesson-plan and "Basal Reader." Perhaps, however, it is the kind of distance that we ought to start to travel when we speak of public schools. Teachers and authors, in trying to deal with schooling problems, attempt to hold their focus tightly on the classroom. To do this is attractive and respectful, but evasive in the long run. It will, of course, always help in certain ways to look into the matter of the lesson-plans and reading programs and the like. I think that it will help even more, however, to look into the words of the Pledge of Allegiance and into the writings of Thoreau. Political considerations are often degraded as shrill, irrelevant, and, above all, unprofessional by educators. I have attempted, in this writing, to speak of matters mainly nonpolitical, but I do not think that pedagogy and politics can quite so neatly be dichotomized as we may wish to think. It is, of course, self-serving to perpetuate this severance: it is an easier and less offensive way to speak about the problems of our public schools. But it is also a way of moving in a circle within fixed limits. I cannot guess what others will do, but I sense, for my own part, an increasing recognition that the subject of school reform in the United States must become a great deal more political, and a good deal less rhapsodic, less "beautiful" and less utopian, than it has been now for some time.

# JUMPING THE TRACK

Happily, schools are springing up across the country which truly attempt to help kids grow up. In the past five years several hundred "free schools" have sprouted up throughout the United States, with a particular concentration in California and the Northeast. In addition, a number of the public school systems have begun to experiment with new educational forms. The schools described in the final section of this book represent the best of these schools, public and private. They vary in form and purpose. Some, like Harlem Prep or John Adams, place strong emphasis on traditional goals of job or college. Others, like Other Ways or LEAP, seem more like a family or club than a school. But all of these schools share a common idea: they are based on a profound respect for the student—his ideas and potential. They all seek to encourage a student to follow his natural impulses and interests, not to stifle them. Hopefully they represent the future.

# Murray Road: Beyond Innovation

## BY EVANS CLINCHY

The Newton, Massachusetts, public schools have long been regarded as the epitome of "excellent" suburban education. Many of the earlier innovations, such as the new math and science curricula, were introduced early on there. So it is perhaps fitting that Newton is the scene of one of the most radical experiments in high-school education.

Murray Road School has no administration, no grades, no set curriculum, and no compulsory attendance. It may very well be the answer to many of the points raised by the Montgomery County, Maryland, students in their critique of that county's system. With student unrest as endemic in the suburbs as in the inner city, Murray Road deserves close attention. It may well be that the comfortable middle-class kids with their "smooth, reasonable, democratic unfreedom" are the greatest victims of high-school education.

Evans Clinchy is president of Educational Planning Associates, Inc., a Boston-based consulting firm.

To THE casual eye it looks like any small, suburban, elementary school—glass, nondescript, beige stone, slightly modernistic in design for an early 1950s building. Surrounding it is the usual collection of middle-class, suburban homes—not rich, but by no means poor—each set in the middle of its own small plot of grass. (This piece of Newton, Massachusetts, happens to be suburbia, even though Newton *in toto* is really a small city of 92,400 with industry, poor people, and a national image as the epitome of nonurban educational desirability.)

The casual eye, of course, is all wrong. The Murray Road School is no longer an elementary school but one of the most unusual high schools in the country. It houses (on and off) 115 students and eight teachers. Students do not have to be there unless they actually have a scheduled class or want to be there to use the facilities or to meet their friends. There is no set curriculum. What "curriculum" there is is devised collaboratively by the students and teachers. There are no grades. There is no principal. (The teachers elect one of their number to handle the administrative chores on a rotating basis.)

The students, at the moment, are tenth-, eleventh-, and twelfth-graders, all from the upper, college-bound tracks at Newton High School. Most of the male students sport long hair. Everyone dresses in casual, "hip" attire. Shoes are not much in evidence in warm weather. The atmosphere of the school could hardly be less formal. The halls are filled with students and teachers moving entirely on their own, going about their business. There is no such thing as a "pass" to go anywhere inside or outside of the building. Classes are held in classrooms, in the hall, out on the lawn under trees, depending upon how people feel at the moment (and upon the weather). Classes are also held at night in homes, if they cannot be squeezed into the schedule. (The school is supposed to be closed at 4:30 every afternoon.)

The school's facilities consist of eight largish rooms. Some are typical, 1,000 square-foot, elementary classrooms. Other rooms are slightly larger and are used as: a) a commons room, equipped with a refrigerator, battered old chairs, and a ping-pong table (the school's one piece of physical education equipment); or b) an art studio equipped not so much for teaching as for students doing their own art projects. There is no cafeteria (students bring their own lunches), no auditorium, no gym, no library, no science labs, no language lab, no guidance suite (or guidance counselors), no football team, no cheerleaders, no industrial-arts or home-economics suites. (Each teacher does have his own small office.) It is not an expensive school to operate, despite its roughly 14-1 pupil-teacher ratio.

Indeed, much of the "operating" is done by the students themselves. After the teachers and students have together decided what the "courses" will be for the coming semester, the schedule is worked out by a committee of three students. There used to be a catalogue, atrociously typed, and put together by the students; but that has been abandoned in favor of a floor-to-ceiling cardboard schedule board with courses and times marked in—again, all done by the students. There is a small central office inhabited by the faculty member selected to be the administrator, but inhabited also at all times by students, many of them using the phone at will.

Within this framework of disciplined anarchy the teachers and the students collaborate on all of the important decisions. Since there are virtually no rules, it is difficult to have discipline problems. There are two major requirements—every student must take something called "English" and, at some point, a year of something labeled "American History" (this is a state law). Seventy-five minutes a week of "physical education" is also required, but this is done on the "honor system." Otherwise, students make suggestions about what they would like to study—computer programming, astrology, the origins of man, child psychology, etc. The teachers set forth what they would like to teach—logic, linear algebra, the Alienated Individual in Literature, Comparative Myths, French conversation, etc. The final catalogue is made up of the compromises worked out by students and teachers. Teachers, however, decide how many "credit hours" any particular course is eligible for. All students must end up with a total of sixty-five credits for their three high-school years, the number of credits required for all Newton High School students. At the end of a course, the teacher and student evaluate the student's performance. Usually, the student and teacher will agree on whether credit has been earned, but if there is any disagreement, the teacher's judgment prevails.

If students cannot find a teacher to teach what they want, they are free to set up and "teach" their own course. They can receive credit if a teacher evaluates their work and pronounces it fit. One student, for instance, is offering a course in film-making that meets twice a week, once as a class and once as a three-hour lab period spent shooting and editing film. This same student, Larry Levy, is making a documentary film about the school to be shown to parents, especially parents of would-be students, and to anyone else interested in what's going on.

Another student, Len Goldberg, a tenth-grade student and something of a mathematical whiz, wanted to get a computer-programming course started. Murray Road had no computer, so Len and another student took on the job of figuring out how to solve that problem *on their own*. For four days they worked solidly, going through all of the computer firms in the phone book, trying to find one that would be willing to arrange for time-sharing, etc. All of the laborious details were finally worked out. Len is now the teacher of computer-programming. In a small room off the commons room there is a large and gaudily decorated box with "Mock II—Desk Top Computer" painted on it. Inside the box (if you are foolish enough to look inside) is a telephone. A wire leads from Mock II to a computer terminal beside the desk.

Len came to Murray Road directly from the ninth grade at a nearby junior high school. He had heard from friends about what high school was like. It made him nervous. But when he saw Frederick Wiseman's film *High School,* that finished him. Much of what he saw in the film was exactly what he saw every day at his junior high. He applied immediately for Murray Road, knowing little more about it than it was obviously nothing like the school in the film. He now finds Murray Road very much to his liking. One possible piece of evidence for this is a large sign placed on the huge communications board in the central lobby. It reads:

> Wanted: One total baseball nut—Some guy who as a kid knew everyone's batting average, etc. I am trying to write a fairly realistic computer program to simulate baseball, and I need an idea how the satistics [sic] work. HELP ! ! !
>
> Len Goldberg, 10th grade

Or, take another example, a black girl who shall here be called Doris and who is not actually a student at Murray Road at all. Doris is enrolled at Newton South High. Last year she was on the verge of dropping out until she heard about Murray Road and began going there whenever she found time (which was, apparently, fairly often at hours when she was supposed to be at Newton South).

School has never been high on Doris' list of favorite pastimes. She grew up in Roxbury, Boston's predominantly black section, and went to her local elementary school. ("I hated it—they were always trying to put us down and telling us how dumb we were.") She also attended the academically selective Girl's Public Latin School, an institution she found hopelessly rigid and old-fashioned ("like a convent"), but for which she harbors a sneaking admiration. An English teacher, she says, once told her that she did not believe in assigning books less than thirty years old, because "they had not yet stood the test of time."

Although Newton South was considerably better than Girl's Latin, it was still not "free" enough for Doris' tastes. (It is also a large school.) Whenever she can, Doris comes over and takes courses at Murray Road and also takes part in the intense social life. One of her "courses" (completely non-credit) is a small group studying Danish with a teacher who happens to know Danish.

Doris is desperate to gain full-fledged admittance to Murray Road next year. Students are selected by the teachers from those who apply. (There will be thirty places next year, and there are already about one hundred applicants.) The criteria for selection are not completely clear, but one is the staff's estimate of whether the student really wants to come and can handle the considerable responsibility of a basically self-directed education. It is perhaps an uncertainty about Doris' ability to handle that responsibility that keeps the issue in doubt. One effect this has had on Doris is that she is attending Newton South regularly and trying to establish an acceptable record there, but only so that she can earn her way into Murray Road.

Another anonymous student's reaction to Murray Road is recorded in a collection of such reactions put out by the school:

> Unfortunately, I succeeded at the high school and without a great deal of work. Without really pursuing things and without really doing excellent work. It's much harder being at Murray Road and it took me a while to really discover this. At the high school I was able to do a great many things, not really as well as I could have and still pull A's, etc. When I arrived at Murray Road I was very excited by all the options and became rapidly overextended. The standards here, which are self-imposed, are much harder to fulfill. To really fulfill them, one must do a few things excellently rather than many things fairly.
>
> Mathematics still doesn't turn me on, but my dislike isn't quite as acute as it was at the beginning of the year.
>
> At first, I thought I was destined to another hell-raising year in French. But soon I realized that teachers need cooperation from the class, and that teachers have feelings as well—which must sound over-obvious, but I never considered teachers' feelings before.
>
> I am much more involved in everything I do and in the school and give much more of myself and am much less tense. Also, I am making decisions for myself and if I am not satisfied, I am learning to try to change. I know that at Newton High School I would be working hard and getting good grades but that would be all. I am working harder this year because I have my own standards to live up to.

Murray Road is technically not a separate school but an annex to, and therefore a part of, Newton High School. As happens with many such wild experiments, it was not started because of a specific urge to make a radical departure. Newton High School in the spring of 1967 was badly overcrowded. The Murray Road Elementary School, about two miles away, was offered as a possible way of handling the overflow.

Given this opportunity, the staff of Newton High and its principal, Richard W. Mechem, took advantage of the situation. If a piece of the school was going to be two miles away, there wasn't much point in trying to mesh schedules and trundle students back and forth. It was therefore decided that Murray Road should operate on its own, and that it would consciously and deliberately experiment with new ideas that might turn out to be useful in the programming and design of a new high school to open in the early 1970s. The main point of the experiment was to test out two ideas: that students could take a great deal more responsibility for their own education; and that teachers and students could collaborate on the establishment and development of "curriculum."

The school was planned to open with 150 eleventh-grade, volunteer students who would represent a genuine cross-section of the student body at Newton High. This did not happen. Only 107 students volunteered, and they were all from the college-bound tracks of the school. Most of them, too, were from the "hip" element of the school. Murray Road, right from the start, has had a reputation as a "hippie" haven, and it has been almost impossible to recruit students who are typical, "straight," suburban kids, or students who come from working-class families.

Originally, it was planned that the students would take their eleventh-grade year at Murray Road, and then go back to the high school for their final year and graduation. After the first year of the experiment, the staff argued against this and won. In 1968, the school had eleventh- and twelfth-grade students. This past year it has had tenth-, eleventh-, and twelfth-graders. The staff would like to go back next year to just eleventh- and twelfth-graders, having learned, they say, that the three-grade span is too great for them to handle in such a small school.

Is Murray Road working? How do people—parents, administrators, the students themselves, other students, and the community at large—feel about Murray Road?

There is little doubt in the students' minds that the school is successful. Not perfect, perhaps, but different from and more rewarding than normal "school." The most casual observation of the school gives evidence of that. The atmosphere is one of great warmth and mutual respect between teachers and students. First names are always used by and for everybody. Seldom does one catch a teacher putting on airs and behaving "teacherish." At one point during an impromptu session devoted to painting all the available glass in the front lobby, several of the students decided that one of the men teachers would look better if he had a racing stripe painted down the middle of his face. After being chased all over the school grounds, the teacher returned with a blue racing stripe painted down the middle of his face.

Another example from that same painting session: after spending most of an afternoon covering every glass surface with imaginative designs, the students suddenly remembered that the school was holding a meeting that night for the parents of students who wanted to come to the school next year. In the course of a fairly heated discussion, several things began to become clear. Some of the students—perhaps all of them—were aware that the school has a "booky" reputation in Newton and that prospective parents, already wary and suspicious, might be turned off if they arrived to find the entrance hall gaudily decorated with bright colors and brighter sayings. Some of the students angrily argued that it would be hypocritical to remove the paint. This is the kind of thing that goes on at Murray Road, they argued, and the uptight suburban parents had better meet it head on rather than find out about it later.

The other side admitted all that, but argued back that it was still the parents who were, by and large, going to decide whether or not the students were to be allowed to come. It was thus better for the school to appear perhaps squarer than it really is, *because it would not be fair to the prospective students if they could not come just because their parents disliked gaudy paint.* The teachers took little part in this discussion. As far as they were concerned, it was all up to the students. At least one teacher sided with the antihypocrites.

But the paint-removers won the argument. Everyone, including teachers and this visitor, was pressed into service to scrape and wash away the paint. It was a painful experience, since much of the work was first-rate.

The students really do seem to *care.* Murray Road is very much *their* school, and they intend to defend it against all comers. Or rather it is a school run by and for students and teachers. There is no organized parents group, nor does anyone seem eager to have one.

The teachers, too, feel that the school is a success so far, not only for the students but for themselves as well. They are a self-selected crew who have really wanted to try something different and who find what they are doing professionally rewarding. Exhausting and often maddening, true, but still professionally rewarding. Although the staff has grown from five to eight, only one teacher has left and gone back to the high school.

The staff as a whole interviews and selects new teachers, whether they be people applying from inside the Newton system or from the outside. They have found that, for the most part, teachers with six or seven years' experience work out best. It takes enormous confidence—both self-confidence and professional confidence—to work in a situation as unstructured as the one at Murray Road. Such teachers, they say with ill-concealed pride, are not easy to come by; and rarely do these qualities show up in brand-new, inexperienced people.

And the parents—what about this neglected group? The evidence seems to indicate that, with the rarest of exceptions, they are pleased by what Murray Road does for and with their children. There have been sporadic complaints, but no serious ones. Getting into college, since almost all Murray Road students are middle-class, suburban and therefore college-bound kids, is uppermost in most of the parents' minds. Eighty percent of last year's graduating class at Murray Road went on to college— exactly the same percent as the comparable group at Newton High. So, apparently, this is not the problem one might have expected it to be.

In addition, many of the parents are actively behind the school and enthusiastic about what it is trying to do. Quoting again from the comments collected and put out by the school, these are parents talking about their own children:

> When my son was unhappy at Newton High School and doing poorly I could never decide whether he was the problem or if perhaps he was right when he said that much of the school did not teach him anything. I feel now he was sincere. This year he cannot get enough of all he is learning—he spends every minute singing the praises of Murray Road, but he does *not* talk about freedom, bull sessions, fooling around and indifference but downright, genuine desire to make papers perfect, an absolutely amazing love for every teacher, an incentive which has focused his every bit of energy toward doing better today than yesterday and suddenly a hunger for many tomorrows which will enable him to do more. It is a miracle. I can't help feeling such an effervescence could not all be caused by the fact that he is a year older. I am so sure this program has what it takes to make hard study a joy and invites an urge to become more seriously involved in meaningful activity to further a student's ability to make every minute count. With less pressure from school routine that was so great at Newton High, my son has pressured himself more, putting study first, and working to conclusions. I believe his scope has broadened —his desire to absorb more and more. I am aware of the need for organization, and the value of certain lines being met, but I feel this is being done by pupils, on their own.
>
> If he had stayed at Newton High School, I see the possibility

of his wings never spreading. I had no idea so much could unfold in so short a time.

Or, less full of enthusiasm:

She does not seem to spend more time studying at home (if anything less), nor does she show overt signs of more disciplined study habits. What does seem to be the case is that her general satisfaction with the Murray Road program re-enforces the whole learning process. *She seems to learn more in less time.* She has not yet seemed to run into "slumps" as she did habitually two or three times a year when she would be bored with and disaffected by school.

And a final crucial question: has Murray Road fulfilled its original aim of affecting education elsewhere in Newton, particularly at Newton High and the planning for the new high school? Or has it remained a little gem of innovation off by itself, carefully quarantined so that it will not infect anybody? "Yes, to the first question, and absolutely not to the second," says Richard Mechem, Newton High's principal and one of Murray Road's originators and constant supporters. Murray Road, he says, has first and most importantly altered the "attitude" of Newton High teachers and students. It has as yet created no wholesale changes in the school itself, but the fact that Murray Road has survived and prospered has caused many people to rethink what they are doing. Mechem characterizes Newton High as essentially a "conservative" school, although he boggles a bit at using the words. Murray Road, he says, has made everyone more "liberal."

"As far as I am concerned," Mechem says, "Murray Road is a complete success. We sometimes feel that the education we offer at the high school is lifeless." What Murray Road has done, he feels, is to demonstrate that education need not be lifeless, that it can have zip and zing, that it can be something that students can respond to.

One direct effect that Murray Road has had on the high school is in Barry House, one of the school's seven houses. Here a group of about 120 sophomores and their teachers have been kept together and given a large block of time in which they organize and schedule themselves. In addition, a group of students all this past year have been agitating and attempting to plan a Murray Road type subdivision of the high school that was to be called the Walnut Street Annex. "Was" because it didn't work. The students thought they had the necessary teachers lined up, but at the last minute the teachers pulled out.

Teachers, says Mechem, are one of the big problems in assessing whether or not Murray Road is having an effect. "Teaching at a school like Murray Road requires total commitment." It is not that non-Murray Road teachers lack commitment, according to Mechem, but that they have many other things they are involved in and interested in at the high school. Most of them do not feel they would be comfortable under the intense pressure that Murray Road forces onto teachers.

If teachers are one of the problems with Murray Road's type of education, Mechem feels that an even more serious one is the fact that the school has succeeded in attracting only one type of student—the more liberal, "hip," college-bound student. He refers to this phenomenon as "psychological stratification." He has tried repeatedly, as has Murray Road itself, to broaden the student body and achieve the cross-section that was originally intended. (these efforts have earned him the more or less affectionate title of "Mix 'em up Mechem" from the students at Murray Road.) He would especially like to see more children of working-class parents attending Murray Road. But these students are just the ones who are put off by the "hip" appearance and the "liberal" reputation of the school.

What Mechem—and many other people around the country —is moving toward is a revival of the old-fashioned notion of *pluralism*, the idea that schools—or even pieces of schools—need not all be the same or even all operate by the same rules and aims. There is no particular reason, Mechem says, why schools cannot be shaped to fit students; no reason why there cannot be a wide variety of different kinds of schools from which students (and their parents) can select the most appropriate model.

This notion of pluralism has nothing to do with the concept of tracks or ability grouping along lines dictated by IQ tests or "academic achievement." It has to do with different *styles* of learning, different kinds of students feeling more comfortable with and responding to different ways of becoming involved with the world of knowledge.

This might mean that Murray Road is not necessarily the perfect school for every student. Indeed, it may well not be. But it appears to be one of the most significant alternatives around at the present. And there is little doubt that taking a trip down Murray Road in the moonlight can be quite an experience.

# Parkway: A School Without Walls

## BY HENRY RESNIK

Philadelphia, under the leadership of Superintendent Mark Shedd, has recently undertaken a number of significant educational experiments such as the Pennsylvania Advancement School, the development of an affective curriculum, and the Open Classroom system, a new model of primary education. Perhaps its most significant venture has been the Parkway School, a new concept in secondary education which makes the entire city the classroom—a "school without walls."

Rather than ingesting predigested blocks of "knowledge" handed down by a teacher standing in front of the class, Parkway students learn by doing—in the city's museums, hospitals, schools, businesses, and libraries. The program has been widely copied and is regarded as a model of how to involve students in a meaningful and relevant education.

Henry Resnik is a free-lance writer and author of *Turning on the System*, a study of the Philadelphia schools.

TINKERING WITH the educational system is generally recognized these days as a poor solution to the problems of America's schools, and one wing of the educational avant-garde has decided that a possible answer may lie in changing the nature of school altogether. Of the several school structures that educators have proposed as alternatives, one of the most consistently popular is the "school without walls." This is essentially a community of learners who may use a building, or scattered classrooms, as a base of operations, but for whom the real classroom—and the most important teacher—is the community at large. High schools without walls are either in the planning stages or have opened in Chicago, Toronto, and Kansas City, among other places; on the elementary level, Hartford has the "everywhere" school, a network of community-oriented classrooms located in several different parts of a new housing project; and two of Manhattan's subdistricts are planning similar elementary schools. But most of these have taken the lead from the granddaddy of them all, Philadelphia's Parkway Program.

The Parkway Program is an experimental high school that has no building of its own, but uses all of downtown Philadelphia as an educational resource. Instead of sitting in classrooms memorizing textbooks, Parkway students learn through direct experience in hospitals, universities, theaters, offices, and the large number of cultural institutions—among them the Museum of Art, the Franklin Institute, and the Free Library—that line the Benjamin Franklin Parkway, an elegant boulevard stretching from City Hall to the art museum a mile away.

The Parkway Program celebrated its first birthday in February 1970 by graduating a class of seven, all college-bound, in a ceremony keynoted by U.S. Commissioner of Education James Allen. A class of eighty, more than half of whom will go on to college, was graduated in June 1970. Although the program started with a Ford grant and a pilot group of 140 students, funding now comes from the Philadelphia Board of Education, the number of students has reached 500, there are thirty full-time teachers and thirty university interns, and the program has been hailed throughout the nation as a brilliant success. The nearly universal popularity of the Parkway Program is probably best embodied in the enthusiasm of its own students. "The thing about this school is . . . I feel like everybody loves each other," one student affirmed in a speech at the February graduation ceremony; others have coined such labels as "the school for kids" and "the ultimate high school."

The Parkway Program is not just another educational panacea —it's a way of life. I happened to be spending most of my days in

Philadelphia when the program was first announced and I was as excited by the original concept as anyone. I followed the development of the program closely from the beginning and became a part-time member of the original community when it finally opened. Long after I'd finished my research, I continued commuting to Philadelphia twice a week to conduct a workshop in journalism for Parkway students.

The program has attracted hordes of visitors, but almost by definition it cannot be neatly or concisely observed. It just *happens*—all day and all week long, summer and winter, within a huge area (by no means limited to the Parkway itself) that keeps growing and could eventually extend to all of Philadelphia. Because the program is highly individualized, the only way an observer could legitimately claim to have an over-all view of it would be to know each student and follow him through his daily or weekly schedule.

A student's typical day might include a course in journalism at the Philadelphia *Bulletin* taught by the newspaper's staff, a lecture in physical science at the Franklin Institute, lunch in a nearby coffee shop, "tutorial" in the art museum (these groups of eighteen or so, which meet four times a week, are the base, something like a family, in which students receive counseling, instruction in basic skills, and evaluation), and a couple of hours' work in a downtown auto shop or a furniture-maker's studio in the little Bohemia of Sansom Street. Parkway students can conceivably spend the morning in an office building a few blocks from the Delaware River, Philadelphia's eastern boundary, and the afternoon at the University of Pennsylvania, forty blocks westward. Obviously, the Parkway Program involves a good deal of walking, but students who need to travel more than ten blocks receive free tokens for buses and subways.

The easy accessibility of downtown Philadelphia is not the only reason for the program's success, however. It's an important factor, but there are several other structural and educational components that may be even more important. Actually the Parkway Program is a synthesis of two educational concepts which sustain and complement each other.

The first was the brain child of Clifford Brenner, an administrative assistant to Philadelphia's school board, who looked out his window in the Board's Parkway offices one day and saw a vision: relief for the severe problem of overcrowding in the city's high schools and the possibility of a completely new kind of school. The Parkway would be the school's campus, the institutions its classrooms. The proposal also included a system of continuous shuttle buses carrying students from one class to another. One of the main gripes about today's schools is the irrelevance of what happens in them; Brenner's idea opened the way for a kind of daily contact with the real world that in most schools is restricted to infrequent field trips. And the four-year school, planned to serve 2,400 students, would save the financially troubled Board $15 million—the cost of a new building.

Eight months after the Board's announcement of this proposal, the other main component of the program arrived in Philadelphia in the form of John Bremer, a forty-two-year-old Englishman who had been selected as the program's director. A deceptively mild-mannered iconoclast whose intellectual convictions have roots in Plato, Freud, and Dewey, Bremer had been developing a unique educational style and philosophy for more than a decade. He had worked in the famed Leicestershire schools —the "infant schools"—of England; he had founded an experimental college; and after emigrating to America he had most recently served as educational director of New York's Two Bridges Experimental School District, a tempestuous venture into community control.

John Bremer is one of the few self-proclaimed educational innovators I've encountered who doesn't sound as if he's selling vacuum cleaners. His appointment as director of the Parkway Program has clearly been, as another program participant once observed, a case of "the right man in the right place at the right time." Indeed, the original concept of the program is an ideal frame for what Bremer has been attempting throughout his career: to create an educational institution that will truly educate. The name rhymes, incidentally, with "dreamer."

It seems to me now that the Parkway Program could not possibly function in any way except according to the "model" that John Bremer conceived for it. During the months of speculation before Bremer's arrival, however, tradition-oriented teachers and administrators warned that the enterprise would require no less than an administrative genius to make it work smoothly. Computers would have to plan every student's schedule in detail, people said; the school administration would have to guarantee that all 2,400 Parkway students wouldn't end up in, say, the dinosaur room of the Academy of Natural Sciences at the same time. Attendance would have to be taken constantly everywhere. Seen in this light, the program was a huge logistics problem that most administrators were glad they didn't have to handle—a mountain of busywork, a nightmare version of the traditional school.

But Bremer is an articulate foe of such routine thinking. He has tremendous faith in the ability of every individual to manage his own life and his own education, and he has made this faith the heart of his school. In our first conversation, for example, he dispensed with the idea that students would be bused up and down the Parkway; they would *walk,* he told me vehemently, or else they'd find their own way of getting from one place to another. "If people aren't responsible for their lives," he said, "you're keeping them children. Without responsibility there's no education at all. My job is to set the limits in which the operation takes place." I seem to have heard Bremer repeat any number of variations on this theme several hundred times; he's made it into a kind of litany. Bremer's ideas are so subversive, often so genuinely shocking, that he doesn't take any chance of his listeners missing the point.

"If you presuppose that what the student is expected to learn is already known by the teacher, or his surrogate, the textbook," Bremer told me during a later session, "the whole thing is an imposition on the student and he'll fight it. He *ought* to fight it." The curriculum in the Parkway Program, he went on, is not a set of known facts that some authority—state department of education, principal, or teacher—has decided the student must learn, but the student's own growth, and the growth of the school and the city as well. A student might learn more in a half hour of walking down Market Street than in several weeks of sitting in a conventional classroom. If he discovers that he wasted twenty-five cents by not buying a subway transfer, that's part of his curriculum. Maybe, on a more important level, he'll realize that a class at the Franklin Institute isn't as exciting as he thought it would be, that physics bores him—that's part of his curriculum too. In the Parkway Program he has the freedom to find out what he wants to learn and to be a responsible adult. Within broad state requirements for the high-school diploma he can actually do just about anything he wants—eighteen courses in a Parkway catalogue, for example, fulfill the state math requirement.

What many students want, of course, is often merely a more humane version of what they receive in traditional schools—college preparation and training in basic skills. Thus, while some prefer to elect such exotic-sounding courses as "Zen Watercolors," others may choose conventional fare like general science, basic English, and typing. The course catalogue lists candlemaking and leatherwork apprenticeships in quaint little shops, but it also includes a conventional lecture in art history at the Museum of Art, home economics, and eleven languages, among which are Latin, Greek, and Hebrew. Some Philadelphians see the program, in the words of one skeptic, as a "place for the weirdos," but this impression is probably the result of the school's tremendous freedom—from dress rules, rigid schedules, and all the usual limitations—for in no way are students pressured to be noncomformists or rebels.

Although the freedom of the Parkway Program can be misconstrued as wild anarchy, in fact, Bremer insists that he has created a tight structure and that this structure is more honest and logical than that of the traditional school, where structure is essentially repressive. At any rate, a basic plan has evolved that differs only in minor ways from the model Bremer began talking about it the early days of his appointment.

The plan calls for separate "units," or communities, with roughly 130 students and sixteen faculty members, half of whom are volunteer interns. Everyone in the unit is a member of a tutorial, which should function as the center of the student's high-school career, and offers such diverse activities as parties and picnics, help with practical problems (if a student has trouble with statistics for a course in basic insurance at the Insurance Company of North America, his tutorial leaders would give him instruction in math, or at least make sure that he found it somewhere else), and an ongoing evaluation. There are no marks—evaluation is done on the basis of pass or fail and a written comment. The whole measuring, testing, grading madness has been totally eliminated, in fact; even admission to the school is decided by the random process of a public lottery. (Parkway is not a special school for "bright" kids or white kids; racially and intellectually, the student body is a heterogeneous mix that includes a small percentage from suburban and parochial high schools as well as representatives of the eight geographical school districts within the public school system.)

Another structural element within the unit is a weekly "town meeting," the closest thing in the program to an actual government, where problems of general concern to the community can be aired. And students can volunteer to be members of "management groups," which are set up when needed to provide services for the program's successful functioning. Among others, there have been management groups for fund-raising, coordinating social activities, publishing a newspaper, printing a course catalogue, and building a school library.

As for courses, students can select either from "faculty offerings" taught by the program's own staff (these range from fundamental basic skills to such pleasures as kite-flying and model ship-building), or "institutional offerings," which include everything taught by anyone outside the staff and cover the spectrum from on-the-job training in local businesses to demonstration-lectures at various institutions (many of these are as dry as the most orthodox classes in traditional schools) to courses run by volunteers in nearby colleges. There are three separate units in the program ("Alpha," "Beta," and "Gamma"), each with its own headquarters and its own catalogue of offerings, and each catalogue lists roughly ninety courses from which students can choose.

One of the most important structural factors is the selection of faculty. Applicants are interviewed by a committee that consists of a Parkway teacher and student, a university intern, and a parent from the community. Naturally, the committees have certain preferences—the Parkway faculty tends to be young, vital,, and friendly.

One might guess that this basic structure would be just as simple in operation as in theory. It's every student-prisoner's dream come true—no more rules, do your thing. But in practice the structure reveals the profound significance of that catchy phrase "school without walls." John Bremer wasn't satisfied just to do away with the physical walls; he removed the psychological walls as well. His real goal is to nourish a new generation of *people* without walls, and everyone who enters the program quickly discovers that the most important learning, as Bremer often reminds them, is bound to be messy.

Some blessed instinct kept me from the messiest, most discouraging kind of learning until several weeks after the beginning of the program. I was lucky; in my role of visiting writer I spent the first week as a participating member of "Cy's tutorial," and I saw more positive change and growth among the students in that week than I had seen in a year of my own presumably dedicated teaching within a more traditional framework.

"Cy" is Cy Swartz, a thirty-two-year-old teacher of English with seven years' experience in the Philadelphia public schools who is now administrative head of community "Gamma" and who was probably at the beginning the teacher best prepared, both in temperament and experience, to work within the Parkway structure. Each tutorial is presided over by a member of the permanent staff and a volunteer intern, creating a teacher-student ratio of roughly eight to one—few classes at Parkway number more than fifteen, and to a great extent this accounts for the friendliness and intimacy of each unit. Cy's partner, Meg Vasey, was an Antioch undergraduate working at Parkway as part of her work-study program. Together they grew into an extraordinarily effective team.

Tutorials were formed on the first day, after Bremer made a few introductory remarks in the main room of the program's second-floor loft at 1801 Market Street. Like the admissions process, the organization of tutorials is utterly random; kids drew the names of their tutorial leaders from a hat, and the groups then assembled in various corners of the huge room. In addition to Cy, Meg, and me, our group consisted of sixteen students, later reduced by two when a new tutorial was formed in order to lower the numbers in each. It didn't seem like a miracle group, but chance was on our side—another tutorial ended up with fourteen boys and two girls, and the racial balance could be an important element of group harmony as well (five of our group were black, lower than the program's 50 percent representation). There was, at any rate, tremendous diversity: two self-proclaimed refugees from the city's elite public high school for girls, two boys considerably younger than the rest, several extremely quiet ones, and a few in beads and fringe. Roughly half were from the inner city and half from the semi-suburban northeast. By the time we were all together, there was so much noise in the main room that Cy led us downstairs for a brief organizational meeting on the sidewalk.

We had all been given a mimeographed packet of information at the beginning of the morning, and according to the schedule, we would be having lunch between 11:00 and 1:00; then tutorial groups would meet from 1:00 to 3:00. It was close to 11:00, and as we stood blinking at each other on the sidewalk it became clear that nobody really knew what we were supposed to be doing. Something prompted Cy to suggest that we walk over to Rittenhouse Square, a comfortable park several blocks away, and make some plans. It was the last time that Cy even came close to telling us what to do.

Assembled again in the middle of the square, after a ten-minute walk in which we'd had an opportunity to exchange fundamental identification signals, we proceeded to stare at each other, to giggle with embarrassment, and then to wonder aloud what was going to happen. One of the kids finally asked Cy rather aggressively, "Where are we supposed to go *now?*" A pixie with a mustache and laughing eyes, Cy stared back and said, "*I* don't know. Why are you asking *me?*"

After several minutes of animated conversation, we agreed that we would just go off somewhere and do whatever we wanted until our designated tutorial meeting at 1:00; the only rule was that everyone had to be with at least one other member of the group. Somebody said, "Okay, let's go," and almost as if it had been prearranged, the group divided into equal halves, one setting off to the south with Meg, and the other, including me, heading toward Market Street and City Hall with Cy.

First we had lunch at a nearby Automat, a block from City Hall. While we were still at the Automat, just about everyone took out cigarettes—even one of the smallest, youngest kids in the program, who borrowed from another kid, choked horribly after one drag, and told us, "I don't smoke very often. I have asthma."

After lunch we decided to go to the top of the City Hall tower and have a look at Philadelphia. Two of the group's junior members, however, apparently feeling overwhelmed by the older ones, wanted to assert their independence by going somewhere else—they'd already been to the top of the tower, they said. No one protested; we agreed to meet them in half an hour or so downstairs. When we saw them again they'd been completely transformed by excitement: not only had they, the younger ones, decided that they wanted to do something by themselves, but they'd actually sat in on a real trial in one of the courtrooms.

Cy's was the only tutorial that hadn't been provided with a meeting place outside of 1801 Market Street (offices, churches, and other institutions often volunteer classroom space in which Parkway staff can meet their students), and when we reconvened at the program's headquarters much of the conversation centered on finding a place of our own. There were also numerous questions about the program itself. "When are we going to start school work?" asked one boy. "We've already started," Cy answered, "but the actual course work will begin in three weeks." The atmosphere was casual and friendly; even the quietest had begun to talk. By the end of the afternoon we had organized ourselves toward finding a meeting place, but one of the boys, who looked as if he'd never been happier in his life, told the group, "If we can't find a place, you can all come to my house."

At the second meeting of Cy's tutorial, on Tuesday afternoon, we proceeded immediately to the business of finding quarters, but the enthusiasm of the day before hadn't quite carried people into the action they'd promised. One of the boys suggested that the group break up at 2:30 and take the rest of the afternoon to canvass the neighborhood looking for a room. There was disagreement, then a heated discussion about procedure. Someone asked Cy if it would be okay for the group to leave at 2:30. "*I* don't know," Cy said. "Don't ask *me*." He was less deliberately naïve this time.

"You're the chairman," one of the kids told him.

"No, I'm not," Cy retorted. "Nobody ever said that."

One boy jabbed a finger at him jokingly and said, "I *appoint* you chairman." But it was a feeble gesture. The kids were beginning to realize that when people in the Parkway Program told them they'd have the responsibility for their own decisions, it was true. It wasn't just another teacher's con.

On Thursday, one of the boys in Cy's tutorial announced that he had decided to leave the program. His conscience told him that it wasn't right for him, he said. The others wanted to know why. There were several digressions, but he finally admitted, looking at the floor most of the time, that he didn't think the program would fulfill all his course requirements for college and he'd better get back to his former high school because he was missing work and would fall behind if he didn't go soon. "We're not trying to force you to stay," Cy said, "but *we* can learn something from talking with you about it if you don't mind telling us your reasons." The discussion proceeded, and over half an hour or so the increasingly lively and involved group systematically convinced the boy that whatever his reasons for leaving the program were, they couldn't really have anything to do with college credits. There was nothing he couldn't get from the program if he wanted it.

Prompted by the boy's abrupt judgment, we took an informal survey of everyone's attitudes toward the program so far by just going around the room. Several called it "a second chance"; with the exception of the lone dissenter, approval was unanimous. This general feeling of solidarity and community led us to question a few of the problems that were already in evidence—kids running wild on Market Street, for instance, and accidentally hitting passersby with snowballs, or behaving so boisterously that they damaged furniture in the main office. The group thought the program was so good, in short, that they wanted to make it better.

Finally several kids suggested that during the first town meeting the following day they would go before the community and propose certain minimal rules and standards of behavior. For the first time since he had voiced his disappointment, the boy who wanted to leave the program nodded vigorous assent. At the end of the session he even handed in a sheet of course preferences, which suggested that he might stay. But the rules couldn't possibly be arrived at fast enough for him, and there would never be enough rules in the Parkway Program anyway. He returned to his former school within a few weeks.

The success of Cy's tutorial, which veterans still refer to as a paragon of the Parkway philosophy in action, represents a skillful balance of affective and cognitive learning. The traditional school, critics of the educational system generally agree, emphasizes cognitive skills almost exclusively, mainly through the memorization of facts, while affective learning—the development of relationships with other people and the emotional growth of each individual within a group—is totally ignored. "The Parkway Program minimizes the artificiality of bureaucratic functioning," says Mario D. Fantini, a leading educational theorist and the program's liaison with the Ford Foundation. "The fact that you're human is the important thing. It used to be that your role was important and the fact that you were human was secondary. . . . In the Parkway Program kids talk about how decisions are made; they question processes. The whole interaction and the openness—it's a different form of governance."

Cy's tutorial was an outstanding example of humanistic education, but it certainly wasn't typical of the program as a whole. In fact, for every minute of intense community that Meg and Cy created there was probably a half hour of misunderstanding and tension elsewhere. Very early in the first session, for example, it became clear that a large number of the students were simply overwhelmed by what they had been offered, too baffled even to reject it. With its vast course catalogues and its emphasis on individuality, the Parkway Program had a decidedly white-middle-class perspective that was bound to turn off the uninitiated (only recently has a group of black boys sought a radical departure: a community-oriented neighborhood project in the North Philadelphia ghetto). The resulting disaffection among many of the students has been a vivid example of the messiness of learning John Bremer often talks about; some students even insist that the school is essentially the same as the schools from which they came, except for a lot of walking. Bremer would say, of course, that they haven't yet learned they can change it.

These issues were fairly clear even at the beginning. When I returned for a week's visit shortly after the program's first anniversary, however, I was not prepared for the deeper malaise I frequently encountered. Students complained to me that tutorials were boring and town meetings a waste of time. Cutting of classes was widespread (some teachers have decided to give only partial credit in proportion to a perennial absentee's attendance rate). A few institutions had suffered property losses at the hands of Parkway students. There were racial tensions within the units. One student actually called the program "the lesser of two evils."

A good deal of the malaise seems quite clearly to be the result of two major crises the program sustained during 1969-70. The first was the departure of half of the original faculty from the first unit (now called "Alpha"), many of whom returned to college or left to work in the other units being established. The original community had been so strong that the loss was deeply felt and resulted in a general lowering of morale.

The other was a lengthy dispute over the newest unit, Gamma, which briefly included one hundred elementary students and functioned as a combination elementary-secondary school in which the older students assisted in teaching the younger ones. In November 1969 a group of citizens protested the recruitment of a large number of the elementary students who were being bused from Philadelphia's Germantown section and who had been chosen, they maintained, by undemocratic means. Bremer has been at odds with the school system's central administration—particularly superintendent of schools Mark Shedd—since his arrival, and Shedd, bowing to the pressure, finally ordered the elementary unit closed.

When I talked with Bremer about some of the problems I'd seen during the week's visit, his response was predictable: "You've got to look to see where a program is *going*," he said, "not what it's like. The problems of the students *are* the educational problems. Now the problem is whether the structure of the program can support them—if the program becomes rigid within, it will be killed. There is disorder, but you've got to be prepared for disorder if there's going to be any real learning. You can't expect them to be neat and tidy and well mannered and literate in a true educational setting."

What about the students' complaints? I asked. Bremer seemed unperturbed. "Saying something's a waste of time is like saying you're bored," he explained, "and boredom is a sign of anger. In the long run I believe in the democratic process, but it's a very painful one. The students have to participate in the governance of their lives—that's tough learning. We've only had students a year and people have been struggling with democracy for *hundreds* of years." In fact, many members of the Parkway community are now vindicating Bremer by recognizing their own failures and re-evaluating the entire program; though painful, the process of growth continues unabated.

Very few professional educators have John Bremer's unyielding faith in human potential, but at times he seems almost blindly idealistic. He insists on letting all the messy learning happen as it will, yet he is fully aware that the Board of Education must commission a detailed and formal evaluation of the program, and that school boards do not commonly invest money in someone else's faith without a guarantee that they can expect measurable results, even though many argue that the cost of the Parkway Program is less than that of a conventional high school.

Among Bremer's private book of maxims, one of my favorites is "Anything that can be measured is educationally worthless." But ours is distinctly a society of measurables. Can the Parkway Program, as John Bremer has conceived it, survive in a basically competitive, alienating society?

"It was a good experience," a former Parkway student who had returned to his original high school told me shortly before I left Philadelphia at the end of my week's visit, "but I wasn't really getting anything out of it. All I really learned about was people. My other school is like a memorizing game—I know that—but the Parkway Program's not what I want. I learned a lot about myself, but I didn't learn the things I'll need for college."

Like the boy in Cy's tutorial who also returned to his original school, my friend was wrong—technically, Parkway satisfies all the requirements. But he was certainly right in fearing that American society may not be ready for the kind of people that Parkway students are preparing to become.

# John Adams High School: Something for Everyone

## BY JOHN GEURNSEY

Murray Road and Parkway are two examples of public school systems experimenting with new educational forms; John Adams High School in Portland, Oregon, is another. Conceived by seven education students while in graduate school, John Adams has attracted wide attention for its imaginative curriculum, democratic governance, and other innovations in staffing and teaching.

John Geurnsey is an education writer for the Portland Oregonian.

JOHN ADAMS High School in Portland, Oregon, is a new and radically different approach to high-school education. Robert Schwartz, the principal, describes Adams as "a school where students want to go, and want to learn because they are curious and interested—not because an attempt is made to force them to learn." He has stayed in the saddle during the bucking first months of the operation, and is now convinced that "the school will gain momentum and support as it goes."

The school has inspired some hot feelings in Portland:

"Adams High does not teach respect for authority, discipline, basic scholarship, or orderly use of time. The school teaches gross egotism, extreme self-centeredness, myopic self-delusion, and general anarchy," says one Portland resident.

"We're learning to live with other races and other people here

263

at Adams," says a student. "And all the math, English, Chaucer, and history teaching in the past didn't teach our parents how to do that."

"My daughter's education is being neglected at Adams, and I am having her transferred to another high school," says a parent who meant it. His daughter now attends a different high school.

"I'm all for Adams," says another parent. "My daughter went to another high school for two years, but this is the first time she has taken the initiative to do studies and projects on her own."

What's so different about Adams that has inspired such diametrically opposed opinion?

For one thing, it's the school's curriculum itself, which is split into general education problem-solving courses and an electives program. The general education part works like this:

All students spend about half of each school day, either the morning or the afternoon, on different teams that study ways to cope with such problems as air and water pollution, unemployment and welfare, reducing student unrest, improving student-adult understanding, keeping the automobile from destroying the metropolitan area, reducing the crime rate, and lessening race-related friction in the school and community.

There is no breakdown by grades or ability in these problem-solving sessions: All study teams are mixtures of seniors, juniors, sophomores, and freshmen.

Teachers attempt to encourage older students to help the younger ones, the faster ones to help the slower ones, and each student works on the part of a problem that is compatible with his ability. The problem-solving tactic also avoids the compartmentalization of subjects: The students do not study English for forty minutes, or social studies, math, science, or history as specific courses; they deal with all these basic subjects as parts of a study of a given real problem during the general education program.

As an example of the value of the general education approach, Schwartz refers to an incident that occurred just as Adams opened in the fall of 1969. Several Portland high schools began the year with serious race-related student problems, resulting in numerous assaults and police action. The most severe disturbances were at Adams, where the philosophy is to bring together students from all backgrounds, representing many ranges of abilities, and where the student body is 22 percent black.

General education study teams jumped right into the action and undertook to develop solutions to Adams' racial problems. In fact, race relations occupied the whole general education program for the first couple of weeks of school. A race relations committee held assemblies where students could talk matters out, and black and white student leaders began to take command of the situation. Since then, although assaults and confrontations haven't ceased altogether, there has not been another major racial flare-up at the school.

Schwartz explains the problem-solving education approach: "Students need to learn what will help them function effectively in society, regardless of what type of work or what further education they plan to go into after high school."

The courses at Adams were put together almost entirely by the teachers, with help from about 100 students, during the summer of 1969. Schwartz would have liked to have had even more of the school's 1,300 students take part in curriculum planning.

The teachers kept several questions in mind while putting together the courses. What should students know and be able to do after leaving high school? What parts of the individual disciplines can contribute the most to the over-all general studies courses?

"The program is tied to something inside the kid that interests him," says Schwartz. "Then it must be tied to something on the outside that is real." By real, Schwartz and his teachers mean the problems of today—race, pollution, crime, and so forth—not material that deals with national problems of 100 or 200 years ago, although they do not ignore historical perspective.

"The important thing is that students should learn the techniques of problem solving and how to adjust to change. These abilities should prove useful throughout the rest of their lives," Schwartz adds.

It is noon now, and half the students have completed their problem-solving sessions. During the afternoon they will attend specific classes—but they take what electives they please—or they can do independent study, meet with student-faculty committees, or even goof off a part of the time. Each student is scheduled for some electives at which attendance is expected.

Of the elective courses, some require a full school year and others are mini-courses that last about six weeks. The mini-courses meet just about every imaginable interest: computer application and technology, astrology, coed badminton, and even such special studies as "From Bach to Bartok." Schwartz explains the large number of elective courses and the free time in which students can study what they wish: "Give kids a chance to try some of the things they're interested in. They must have the chance to be curious, to explore adult roles and have meaningful choices."

Schwartz also points out that the academic and college-bound students can use the elective periods for taking in-depth and continuous studies in math, sciences, foreign languages, and other college-requirement courses.

Adams is well tuned to the fact that, on the basis of national statistics, of each ten students who begin as freshmen in high school, only about two will go on to complete college. Consequently, the $5.8 million high school has strong and wide-ranging job-related programs in which a good percentage of Adams students are enrolled.

Schwartz and his staff plan to encourage business, industry, and the professions to participate in the school's training program and to sponsor students in half-day on-the-job-training apprenticeships. They also hope to invite business and industrial representatives as guest lecturers and assistant teachers, and they plan to arrange for some vocational-technical classes at outside plants during the evening.

For sixty students who don't really seem to be turned on by

the academic or vocational program at Adams, there is a mobile school where they spend most of their general education time. A big bus, accommodating about thirty youths each morning and afternoon, roams the metropolitan area on scheduled visits to industrial plants, art museums, city and county operations, conservation projects, airports, and the like. In an attempt to add relevancy, Adams uses the community itself as a basis for these youngsters' education. On returning to Adams, the students write, tell stories, or make movies concerning their outings, and teachers try to motivate them toward more concrete learning experiences.

Some parents, especially those whose youngsters are headed for college, are uneasy about the school's relatively lax requirements that specific courses be completed in order to qualify for graduation. However, college officials have assured them that their children will not be denied college admission because of that. Grades are optional at Adams. At the beginning of each course students can, with their parents' approval, choose to receive either a regular letter grade or a pass-fail notice.

Another of Adams' major educational tenets is that students learn better and teachers teach better when the students and teachers have a close understanding of one another via more personal contact and less formal relationships.

To combat the impersonality of largeness, Adams operates as four smaller high schools in one—at least for the general education program and for administrative purposes such as counseling and disciplining. Each smaller school—known as a house—has about 300 students, mixed as to age, race, and social and economic background. Two teams of teachers work with the students in each house, and the same teachers stay with the same students as much as possible for more than one academic year.

Counselors are part of each house team and work with the students and other teachers all day long. In this manner the counselors get to know the students better and can do more to help them with their problems. They also help teachers improve their counseling abilities.

One of the most innovative changes at Adams is in the area of school policy-making. While the ultimate responsibility for the operation of the school rests with the principal, Adams is experimenting with a mechanism to permit majority rule voting by students and faculty members on some issues. The Adams operation duplicates in some respects the functioning of the U.S. Government.

"The whole issue of decision-making in conventional high schools is wrong," says Schwartz. "The students and faculty members want more voice, so we're experimenting with the delegation of authority."

At Adams there is a school legislature made up of a student-elected student senate and a faculty-elected faculty senate. Joint committees representing these bodies meet on such issues as curriculum and grading, or on policies that most directly affect students and teachers.

In other cases the senates function separately. If the issues involve student funds, for example, the policies are made and enforced by the student senate. If they involve working conditions and other areas of primary interest to teachers, they are dealt with by the faculty senate.

Schwartz and other administrators make up the executive branch of the school government. Changes or new policies developed and approved by the senates, jointly or separately, require the principal's signature before they can become school policies. Although the principal has veto power over bills sent to him, the legislative bodies have been empowered to override the principal's veto by a two-thirds vote.

Adams also plans to set up a judicial branch which will probably be some sort of appeals body made up of students, faculty members, and administrators. However, Schwartz and his staff have found that there are many legal implications involved that require careful study. "A school is not a court," said Jerry Fletcher, coordinator of research and evaluation at Adams. "We have to be very careful in setting up quasi-judicial procedures."

In addition to introducing changes that could make education more interesting and relevant to students and teachers, Adams includes numerous clinical programs to influence teacher preparation, teacher enthusiasm for teaching, and community involvement. Schwartz and his staff feel that the clinical approach is one of the most important aspects of the experimental school. They challenge the long-standing education concept that college and university campuses are the best places for training teachers and performing educational research.

"The truth is that a university is just not a very relevant setting for training teachers and doing much educational research," says Schwartz. "As it is now, a college student training to be a teacher does not get into a regular school classroom until very late in his training—the last part of the senior year. He gets far too much of his material from theory and hearsay from a professor." So Adams has worked out an arrangement with officials of Reed College, Lewis and Clark College, and Oregon State University that permits junior-year teacher trainees to receive college credit for working in Adams classrooms. Nearly all of Adams' eighty-member faculty is made up of experienced teachers, but the school also has a great many trainees. They are teamed off with regular teachers so that the inexperienced learn from the experienced in actual classroom situations.

Some of the teachers at Adams also hold assistant professorships at the colleges with which the high school cooperates. Schwartz views this as a very necessary advancement in education. "There must be closer educational ties between the four-year campuses and the grade schools and high schools," he stresses.

In one training program that Adams carries out in cooperation with Oregon State University, eight interns, most of them black, are being trained for teaching in inner-city schools. The interns either have no college degrees or majored in something other than education. They are learning on the job at Adams, getting a full year of actual classroom experience and taking training for college credit from the Adams teachers who double as professors. Schwartz hopes that the experiment, sponsored under the Education Professions Development Act, will result in more blacks with teaching potential being able to enter the teaching field.

Schwartz believes the on-the-job training for both blacks and whites without college training in the field of education can have two major impacts:

1. Elementary schools and high schools throughout the nation want more black teachers than they can find, because not enough blacks have college backgrounds—especially in the field of education. On-the-job training like that provided in the Adams-OSU program could qualify many more in a hurry.

2. Preparing teachers without an overload of educational theory courses could modify long-standing teacher credential requirements which deny schools the use of many persons who are experts in their fields and who would like to teach but will not take the methods courses necessary to qualify. Adams also hopes to add to the significance of educational research, since the school has its own researchers and evaluators right there on the job as part of the teaching teams. "Research is much more meaningful and reliable when conducted in and around actual classrooms," Schwartz emphasizes.

John Adams High School is the creature of Schwartz and six other secondary-school teachers who, in 1967, were in their final year of study at the Harvard Graduate School of Education. They set out to develop a model for a school program that would make possible the achievement of many of the educational objectives that were commonly voiced by educational and social analysis but had not been established in practice or adequately tested.

The Harvard graduate students envisioned a clinical high school—one where instruction of students, curriculum development, preservice and in-service training, and research could all go on simultaneously. A high school, they believed, might be made to function somewhat like a teaching-hospital does in medicine.

"We realized that our individual voices would be drowned

out, but if we had our own high school and worked as a team, we could make the changes we believe are necessary," says Schwartz.

The seven graduate students developed a detailed plan of how they believed a high school should operate. Then they sent a proposal to half a dozen metropolitan school districts and kept their fingers crossed that they would get a taker. They got several but were most impressed by the enthusiastic reply from Portland school officials and school board members.

Adams won't claim that it has solved all attendance problems or convinced 1,300 students there to love school. But many of the students obviously do like Adams, and their enthusiasm has been instrumental in quieting down a large number of questioning parents. As one parent put it: "I still don't understand the damned place, but it's the first time my kid has actually been excited about going to school. So how can I knock it?"

Some students feel they are learning more at Adams. Others like the school because they have more voice in what they will study or a chance to be on their own. Then there are some who really don't know why they like it more than other high schools. "We just feel better here," they'll say. But most will tell you, "We're getting more out of school here because our teachers are more than teachers—they help you with all kinds of problems."

Since Adams teachers have less time scheduled in classes than teachers at other Portland schools, they have more time for other contacts with students. "A very positive point," says Patricia Wertheimer, coordinator of social services at the school, "is that the teachers have a genuine interest in their kids. How many other schools do you know where teachers visit a student's home or phone if the student is absent too many times?"

A visit to the school at 3 P.M. verifies this. People aren't stampeding one another to check out and leave for the day. Many students and teachers stay until five, six, or seven because they're working on something—or with somebody—they're interested in.

# Harlem Prep: An Alternative System

## BY ANN M. CARPENTER AND JAMES ROGERS

Harlem Preparatory School opened in 1967 as the first high school in Harlem designed to serve the real needs of the community. It is an independent nonsectarian school supported by private donations. Harlem Prep, along with the Street Academies from which it draws many of its students, constitutes an alternative education system demonstrating that schooling in the inner city can work if a meaningful curriculum is combined with open and honest respect for students.

Ann M. Carpenter is chairman of the English Department of Harlem Preparatory School. James Rogers, a graduate of the school, is a student at Fairleigh Dickinson University.

ON JUNE 11, 1969, the community of Harlem paused from its routine activities to act as host in an unusual ceremony: the second graduation exercises of the recently founded Harlem Preparatory School. Days earlier students had passed out flyers inviting parents, housewives, local businessmen, churchmen, doctors, policemen and passersby to the open-air graduation that was to be held on the sidewalks of 136th Street, between Eighth and Edgecombe avenues. In addition, invitations were mailed to every person who had made a financial contribution to the school or had served in any other way since its opening in October 1967. The result was a gathering of people of diverse educational, social, economic, religious, racial and ethnic backgrounds, united in honoring the graduates and giving recognition to the record of achievement of Harlem Prep. That record includes:

—October 1967: Harlem Prep opened with forty-nine students; by February 1968 its enrollment had reached seventy students. In its first graduation, June 1968, thirty-five students were graduated, all of whom were accepted by accredited colleges and universities.

—September 1968: enrollment was up to 181 students; in January 1969 Harlem Prep opened up evening programs in adult education; and in June 1969 seventy-five students were graduated, all of whom are now enrolled in accredited colleges and universities.

Harlem Prep was created to provide an educational milieu which could meet the needs of the youth of Harlem who had rejected traditional educational programs. These youths, coming from an area of New York City that has a high level of poverty, population density, and many social, physical and mental pathologies, have been labeled in school as "deprived," "different," "disadvantaged," and "disaffected." Many who remain until high-school graduation find that they are unprepared to enter a college, technical school, or any other institution beyond the secondary-school level. These are students who are able, intelligent and "good"—they do their homework; they diligently copy notes from the blackboard; they answer the teacher's questions in class; they pass the weekly tests—yet they emerge from high school under-educated and disillusioned. A great number of others do not last until graduation and drop out, disappointed and angry.

In late spring 1967 Dr. Eugene Callender, then the executive director of the New York Urban League, met with the administration of Manhattanville College to formulate plans for offering these youths a different kind of education. Before any considerations of faculty, curriculum or philosophy of the program were made, it was noted that at the time there was no public high school in central Harlem; graduates from junior high schools in the area were sent to other parts of the city for secondary education. Therefore, it was essential that the new educational program be located in central Harlem. This program was viewed as a means of counteracting the alienation, disillusionment and anger which grew out of the poor education some youth of Harlem received in traditional educational programs. Harlem Prep was created to break the old patterns of failure and rejection and establish new means of growth and success.

On July 28, 1967, the New York State Department of Education granted the school a provisional charter for the following purposes:

"To establish, conduct, operate and maintain a non-sectarian, private college preparatory school for boys and girls between the ages of 16 and 21 who have dropped out of school and who, in the opinion of the administration of the school, can be motivated to complete secondary education, to provide such education for such boys and girls, and to develop liaison with a number of colleges eager and willing to accept such graduates."

The headmaster and vice-principal were charged with recruiting the staff and developing curriculums to achieve these purposes.

In hiring teachers the headmaster consciously sought individuals who presented varying experiences and backgrounds; thus a diverse staff of white, black, and Indian races, and Catholic, Protestant, Jewish, Buddhist and Baha'i religions resulted. Educational backgrounds varied from the Ph.D. to undergraduate status; the range of teaching experience extended from twenty years to three months. The common characteristic of the faculty was a sincere commitment to the idea that it was possible to take capable young dropouts and offer them a different educational experience which would enable them to complete high school and be accepted for admission to college; furthermore, they believed that these dropouts could make a significant contribution to society. Other requisites for a successful teacher at Harlem Prep were the ability to be flexible in adapting teaching methods and subject matter to the changing needs and interests of the students, and the ability and strength of personality to accept strong student challenge, open criticism and incisive questions.

Individual interviews with these youths indicated that they had dropped out of traditional school systems for various reasons: they were lost among great numbers of students in classes in which teachers did not even know their names; the courses they studied were not related to problems of their daily lives; they had no power in making decisions that affected them, such as what was taught, how it was taught, or who taught it; they were continually forced to conform to a system of values which they had no part in forming and which they did not honor.

After a period of consulting on the principles on which Harlem Prep's curriculum would be based, courses of study were drawn up. The subjects which were taught included basic mathematics, algebra, geometry, trigonometry, analytic geometry and calculus, writing skills, comparative literature, reading skills, speech, drama, mass-media analysis, creative writing, African studies, Egyptology, Caribbean studies, political science, sociology, contemporary problems of democracy, comparative economics, biology, chemistry, physics, logic, film-making and video recording, art and music.

The orientation of the courses was toward the development of skills and knowledge, the stimulation of intellectual curiosity, the development of individual research techniques, the development of standards of evaluation, and the development of tolerance to accept different opinions, criticisms, and evaluation from others. Traditional subjects were taught with a view toward applying their theories to contemporary social problems; wherever possible, interdisciplinary approaches were used. In all areas individual assignments and research projects were provided.

With the recruitment of staff, the establishment of the curriculum and the agreement upon purposes of the school, the headmaster and vice-principal set the opening date of Harlem Prep at October 2, 1967. Classes were held in an auditorium and two rooms of the 369th Regiment Armory on Fifth Avenue at 142nd Street. Forty-nine students were enrolled. In February 1968 enrollment rose to seventy. About two-thirds of the students came from the New York Urban League's Street Academies Program; others, from churches and individual or public-school recommendation. These students represented the various political and religious ingredients which may be found in the ghettos of the city. There were black, Spanish-speaking and white students of Catholic, Protestant, Jewish, Muslim, and Baha'i religions. The political views of the students included nationalists, Garveyites, Five-Percenters, followers of the late Malcolm X, incipient Black Panthers, and peace marchers. The student population was as varied as the faculty; in both cases the important thesis was that from diversity the school could achieve unity.

In June 1968 thirty-five of the seventy students were graduated and admitted to colleges across the country. The graduation exercise was the occasion for illustrating that the aim of achieving unity from diversity had been accomplished: members of opposing groups in Harlem met in harmony to honor their youth; students of different political and religious ideologies embraced each other as brothers; students and faculty reflected the image of a family. The gift of the first graduates was the school flag with its emblem and motto: MOJA LOGO—UNITY, BROTHERHOOD.

The themes of unity and brotherhood are important developments in the lives of typical ghetto dwellers; they are particularly vital in view of the global village concept. No longer are peoples of the world isolated by great distances from each other; the modern need in education is to prepare youth to live peacefully in a society that comprises people of different racial, religious, ethnic and political backgrounds. In purposely bringing together a faculty and student body of richly varied backgrounds the headmaster established the setting for great student growth. In such a situation these youths have an opportunity to interact intimately in a favorable milieu and, through their interactions, test their biases, become aware of their false assumptions about each other and begin to eliminate their prejudices. This process is necessary for achieving harmony in our society; the presentation of the school flag and motto assured the faculty that the first graduating class had developed an awareness of this need.

In September 1968 Harlem Prep moved to its permanent home, a remodeled supermarket with an area of ten thousand square feet. The faculty and headmaster consulted at length on the question of the best physical arrangement for establishing new behavioral patterns. The resulting organization reflects their concept of the structure which is best not only for achieving students' academic progress but also for enhancing their social development and stimulating their intellectual curiosity.

The cinder-block walls have been painted and paneled. Acoustical tiles have been installed against the ceiling; blue-green outdoor carpet now covers the concrete floor. No walls or partitions have been erected.

A visitor entering Harlem Prep sees a vast, open area. Classes are defined in clusters—chairs grouped in circles, portable blackboards stationed where needed. At times teachers may be indistinguishable from students because they are not in their traditional places at the front of the group; more often they are just another member of the circle. Because there are no separations between clusters it is possible for students to see and hear what is happening in classes around them. This setting is permitted because the faculty felt that this arrangement would provide a therapeutic atmosphere for the students.

First, it gives everyone in the school a sense of "elbow room." In an area of the city where people are physically crushed together constantly, this expansiveness can provide great psychological relief to all who enter. Secondly, the openness permits students to observe learning activities of other areas as well as their own, and allows them to choose which one they take part in. Students are free to visit other classes whenever they choose; they agree, however, to make up work they miss in their own class. The open structure also acts as a stimulus to teachers—their realization that students are free to sit in on other classes serves as a reminder that they must prepare meaningful material that is adapted to the needs of their students.

A basic premise on which all activity at Harlem Prep is founded is that the school is preparing leaders of the future. Thus students are given chances to develop and strengthen their leadership abilities as often as possible. Along with their teachers they plan and evaluate material to be studied in class. They organize and elect their own student council and write their constitution. They elect a student representative to the Board of Trustees. They maintain a speakers' bureau and help to raise funds for meeting the school's budget. They also administer funds in the student welfare account. Student representatives attend faculty conferences, share in evaluating the curriculum and make suggestions for improving various aspects of the school's operation. In addition, the council hears all student grievances and makes recommendations for action.

Traditionally, groups who have been enclosed in a ghetto have used education as a means for escaping. At Harlem Prep the students are aware of this characteristic of education, but they believe in a greater purpose. Those who enter the school do not seek to flee from the ghetto but to develop themselves fully so that they may return to render service there. In this way they will break the pattern of flight from impoverished areas; by returning to serve they will act as positive-role models for children and adolescents and will share their education and accomplishments with the community. The leadership training experiences they gain at Harlem Prep are a critical step in their growth.

In the brief time that it has been in existence Harlem Prep has already been responsible for institutional change in colleges and universities. More than one hundred and fifty of them have corresponded with the school in search of candidates. Prior to the school there was little if anything a dropout could do to re-enter educational circles; colleges were unwilling to consider candidates with records of failure in traditional systems. Those who recruit candidates from Harlem Prep, however, willingly disregard the previous transcripts and consider students on the basis of their achievements at Harlem Prep. This is a new move in education.

To date graduates of Harlem Prep have entered schools such as Fordham University, New York University, Harvard, Vassar, City University of New York, University of California at Berkeley, Diablo Valley College, Lincoln University, Shaw University, Hampton Institute, Marist College, Wesleyan University, Long Island University, University of Wisconsin, University of Massachusetts at Amherst and the State University of New York at Buffalo, Stony Brook, Oneonta and New Paltz. Students are encouraged to apply to a range of schools so that they are dispersed across the nation. In this way they will have differing experiences to bring back to their areas of service.

This report details the success which Harlem Prep has attained after two years of operation. Further determination of its achievement may be made after a lapse of one more year, when members of its first class will have graduated from college. Until then, the faculty can only point to the number of people who have been educationally revived—not only the students who have actually attended Harlem Prep but also their parents, who were inspired to organize and open a school of their own, and the thousands of other young people to whom these youths will be examples.

For those who have been placed in college it has been a long road back. The statement made by John Bell, who was graduated in 1968 and accepted at the State University of New York at Oneonta, expresses the feelings of many students: "I am bringing myself out of the strain of the doing, into the peace of the done; for I have done so much with so little for so long that now I can do anything with nothing at all."

## . . . A STUDENT VIEW
## BY JAMES ROGERS, CLASS OF 1969

MOJA and LOGO are written on the wall at Harlem Prep. These two words of African origin for unity and brotherhood have as many meanings as our school's students have diverse experiences. But each of our lives is united for one immediate aim—to go on to college. As a family helps its members get a start in life, we students help each other toward our common goal.

Harlem Prep really is a family—and not one just in name. People at the school I formerly attended spoke of being a family, but what was projected was the coldness of an institution that paralyzed creative thinking. The difference between that school and Harlem Prep is the difference between my turning out to be a graduation statistic or a creative thinker in whatever field I might choose.

The fact that everyone knows everyone else adds to Harlem Prep's personal character. Even the person with the most contrasting point of view is my friend—better yet, my brother. Brotherhood—it's written on the wall, and it's practiced by students and teachers alike. And when you have a school where teachers and students work together, you have a family.

To all of us, Harlem Prep is a second chance, whether we dropped out of school or just managed to graduate. We know we are the lucky few who have this precious second chance. In order to make it, we have to meet these standards: "For graduation, students must have demonstrated the power to do college work; they must be proficient in verbal and writing skills, as well as in mathematical skills. They must have acquired a firm grounding in social studies. . . . The aim of Harlem Prep is not only a diploma, but to place a student in college. He must have a record for consistent attendance and punctuality and show his ability to live up to the spirit of the school, which presupposes self-development and service to the community."

Located in a dreary armory near the Harlem River for its first year, Harlem Prep ushered thirty-five students into U.S. colleges and universities. The spirit of Harlem Prep was born in that armory. Now located in a remodeled supermarket that is undergoing metamorphosis into a school building, the spirit of Harlem Prep is carried on by us.

It's not the same place for more than a week. When we first came to the building, there were no blackboards, or study tables, or even, to some extent, books. The school was one spacious room, contrasting drastically to the large, many-cubicled standard secondary-school buildings. You can imagine it: a supermarket, minus the shelves and counters. But that was the first week. For a while, book-shelf partitions were erected between classroom areas, where once only space made one class distinct from another. Now the library is shelved on lower bookcases, and once again there are no physical dividers between classes. The atmosphere of the building has been softened by a new acoustical ceiling and a black-flecked green carpet covering the entire school floor.

Many people believe that classrooms and textbooks are necessary to education, but Harlem Prep can testify that they are not. What makes a school is what goes on in the classes—and in each individual student. Our interests are so deep that outright questioning, even with anger, is common. Anger in my old school, even when it was directed at the lesson, was attacked as a lack of discipline. This made many students apathetic and kept them from taking part.

Harlem Prep, on the other hand, does not suppress response, no matter how strongly it is presented. Because we show our interest this intensely, it suggests that we are academically inclined. The teachers understand this. They react in such a way as to keep the lesson on topic, as well as to let us speak our minds. Moreover, the faculty is not just a body of teachers but a group of human beings who look at students as other human beings. This is what I think differentiates a Harlem Prep teacher—he accepts a student who questions as being involved rather than being a "disrupter of the class."

Smoking was a major reason for being expelled at my old school. At Harlem Prep, this rule, along with a few others, has been left out of the book. Eating in class was allowed—until the students themselves voted to dispense with it because it interfered with the educational process.

We can also attend the classes we choose. If, for some reason, the teacher fails to show up, we can sit in on any other class—or sit alone and study. By not having a substitute teacher in front of the class, we are assured that Harlem Prep feels we are old enough and responsible enough to make independent decisions and judgments.

A project the faculty members want to undertake is to put their work into textbook form. Since our curriculum is so diverse, there are no textbooks that fulfill our requirements. For example, one instructor handles algebra, trigonometry, geometry, and computer math in the same course. To do this, he has to hand out worksheets nearly every day. All science classes include two or more sciences, such as chemistry and physics, or chemistry and biology. Clearly, the faculty members are developing new approaches.

When I said that textbooks are not necessary for classwork, I meant it. Textbooks are nothing compared to a faculty with interesting ideas. But this isn't all. At Harlem Prep, students themselves are encouraged to contribute ideas for improvement. It's a good feeling to have a teacher ask, "What do you think we should do?" And this has happened to me. Unlike ordinary schools, we don't have something pushed on us or have to fight for a say. We keep close touch with the administration.

The three administrators, including Mr. Carpenter, the headmaster, teach and extend themselves as people. They are looked on by everyone as individuals.

There is a tree planted in front of Harlem Prep which, in a way, symbolizes our individualism. It is dedicated to Vic Gomez, a student who died striving to fulfill his goal. Many of us did not know him, but Mr. Carpenter did. He says: "Brother Vic was slight, intense, driven. He had three wishes: to attend Harlem Prep, to visit Africa, and to enter college. He died fulfilling his second wish; he was drowned while on safari in Africa. But the honor, dignity, and pride that he possessed are carried on."

The administration does not work alone. Along with the Board of Trustees, it works very closely with the Parents' Committee. In fact, five parents and the president of the Student Body serve on the Board. But this is not all the parents do. Since many potential college students work during the day, the Parents' Committee of Harlem Prep decided to open a night school. They engaged the faculty and manned the registration for subjects such as psychology, logic, English, math, Swahili, typing, and investment banking. Classes meet from 7:00 P.M. to 10:00 P.M., Monday through Thursday. Here are some reactions of the school's night family: "Harlem Prep is a challenge, a pioneer, and a godsend. A challenge to the establishment which has discarded those who wish to be educated and economically better off. A pioneer in rendering educational assistance to these people. A godsend because we all ask where would we be without Harlem Prep?"

"If Harlem Prep doesn't do anything else for me, or even if I don't make it to college. Harlem Prep has given me self-confidence. A man won't take the first step if he knows he is going to fall."

Not only the parents but also the daytime students show concern for the community, and we try to demonstrate the feeling of unity inspired by Harlem Prep. In our free periods, many of us tutor children in the public schools in the neighborhood. During the teachers' strike, we helped out with elementary school pupils. We find that tutoring is richly rewarding for both tutor and pupil.

Though I think very highly of Harlem Prep, it has its weaknesses. Because our building is still being modified, we lack many things that established schools have. For example, laboratory and lunchroom facilities are still in the planning stages. Obviously these have priority over a student lounge and other luxuries, so they must be built first. But the amount of construction is relative to the amount of money the school has. Many good things will not be completed by the time I graduate. If more funds appear, more construction will be undertaken.

Enough about buildings! If the spirit of Harlem Prep could be introduced in large public schools, they would be making giant steps, not only in education, but giant steps toward real personal relationships. And that's what it's all about—unity and brotherhood. That's the writing on the wall!

## Shule Ya Uhuru: Freedom and Manhood

Founded by student initiative in 1968, the Eastern Freedom School (Shule Ya Uhuru) is an annex to a regular public school in Washington, D.C., from which students receive credit for the courses taken at the Freedom School. Shule Ya Uhuru doesn't attempt to cover all courses, but focuses on Black Studies through offerings in Black History, Third World Studies, Community Organization, Black Literature, etc. In addition to exemplifying an educational program devoted to the true liberation and humanization of the individual, it also illustrates how a curriculum can be both relevant and rigorous. Mamadou Lumumba, Director of Curriculum at the Freedom School, coordinated preparation of this article, which is written by several teachers and students at the school.

### THE ORIGIN OF THE FREEDOM SCHOOL (SHULE YA UHURU)

Up you mighty race you can accomplish what you will!!
—Ndugu Marcus Garvey

In November of 1968 approximately 110 Eastern High School students and Washington school-system dropouts filed into a church building in northeast Washington. These 110 black people were about education—more specifically, a black education. And so they filed into their nine selected selected classes, and the year went on. . . .

All of this started a year before in an Eastern High School English class when students discussed the condition of the Washington, D.C., school system—and more specifically Eastern High. It seemed that Eastern was receiving less money than some of the schools that had a substantial enrollment of white students. These black students found that they were receiving hundreds of dollars less per pupil than the white students. They found that they had more temporary teachers, fewer textbooks, and most important they found they were receiving a white education. The result of all this was one of the lowest reading and math scores in the country.

When this was brought to the attention of the principal of the school he said that Eastern had (1) the best cadet corps in the city, (2) the best athletic program in the city, (3) an active "Negro" History Club, and (4) a variety of students, some from homes that "you know, don't come from a learning environment."

These were not satisfactory reasons for such a low academic atmosphere. It seemed that "Johnny can run fast, shoot fast, shoot straight, participate in a variety of clubs, but can't read or count to ten."

A student organization was formed called the Modern Strivers. We found that a food steamer (brand new) had been sitting in the cafeteria for almost two years, waiting to be installed, while the old one, barely functioning, had been taken off an old tramp steamer long since destroyed. After investigation we found that the new steamer was not in operation because they would have to close down the cafeteria to install it, and there was a shortage of funds.

This was an issue that nobody could oppose, because teachers and students had been complaining about the food for years. A boycott of the cafeteria was called and was very successful. The press had the story, and our organization was well known even though the principal still refused to recognize us. We met with the dietician for the public schools the following week and it was agreed that the steamer would be installed during the next holiday.

Next we met with the principal and he agreed to offer two new classes "if" we could find teachers willing to teach and students willing to take the courses. At the start of the next semester Negro history and social psychology were being offered.

Then in January 1968 the Strivers took their demands to the Board of Education: a school with student control and a black curriculum. The Board said that they had no money but that they would not impede our activities if we could raise it. The original plan called for the Freedom School to be housed at Eastern in what is now known as the woodshop complex. This is an indoor swimming pool that had been filled with cement. An architect's conservative estimate of $80,000 for renovation crushed that idea.

Meanwhile the administration was working hard themselves. The faculty adviser for the Strivers received a letter from his draft board informing him that he was now 1-A! It was learned that the principal had written his draft board and, "as a patriotic gesture," had requested that his deferment be withdrawn. The students of Eastern staged protests and with support from the Washington Teachers Union the principal was forced to resign.

We now started visiting various people and organizations in Washington, D.C., in an effort to raise funds for our school. We were finally offered a grant of $350 by the Washington School of Psychiatry.

With this we traveled to New York, visited several of the large foundations and requested funds. They all told us that they would consider our application and would be in contact with us. We started planning and formed the Eastern High School Freedom Corporation. We were established as a nonprofit educational organization. One of the senior members of the Strivers had worked at a church that summer and arranged a meeting with the pastor. He was very excited about the idea and agreed to lease us a portion of the building rent free.

We then "put out the word" that we were looking for teachers, and scheduled meetings. These "rap sessions" proved to be very successful and we talked about many topics concerning black people. No résumés were required, but we all agreed that only black people would be considered. The reasoning for this was that teaching black people required black people, people who had the same experiences in life as we had.

There was not much chance of any white students attending, because in a school of 2,400 only one student was white.

In September 1968 the money finally started to come in. The Secondary Education Office granted us full accreditation for all of our courses. Because of all of the beautiful knowledge that we found in Washington, D.C. we went over our budget in hiring teachers and hired twelve instead of eight.

Approximately $70,000 was secured by the students through private donations and foundation grants. We spent hour after hour renovating the building and many of us spent the night working, and took time out only to attend our classes at Eastern. At times our parents didn't understand our total involvement in something that they didn't agree with totally, but in the end we all got together and had African feasts and gatherings that brought many of them into the school to work hour after hour.

—NDUGU WILLIS BROOKS, co-founder of the Freedom School (Shule Ya Uhuru)

SCHOOL OPERATION

Because we believe that a clear understanding and knowledge of history will enable us to build a better future, that is the one compulsory course at Shule Ya Uhuru. Students may select two others from a list of eight subjects which cover a broad scope. They include literature, Ki-Swahili, contemporary problems, community organization, philosophy, music, economics, and communicative skills. Whenever students desire assistance in math or science, someone on the staff is available. All courses are accredited.

Shule Ya Uhuru tries to create an atmosphere that will truly be conducive to learning; therefore, we have disposed of the rigid schedule and adopted a more flexible program. Rather than be shaken by the disruption of an impersonal bell system, our classes end with the recordings of our people. Whether it be the dulcet tones of sisters Miriam Makeba Carmichael or Nina Simone, bringing us to the realization that African peoples throughout the world suffer and enjoy similar experiences, or the kingly voice of brother Malcolm X teaching us the methods to overcome the problems we face as a people, each formal class period is ended with yet another learning experience.

In order to operate a school that will educate and re-educate students as well as reorder this country's traditional structure of education the participants must have, foremost, a spiritual bond. What we are about is establishing a new concept of education for African peoples in this country and indeed around the world.

The different responsibilities, disappointments, struggles, accomplishments, confrontations, etc., can only be borne by a united group lest the entire effort disintegrate. Only a small percentage of teachers or students ever achieve this state while in the public school system. We at Shule Ya Uhuru have a much better than average record.

During the past eighteen months there have been many students from all over the country as well as the Washington metropolitan area who have visited our school and shared in the learning experiences. It is therefore realistic for us to say that our program has had an effect on students and school curricula in many cities. Each of these groups has left with a true inspiration to develop something that is similar to Shule Ya Uhuru in their area. Many have since contacted us to let us know their progress.

Nearly everyone who desires an opportunity to develop his social and political consciousness may do so by attending community meetings, discussing programs with city representatives and other Federal government employees. We emphasize the need to attend such meetings and make an input toward solving problems based on knowledge gained at the Freedom School. Our emphasis, in other words, is on action, and we allow ample opportunity for students to put theory into practice.

Aside from the obvious advantages of education while attending Freedom School, there is also the opportunity for each of us to develop management skills which can be applicable to other organizations. For example, as a legally constituted corporation, we have an elected five-man board of directors which includes three students. We have studied the laws concerning non-profit organizations and corporate structure which will enable us to make the practical applications to any other group venture we might participate in. Students who are predominantly responsible for the entire operation of the school have gained some very valuable skills. They make decisions involving thousands of dollars, with a mature, responsible nature that would exceed that of most students and many adults. One can note the over-all seriousness as the Freedom School students are about making our program work.

Students from four area high schools presently attend Freedom School and, hopefully, the number of different schools will increase. After all, in 1968–69 only students from Eastern High School were attending. We have plans for a nursery-school program which is to be implemented very shortly. Although our after-school and evening programs have never enjoyed the stable, precise structure of the day program, each is working to the extent that many more brothers and sisters can be involved in some aspect of the new learning for African peoples.

Special projects are emphasized during the spring and summer months which allow for the logical extension of our program of education for self-reliance. In the planning for this year are a cultural exchange program with the country of Guyana and a farm development project in Tennessee. Each will involve a great deal of hard physical labor (i.e., commitment) in order to succeed. We know the spirit and determination of our ancestors will give us the strength to accomplish these things.

Certain activities are incorporated into the school program; for example, the music class has trained drummers and dancers who perform at various events around the city. Programs at other schools or sponsored by various community organizations are included in the scope of Freedom School activities for our drummers and dancers. The literature teacher and music teacher frequently join their respective skills to produce a program for public presentation.

A student who becomes director of the school has many opportunities to develop leadership expertise in the daily routines of the school. He chairs the corporation meetings, represents the school, along with other students, at meetings, conferences, and other public events. Over the first two years of operation we have had four students in the capacity of director, two co-directors each year. One of last year's directors is presently enrolled in NYU. This year a co-director is a former student who presently is attending Federal City College. The other directors are still in high school. This arrangement facilitates developing new leadership as well as sustaining that which we have.

The school office is manned by both staff and students who serve as clerk-typists. There is no professional secretary at this time. Staff members leave work to be typed and the students do it, thereby gaining practice.

Evening and weekend events at Freedom School primarily consist of providing space for meetings and community dances. Youngsters of the neighborhood come in daily for history instruction and art work. Most of them are in grades 2–5 and attend other schools in the area of the Freedom School. In cooperation with a nearby northeast community organization, CIC, we have provided students who tutor in reading and math at a local elementary school. This program is completely voluntary and our students are therefore motivated by desire and love wherever they see a need for a particular skill in the black community.

The District of Columbia public-school system has provided a modicum of support until recently. Previously, the only genuine support came from Mr. George Rhodes, assistant superintendent of secondary schools, and a few members of the Board of Education. He has been helpful in getting materials reproduced for our use in the school. We have not had the funds to purchase the needed books and other materials and equipment for class presentations. In lieu of this, we find various means of reproducing articles and other pertinent information for distribution to our students.

A group of Freedom School representatives met with acting superintendent of schools Benjamin Henley and school board president Mrs. Anita Allen for the first time since the school has been in operation. Many areas of cooperation were discussed although no firm commitments have been made as yet by either side. At least two additional Board of Education members have visited the school recently in further attempts to gain more information about Shule Ya Uhuru as well as offer any assistance possible for recruitment and liaison work between us and the central administration of the school system.

At the same time we have been expanding and improving our relations with Africans outside the U.S. and in other parts of the U.S. We sent delegates to the Seminar on Pan-Africanism and Black Revolutionary Nationalism held in Georgetown, Guyana, on February 24–26, 1970. Out of this historical meeting we became connected with several black liberation schools throughout the Caribbean, other parts of the U.S. and Africa under the umbrella of the newly formed Pan-African Educational Council. On April 3–5, 1970, we held the Onward to the Black Past: New Perspectives Conference at the Freedom School in which we had four workshops: 1) Black Studies for Black Workers, Black Youth, and Black Parents; 2) Black Studies for Black Teachers; 3) Black Studies for Black Organizers; 4) Black Studies for Black Scholars. In this conference we were able to freely exchange our experiences with *all* levels of the black community from various parts of the U.S. and the world. From this perspective we were able to vote on a set of resolutions which, we believe, will revolutionize the concept of the black studies; which we are about and determined to do in the everyday operations of our school.

—by DADA FOLAYAN and
NDUGU CHARLES ROBINSON

## THE PHILOSOPHY OF THE SHULE YA UHURU (FREEDOM SCHOOL)

### A STUDENT'S VIEW

An oppressed people must look to no one but themselves for answers to their problems. It was a mistake for the slave master to free him from bondage, just as it was a mistake for the colonial to look to the colonizing nation for his freedom. The white Anglo-Saxon Protestants (WASPs) who were in the forefront of the so-called American revolution did not look to England for an answer to their problems; they began to define things for themselves and then acted to free themselves. Black people in the colony within America must take this lesson to heart and begin to redefine and then solve their own problems.

One of the major errors of the civil-rights movement was that black people were asking white people for rights that any human should have automatically. There is a great difference between civil and human rights. Civil rights are granted by governments and can be taken away by governments; human rights are inalienable! Activists in the civil-rights movement were doing nothing but begging a government, one they had already said was superior to themselves, as far as rights were concerned. In order for someone to grant a right, he must be in a position superior to that of the person who is doing the asking. Civil rights was just the slave asking the slave master for his freedom.

The principle of defining things for oneself also applies in the field of education. Black education is geared for black students and directed to solving the problems of the black African nation inside and outside the United States.

Black education courses cannot be organized and taught by people who are now professional educators because they have been trained to educate white students, not black students. Black education has to come from the streets of the black community.

No person, black or white, can sit in Harvard University and come up with a black studies course. Black education must deal with the problems of black people—the problems of black people that the social scientists have overlooked in writing their books (certainly one of the major problems is having white persons define what the problems of black folks are). Black education is a grass-roots education, created by and for the grass-roots black people.

Some people say, "We have Negro history courses. Why do we need black studies?" The answer is simple: The study of "Negro" history is nothing but a look at the good things (as white people have defined them) that some Americans who just happened to be *colored* did, as individuals, for this great land of the WASPs. For example, teachers of Negro history talk about Charles Drew, a black brother who invented blood plasma and the blood bank. They talk about how he went to Amherst College and how he died in a car crash. But do they tell you that Drew was not killed in the crash but that he died on the highway because a white ambulance driver would not drive him to the hospital? Dr. Drew—just another nigger—*bled to death* on the cold, wet highway that night.

> —NDUGU ROGER NEWELL, co-founder of the Shule Ya Uhuru (Freedom School), presently a student at Columbia University

## PHILOSOPHY OF FREEDOM SCHOOL (SHULE YA UHURU) PART 2

### A TEACHER'S VIEW

What is a Black Studies program? What is it students seek when they cry out for Black Studies? In a Letter to the Editor (*Washington Post*, summer 1968) a suburban housewife suggested that if Black Studies were instituted in the District of Columbia public high schools, white students would probably be the ones to excel. She was convinced that black students were not serious in their appeal; were not willing to study. With few exceptions, our observations have shown this woman to be at least partially correct. But not for the reasons she suggests. Most of the Black Studies programs operating in the Washington area simply do not meet the needs of the students. For the most part young blacks are not concerned with the individual intricacies of the individual lives of long-dead individuals, nor are they concerned with sterile statistics: birth date, years of reign, death date, etc. What black students are after is archetypes, both heroic and celestial. They seek basic patterns, manifestations of Truth, if you please, after which to mold their lives.

By heroic archetypes I mean figures like Sundiata as portrayed in D. T. Niane's *Sundiata: An Epic of Old Mali* (London: Longmans, Green and Co. Ltd. 1965). *Sundiata* is a mixture of cosmology, history, geography, genealogy, songs and proverbs all woven into a highly suspenseful, extremely entertaining story. Coming out of the North American experiences, archetype Stagolee is perhaps more familiar to us. Julius Lester's version of the ballad-folktale in *Black Folktales* (New York: Richard W. Baron, 1969, pp. 113–135) is a classic. The tale deals directly with the concepts of good and evil, death, and God as they relate to black people. Aside from all that, the story is a thigh-slapper. I have seen students hang on every word from the beginning ("Stagolee was, undoubtedly and without question, the baddest nigger that ever lived") to the very end.

Story-telling and proverbs should, just as in traditional times, be an integral part in the education of all black young people, not just in the primary grades but at every level, including college. Stories like "Stagolee" and *Sundiata* were meant to be read or spoken aloud. Griot (oral historian) Mamoudou Kouyate, whose text we read in *Sundiata,* castigates those who rely exclusively on books for knowledge: "They do not *feel*[1] the past any more, for

---

[1] My italics.

writing lacks the warmth of the human voice. . . . What paltry learning is that which is congealed in dumb books!" [2]

Unfortunately, most Black Studies programs are set up around reading lists. In a city like Washington, D.C., where most high-school students have reading problems, the situation is tragic (and perhaps designed to be so). The solution seems to be either to teach black students to read or to devise some other method of disseminating information to those students.

My belief is that it is in the spirit of the students' demands that we opt for the New. Enough of this (old) form without substance. Most Black Studies programs have been victimized by the same forces of confusion and bad faith that have virtually destroyed the intent of the 1954 Brown Board of Education decision. William Raspberry on the present condition of the latter:

> Much of the confusion today stems from the fact that the means has now become an end in itself. Suits are being brought for integration, boundaries are being redrawn, busing is being instituted—not to improve education but to integrate classrooms.[3]

Likewise, Black Studies has become "African Studies," "Afro-American Studies," "Afro-Caribbean Studies," "Afro-Russian Studies," "Afro-Jewish Studies," *ad infinitum.* And each of these compartments is further departmentalized in classes labeled "history" as separate from "art" as separate from "literature" as separate from and distinct from "science" and so forth. Human knowledge is a unified whole. "Educators" in setting up Black Studies programs have mainly employed the same fragmented and fragmenting methods employed by Western "education." Each segment is considered separately as a whole in itself. Students are not taught language but the structure of language. They are not taught how to live, as Dick Gregory often says, but how to make a living.

Furthermore, the goal of Black Studies should not simply re-

[2] D. T. Niane, *Sundiata: An Epic of Old Mali,* p. 41.
[3] "Concentration on Integration Is Doing Little for Education," *Washington Post,* February 20, 1970, p. A31.

veal to black students the true identity of the man who "discovered" the North Pole. The students must explore and re-evaluate two basic concepts: life and death. They must learn from every conceivable angle what it really means to live. They must determine whether death is a black-clad angel, a deep pit, a mere continuation of life, or something else.

Enter the celestial archetype. Who or what are we? What, if any, is the purpose of our existence? What is our relationship to the universe? I remember asking a class if, from the beginning, there were not need for men and women to reproduce, would humans still have a sex drive. The answers the students gave were overwhelmingly affirmative. "Promiscuity would be rampant," they declared. But can we really separate sex from procreation? Is man a part of nature or apart from nature? Black Studies programs must be prepared to deal with these questions if these programs are to be of any benefit to students.

We object not only to the fragmenting tendencies of Western scholarship but also to its lack of humor. Chinese philosopher Lin Yutang, while acknowledging the inadequacy of scientific method applied to human conduct, gives as a formula for Wisdom: "Reality and Dreams and Humor." [4] These three components are, at once, necessary ingredients of any Black Studies program and characteristics of Black Group Consciousness. If we accept, with some reservations, the "recent findings" of Western scholarship that black folks probably founded the first civilizations, we can see how long blacks as a whole have had to develop this wisdom. Students of Black Studies programs should, therefore, not take themselves too seriously. Their duty is not to make black people wise but to inform themselves and others of our wisdom. And when these students-turned-teachers run across blacks who are indifferent to what they have to offer even with the innovative methods of instruction and the supposedly "deep" content, hopefully these students/teachers will realize that there are those

[4] Lin Yutang, *The Importance of Living*, pp. 4–5. (London: William Heinemann Ltd., 1938).

among us who are wise enough to know that even those things (Black Studies, the Black Nation, and things) are, in the long run, much too parochial for serious human consideration.

Self-Sacrifice is the reinforcement of the direction and continuity of ancestral life-forces, through the co-ordination of our lives with the lives of slain Black leaders and through the co-ordination of our principles with the principles of Blackness, that have been preserved for us through the struggle of our worthy ancestors. . . . As we continue to fling our personal resources into the Black pool of power, mystery and love, the level rises; encompassing all in the powerful medium in which only the human and soulful can survive.

—DADA MALAIKA LUMUMBA

—NDUGU CHARLES FRYE

## PHILOSOPHY OF FREEDOM SCHOOL (SHULE YA UHURU) PART 3

### AN ADMINISTRATOR'S VIEW

. . . the shortest way to the future is always one that involves a deep understanding of the past.

—NDUGU AIME CESAIRE,
famous black poet and teacher
of Frantz Fanon

*What Is Education?*

We at the Freedom School understand education to be the application of all one's knowledge for the collective, which in turn will benefit each individual within the group. We might add that when we say "the collective" we do *not* mean for the benefit of one or few socioeconomic classes within a particular society, nor do we mean for the benefit of only the *living* members of a society. We mean by "the collective" the grouping of people that encompasses the living, the dead and the sons and daughters forthcoming which emanate from a common set of ancestors. This, in an African view, is the nation (Muntu).

Therefore, what must constitute the basic part of one's education is the understanding of people more than things/property. We have realized that once people understand themselves, their knowledge of things is facilitated, that the exclusive knowledge of things does *not* guarantee knowledge of people, and in fact contributes to the erosion, disintegration and destructivity of the creativity of man.

Thus our guideline for education—in fact all activity—is: The people do not possess the truth; they *are* the truth!

*The Miseducation of the Black Man*

We as Black Africans colonized by the European and his descendants not only have had an "education" where we have been taught that things were more important than people, we have been taught (even by many so-called black radicals unduly influenced by the white "left") that it is not desirable to understand ourselves as a people. The fact is that all successful revolutionaries master an understanding of their people before they thoroughly study contemporary revolutionary thought (i.e., "Marxism-Leninism"). Did not Toussaint L'Ouverture understand his own people before he grasped the meaning of the "French Revolution"? Did not Mao Tse-tung master the Confucian classics and the military writings of Sun-Tzu *before* he mastered the writings of Lenin? Had not Amilcar Cabral in Guinea-Bissau mastered the Ballante peoples' language before mastering the writings of Marx? The fact is that *all* great Third-World Pan-Africanist revolutionaries understand themselves as a people before understanding and mastering so-called contemporary revolutionary thought and practice.

We at the Freedom School understand that if we are to reclaim our rightful position in this universe we must understand (not just *know*) that: 1) We are all products of a culture and civilization which from our earliest days in school (and on television) have been misrepresented, confused, distorted and lied about. Therefore, we need the fullest and most precise knowledge of African people, their culture and achievements in order to obtain our own Self-Appreciation. 2) Though economic redistribution of goods, services and resources provides the answer to the economic and political problems of the world, it does *not*, in itself, for a people who have suffered not only from economic oppression but also from *racial* subordination provide the answer to one of their most basic fundamental needs—the need of self-respect. African history and culture are essential tools for obtaining this for *all* African peoples—especially Africans colonized/enslaved in north, south, central America and the Caribbean. 3) Europeans in the Americas enjoy a background of cultural and historical continuity. However, people of African origin in *both* South and North America have suffered a disruption in their cultural and historical sequence as a result of more than 350 years of slavery imposed by Spanish, Portuguese, French, Danish, Dutch, and Anglo-Saxon slavemasters/oppressors, and this gap must be filled!

BROTHERS AND SISTERS: It is necessary *now* to scrape clean from our minds and hearts that residue of white pus inflicted upon us by white Western miseducators/slavers—regardless they are from the right, left or center of the white/honky world. If we do not *completely* do this there will be no *black* revolution. At best we will be merely cannon fodder for the "inexorable" rise of the Western white proletariat to the top of the ashcan of white empires. At worse, we will see our own women giving birth to our own children in the mud/hot sands of George Wallace's plantations/concentration camps! Either way our ancestors have every right to throw us out of the gates of the garden of eternity, and fling our carcasses into the hot sands of the Sahara, and then spit upon our wretched bones!!!! Umoja (unity)!!!

—NAUGU MAMADOU LUMUMBA,
Curriculum Director of the Freedom School (Shule Ya Uhuru)

# Other Ways: Resource for a System

BY HERBERT KOHL

Other Ways, in Berkeley, California, was founded by Herbert Kohl, author of *36 Children* and *The Open Classroom*, and Allan Kaprow, the artist who invented the term "happenings." One of the most notable aspects of its operation is that the local public school system has given Kohl the status of principal, thus partially incorporating Other Ways into the school system and permitting Kohl to travel to other schools and hold workshops for teachers.

The following description of the school was written by students and teachers and is a montage of ideas, descriptions and plans. This documentation is from the second year of the school and, subsequent to these writings, in Year Three, the Other Ways staff changed, grew and defined the school's program more sharply and fully.

IN 1968 Other Ways started working with students several hours a day, two days a week. For the rest of their time, our students attended the regular schools. We all found four hours a week inadequate. Things would just get started when the hour rolled up. Students and staff alike complained that there wasn't enough time to get involved in learning. Some of our students did very well academically, yet were restless and bored by school. They wanted the time and the facilities to pursue their interests in depth and were frustrated by our limits. They were even more frustrated by the limits of fifty-minute periods at their regular schools and began suggesting that we consider developing a school of our own.

Other students didn't do so well in school. They spent most of their time wandering in the halls or living from suspension to suspension. Some of them began to hang around Other Ways and ask us to teach them. It became clear after a while that we had to become more than a twice-a-week project. However, we did not want to become a private school. Rather, by creating a context which was important for students and teachers alike, we hoped to develop a program for change within the context of public education. This is what we are trying to do this year. One of the students who is with us suggested a curriculum for us.

*THE SCHOOL THAT OUGHT TO BE*

SUBJECTS

Pleasurable Human Behavior

Historydrams

Naturemath

Creative Cookery (on a budget)

The Long Neglected Art of Observation

  "   "   "    " " Walking

  "   "   "    " " Thinking Clearly

  (meditation)

Mastery of the Elegant Insult (optional)

Examination of Fantasy

These classes require small classes in large rooms with easy access to everywhere.

The school has about seventy students. About half of them are full time; the rest of the children take one or two classes at Other Ways, or, more typically, take all their classes at Other Ways except for one or two subjects. For example, we presently do not offer chemistry, physics, foreign languages.

The children range in age from twelve to eighteen, and most are between fourteen and sixteen. A couple of kids come from elementary school, a larger group from the local junior high schools, the largest group from Berkeley High School. Our racial makeup is about half black and half white. Some of the students come from fairly well-off families, some from very poor families. This causes some friction, but not as much as one might suppose. As the students have worked together through the days, they have become friends. There are definite groups, but there is more mixing than there was in September.

Our main idea has been to attempt to create an atmosphere in which students are accorded the respect that they merit as human beings in combination with the opportunity to interact freely and naturally with other kids, to allow students to develop and gain self-respect, self-understanding, pride, and recognition.

To help bring this about Other Ways offers as rich a program as possible, with many alternatives and much diversity. Being free to select and pursue those things that he feels to be relevant, for as long as they remain relevant to him, the student is able to develop an understanding not only of subject matter, but of himself and his relation to others.

To me, informal education outside the classroom means meeting the students on a personal level and relating to problems which they encounter at home, on the street, and as a result of interaction with other persons. By giving the students such attention, I was able to gain a better perspective of where the students' interests and talents lie. Also, it helped me to see the kind of help various students needed to foster these talents and interests and the kind of support needed to overcome or withstand some of the obstacles which they will encounter in the pursuit of goals instead of being snowed under by them.

My first encounter with informal education outside the classroom came about when four students from Other Ways came by my house. We talked about various things, *e.g.*, drugs, families, the public school, how I became a part of Other Ways, things that I like to do, what they like to do, whether I could take them various places.

This discussion reinforced my belief that most teachers (in the public schools) don't have, or will not take, the time to talk to the student but place him in a position where he can do nothing but develop a hostile attitude toward the teacher, the school, and (unknowingly) toward himself.

To implement our goals, we have used informal and formal methods. Formal classes have provided continuity and basic structure. Informal projects and outings have served to reinforce and expand class topics. They have also proved useful by exposing our students to people and experiences outside the normal school curriculum.

*OTHER WAYS CLASSES*

| Class | Teacher | Times/Week* |
|---|---|---|
| Computer Science | Dave Stonerod | 2 |
| Poetry Reading | Gary Hall | 5 |
| The American Indian | Peggy Cogswell | 2 |
| Running | Mike Spino | 3 |
| Swimming | Mike Spino | 4 |
| Sports in Society | Mike Spino | 1 |
| Photography | Paul Cantrell | 3 |
| Shakespeare and the Renaissance | Norm Rabkin | 1 |
| Yoga and Meditation | Shri Jaya | 2 |
| Making of Mandalas | Shri Jaya | 1 |
| Civics | David Conley | 1 |
| Ecology | David Conley | 1 |
| Skin Diving | David Conley | 1 |
| Sociology | David Conley | 1 |
| Humanities | Alta Simon | 1 |
| Poetry | A. Simon & A. Curry | 3 |
| Mathematics | Herbert Kohl | 2 |
| Reading | Herbert Kohl | 1 |
| Human Behavior | Darryle Totty | 2 |

* The indicated meetings per week are formal class sessions. The sessions are usually between two and three hours in length. Section meetings for discussion, projects, study on a topic peripheral to the main subject, private talks with the instructor for advice about further, more concentrated study, etc., are arranged with the instructor. Such ancillary meetings may involve only one or two students, sometimes the whole class. Thus, students spend more time on a subject than is indicated by class sessions.

| *Class* | *Teacher* | *Times/Week* |
|---|---|---|
| Journalism (Graphics) | H. Kohl & R. Freeland | 1 |
| Guerrilla Theater | H. Kohl & S. Chappell | 1 |
| Oceanography | Lewis McClenton | 2 |
| Sculpture | Sean Chappell | 1 |
| Drama | G. Hall & A. Curry | 1 |
| Drama | Sean Chappell | 1 |
| Non-Verbal Communication | Jerry Kramer | 1 |
| Cinematography | Sheldon Renan | 1 |
| Body Movement | Dervica Bryant | 1 |
| Trash Can Films | Catherine Cardwell | 1 |
| Music Theory | Ellen Hoffman | 1 |
| Guitar | Nardy Lovell | 1 |
| Experiments in Music | Schuyler Hoyt | 1 |
| The Individual versus Society in Western History | Peggy Cogswell | 1 |

Also, tutorials are available for math and musical instruments.

## SPECIAL EVENTS & PROJECTS

*A trip to Sonoma State*—The students had an opportunity to see the campus, talk to the students and faculty, gather information on courses and degrees firsthand.

*A trip to Santa Barbara/Pasadena*—Gary Hall, Phillip Harris, Alvin Curry went to give Poetry Readings and talk to others about poetry.

*Maurya and Meta Metal*—a visit to a Quaker School in Los Angeles.

*Jon Otis*—a visit to an observatory in Los Angeles to pursue an interest in astronomy.

*Sean Chappell*—teaching at LeConte School in a special Other Ways project.

*Lisa Moffet*—taking courses in Chicano literature and culture at Merritt College.

Norman Rabkin  
Jo Miles } professors at U.C. offering courses to Other Ways students.  
Brady Williamson

*Richard Hourula and Becky Voight*—working for Books Unlimited.

Ernest Blodgett
Gerald Sims } working on an automotive mechanics project.
Sonny Saunders

*Anne Howard and students*—participated in radio programs at KPFA-FM.

Basketball Team

Singing Group

*Darryle Totty, et al.*—participated in a discussion on education on KQED-FM.

*Poetry Readings*—Daly City, Pleasant Hill, Los Angeles, Pasadena, San Francisco.

Flying

*Peggy Cogswell, et al.*—visited an Indian reservation near Santa Cruz.

*Alta Simon, et al.*—prepared a map of BART land, with technical assistance rendered by a professional at People's Architecture.

## TEACHERS TALK

## HERB KOHL

*Journalism*

The journalism class is broken down into three sections: *poetry* with Alta Simon and Alvin Curry, *comics* with John Allen, and various forms of *writing* with myself.

The class has about eighteen regular students and they wander from group to group periodically. At first, most of the black students were shy about writing and reading. But as they saw that the emphasis is on learning and doing, they have become more relaxed and more interested in learning than in trying to hide their lacks. Since we are always ready to assist the students with technical and mechanical problems, they are free to express themselves. Soon they want to do the projects with a minimum of help and this means that they learn the spelling and the set-up, etc., so they can do what *they* want.

We have had some problems—we need more space, kids like to spread out when they write. We need supplies such as typewriters and colored pencils, more kinds of paper for the kids to play around with. We need more staff. All the students seem to need a lot of attention at the same time. There was also some racial/socio-economic stress. This has pretty much worked itself out.

It's hard to make a general assessment of the class; some students gained immensely, others' needs were just beginning to be met at the time of the holiday break. A couple of the kids are still a little uneasy, but I think I can see success ahead for them too.

## Mathematics

What started out as one math class has turned into four: an advanced class; two classes in games; systems and set theory; an algebra tutorial.

I have been groping for a new way to teach math—to have students understand it as a way of thinking not without its poetry and beauty (terms used); and as an activity of men, not an absolute given. I have been trying to communicate basic concepts: to set problems and get students to start thinking, both collaboratively and individually.

This class has worked best with students who hate math, so I needed a more advanced class, which is using Quine. Students attend, so the class size is reasonably stable and most people do some thinking.

### Guerrilla Theater

Guerrilla Theater is the most fun of all my classes and the most integrated. There are black and white students from Other Ways and four Community High School students.

The class has done a series of improvisations on set and chosen topics. They have also gone out into the community to do events: interviews about the Moratorium; a visit to San Francisco Airport; a Theater Conference at Berkeley High School.

### DAVID CONLEY

### Civics

The traditional civics class has normally examined the structure of the institutions that make up government and society while ignoring, in many cases, the manner in which these institutions function and the nature of the society in which they exist. This civics class has attempted to avoid creating a dichotomy between the institutions and their setting and function in society.

Class meets one afternoon a week. We have been spending usually two or three consecutive meetings doing some sort of field work and then one or two meetings discussing the results of our field work. This field work has included trips to small claims court (and a free unsolicited lecture from the judge), a trip to the financial district in San Francisco to interview people who fit the businessman stereotype, and a trip to the Town and Country Village shopping center to examine the newly emerging institution of the surburban shopping center.

Students have compiled the results of taped interviews, questionnaires, and photographs to create audio collages (combinations of music and dialogue that are similar in concept and effect to visual collages), poetry, composed their own musical scores for urban settings, and photographic essays about people in general.

## Skin Diving

Skin diving meets Tuesdays from three to five at the Willard Swim Center. Students use mask, snorkel and fins in the pool.

The purpose of the class is to acquaint and familiarize the students with basic skin-diving equipment and techniques. In addition to skin diving, students are free to swim and dive on their own. Much of the instruction in this class consists of one student passing on his techniques and tricks to other students who are not as proficient at skin diving, this in spite of the fact that, besides myself, the regular swim-center instructor is available to help those who desire help.

Eventually, when students acquire proficiency and increased endurance and when the ocean warms up a little, we plan to take weekend skin-diving trips to the Monterey area.

## Ecology

This class has consisted of Other Ways students teaching twenty-four fourth- through sixth-grade students at Longfellow School. It also rates as the biggest disaster of my teaching career. We were hampered by difficulties at Longfellow which included inadequate space in which to work (*i.e.*, the book room), poor or no communication between the Longfellow faculty and the ecology staff, and breaks in continuity of up to two weeks due to testing and record-keeping which prevented kids from coming. In addition, we created some nearly disastrous problems ourselves. The idea was for the ecology staff to explore and learn ecology with the kids. However, we became trapped by our definitions of what a teacher is, viewing ourselves as an oracle from which all knowledge flowed. The Longfellow students then lost all confidence when they realized that we knew little more than those we were "teaching" and became unable to learn with us. I still believe the idea behind the program is sound and that my mistake was in choosing a subject that was so totally unfamiliar to all involved.

We no longer work with the kids at Longfellow. However, the class still meets at Other Ways and is *beginning* to take a turn toward the better as we explore the environment in which we exist through field trips and readings. We recently visited the San Francisco Bay Model in Sausalito.

Texts have come from the Ecology Center Bookstore. Typical are *The Population Bomb* by Paul Ehrlich and *Human Use of the Earth* by Philip Wagner.

## Sociology

Sociology meets Friday afternoons at Other Ways. Classes consist of open-ended discussions covering topics ranging from small-group behavior to the history and background of the American family. We also explore the music, literature, and media of our times for clues to the nature of our society. Students have been extremely interested in examining their everyday patterns of interactions, such as dating rituals. The class often moves from the realms of sociology to psychology as people attempt to examine the relationship between the individual and organized society.

### SEAN CHAPPELL

I have spent most of my years in school studying drafting, sculpture, guitar, human-form drawing and painting (oil acrylics), writing poetry, and short stories. For two years I have been studying photography and dramatics. (I worked at The Theater in Berkeley for about six months.) Since last year I have been illustrating *Stuff*, which is edited by Herb Kohl and Victor Cruz; World Books is the publisher. *Stuff* is an anthology of young people's writings. Some of my writing is in it.

Also I have been doing posters and flyers for ballroom dances in the Bay area. And since I have acquired a Volkswagen, I have become quite knowledgeable about repair and have done body work, engine work, and upholstering on many VWs. Lately I have been doing stained-glass windows and much pottery work.

My most recent experience is starting and running an Other Ways School Center at LeConte Elementary School. The class is now being reorganized and we hope to obtain a better room in the school.

Teaching well is one of my important goals; I hope I reach it.

*Human-Form Drawing*

This is a very loosely structured class. I act as a resource for students concerned with human form and movement (basic anatomy). I also help them put their ideas on canvas or paper.

The materials used include oils, acrylics, charcoal, pencils of various grades, paper, duff cloth (canvas substitute), brushes.

*Sculpture*

The purpose of this class is to study form, movement, mediums of material, and methods, then incorporate these in our own ideas. This enables a student to see his own perception of life, and his ideas are also available to other students for examination.

The materials used include clay, plaster, wax, wood, driftwood, lead, metal, paint, glass, mud, asbestos, cloth, plastics, and a bathtub.

**PEGGY COGSWELL**

*American Indians*

There are two sections of American Indians. Each section consists of an hour lecture followed by an hour of discussion. My lectures have been mostly ethnographical, and, since my own interest is in world-view, revitalization movements, and legal systems, the emphasis with each tribe or group of tribes has been in one of these areas.

We have had guest lecturers; Conn Halliman spoke on several occasions. His specialties are the League of the Iroquois, Plains Indian culture, and the Indian Wars. George Csiosery, whose specialty is religion, gave a lecture on Great Basin Indian religion, both before and after white contact.

In January, Professor William Simmons from U.C. will give two lectures on the history of American Indian revitalization movements and another on witchcraft, magic, and sorcery. Some of my students have also been attending his course in American Indians at Cal on Mondays, Wednesdays, Fridays at 11:00.

The other guest lecturer we have scheduled is Dale Valory, who has done two years' research in Yurok shamanism. I did two lectures earlier in the semester on the Yuroks and some of their culturally similar neighbors.

I have not assigned any reading for the whole class, but most of the students have read things in their own field of interest and I have discussed the reading individually with them. They have also contributed much of the interest in the class discussions, drawing from their own reading.

### LEWIS McCLENTON

*Malcolm X, The Man and His Times*

The objective of this course is to give the student a better understanding of who Malcolm X really was and what he really stood for.

### ALTA SIMON

*Poetry*

The poetry class is limited to ten students. We have used the tapes and the writings of local poets and have invited poets from the Bay area to our classes. The visitors have read their poetry to us and then have participated in a general class discussion about their work.

The students in this class are particularly interested and talented in poetry, so much of our class time is spent writing poems ourselves and reading them aloud. We have been experimenting with combining reading and dance, reading and music.

The students have become more aware of words and their beauty. They have learned about poetic forms and uses. They have learned that writing a poem takes effort and found that they enjoy the challenge.

*Humanities*

This class is limited to ten students. In this class we experiment with many art forms and topics around a central theme of city living. We have had classes in psychology, stressing the function of an individual in modern city life. To this end, we also had a class on yoga.

Several periods have been devoted to city planning. We have studied and reviewed Berkeley's Master Plan and drawn maps of our own. We devoted a couple of sessions to improvisational theater—students have developed and acted out typical scenes in contemporary family life. The acting, together with a rather thorough discussion, has given them some insight into group dynamics, role, and some of the stresses and problems of modern urban family life.

Coming classes will include draftsmen's demonstrations of handicrafts from other cultures. This will give them more experience in design forms, and discussing the relation of a culture's artifacts to the culture as a whole should help the students develop some insight into the complexity and the variability of human culture.

TIM O'NEILL

*Computer Science*

The main objective of the course is to teach the fundamentals of computer programming. Once these are learned, the students can choose their own projects and work on them independently, with my role being mainly that of a consultant for any problems that arise.

At present we are working on a program similar to the Czech movie at Expo '67. The students are writing stories with a number of possible endings. The computer will print out the first paragraph and then give the reader a choice of two possible outcomes. The reader will then make his choice and the corresponding paragraph will be printed out with another set of outcomes—and so on to the end. We will also be working on a program for computer dating by astrological sign.

Since the computer has been removed from the Lawrence Hall of Science, I am looking for another facility. I already have permission from the Cal physics department to use the IBM 1620 in Birge Hall and I am exploring the possibility of a terminal setup to be placed in the Other Ways building.

DARRYLE TOTTY

*Human Behavior*

Before I explain why I am doing certain things in my classes, I must go back and explain some of the black students who comprise the majority of my classes.

The problem of black students is their inability or unwillingness to live in two different worlds. (In most cases it is their unwillingness.) Most black students totally reject the schools (others simply tolerate them) because the school system, not understanding the pressures black students live with, is unsympathetic to their reactions to the environment. Since black students live outside the establishment, they resent the fact that adults are forcing them to live hypocritical lives by attempting to mold them into typical "problemless" children of the adult establishment. What I mean by this is that the school system's rigid and authoritarian structure tries to force the students to act in a way that is unnatural to them. This denial of expression causes the students to be hostile to teachers and to fellow students.

We, as adults, are to blame for not supplying real leadership or concern for young people. The examples set up by our adult society have created a generation of young people who have little concern for themselves or for anyone else. They are willing to destroy themselves with drugs, crime, etc. I am attempting in my classes to rebuild the confidence of young people through adult example and through giving them the freedom of expression I feel they need. As the students begin to examine and analyze their own behavior, they gain insight. As they begin to understand their own emotions, they come closer to self-honesty and self-acceptance. Realizing that I accept them helps students accept themselves.

My final goal is teaching the students to learn to *deal* with and function effectively in this society.

## STUDENTS TALK

### DIARY

I like an English class that teaches spelling in a fun way.

MATH. I don't know division at all and barely know my times tables. I think a lot of kids might be behind things, so you ought to get them to tell you what they (as far as education goes) know and what they don't. And ask individual people what they want to learn. You ought to find out where they are behind in subjects and help them. Help them help themselves to get up to where they should be.

We should get a work shop (if possible) for kids to be creative with. I do like to get most of my classes with Other Ways.

Get the kids with each other more. Teachers are just fine. I don't know what to say about the schedule because I don't know what it is.

I myself feel satisfied about the way things are going. So far I have not been pressured into participating in anything—which is not to say that I have not been participating. I enjoy taking more than one class from a teacher (Dave Conley) because I find that in an informal atmosphere and with a limited number of people, the subjects relate.

I suppose things could be progressing faster, but if more pressure were involved, it would completely blow it. I feel like I've become more involved with people here in the last month than I did at Berkeley High in the last two years, simply because it was my choice to.

*Dum-dee-dum-dum da*
*Friday, 10 de octobre*

Other Ways is a mellow place, it's relaxing. Why? Because you can knock over things and not wound them. I have too much free time, but it isn't bad. It's not fair that all the other guys (the 8th and 9th graders) are all friends and I'm not a part of them, but I really don't want to be. Herbert Kohl cares about me. I mean he cares about people and you can't believe rumors people have said about X and Y being snobs. But it doesn't matter and I feel understanding. I got too much understanding.

I didn't want to go skin diving Tuesday because I FEEL pretty BAD in SPORTS.

M and O are so beautiful. I wish I could be free, just floating free.

AMERICAN INDIAN needs organization. Nothing like being relevant. It might get better.

This week has been nice, but I haven't gotten anything done. But now things are getting smoothed over and getting a little more organization—I mean myself. I can start doing things like trying skin diving and reading books for American Indian and all.

I have given up my running class because I'm too lazy.

Herb reminds me of my father and sometimes I get an urge to sit on his lap.

The American Indian and Civics classes need more continuity. But it seems like so long since I've been to any of them. I wish I had Civics and Sociology more than just once a week.

I am getting to like it here more, my second home. Sometimes I wish some of my other friends were here, but not having them here gives me the opportunity to make friends when otherwise I might not.

I like the people and the place and the atmosphere. I don't know how to evaluate this, but this is gonna do fine.

I enjoy LeConte thoroughly—we are just starting and it feels good. I feel I am not wasting my time and I am putting my energy into good places. I feel respected at that school—and the responsibilities are good for me.

My Animal Behavior class is small, personal, and Mr. Ritchie, although very different in his head than me, has much to teach. I am learning more and more that I enjoy listening more than talking.

My American Indian class is beautiful—it is expansive and is teaching me more than anything else I have ever learned.

I feel that this year many people care about what happens to me. I have people to laugh with—and people to share my feelings. This is just the beginning and feels pretty fucking good.

Worked my head off at Books Unlimited. In Civics decided upon my weekly reports. Ran like hell in running. Saw a court trial Tuesday. Lost track of time and missed Journalism which doesn't please me. Did some heavy figuring in math. Made "Sports in Society" class and heard an interesting guy named Dave who really opened aspects of sports. Played basketball at King with Spino and co. American Indians was terrific. We had a guest speaker and he got onto stuff that really interested me.

I've been getting so involved, I think I'm gonna have to quit going to class cause it takes too much energy. All of the regulars from last year have been playing basketball. Lewis, Darryle, Alvin, Mike and me. Logic class really gets my academic ass moving.

I wrote the basis of my first epic poem about hippies and why I ain't innocent no more and drugs. Seems like I come and just have continuous mental orgasms.

This week, on Monday, I went to a lecture by some Indians up at Cal. I like Indian History because I have some Indian heritage and I don't know much about it and no one else in the family knows either. Tuesday and Wednesday I was sick.

Today I went to the Indian class and like the instructor knows what she's talking about. Wow! I would like to hear more rap like that. The more I know about my society and country, the more I'm ashamed of it.

I'm not too hip on what is happening on my program because nothing has been done. I'm very tight inside right now and when I get tight, I break down.

## WHAT HAPPENS

### GARY, MARY, AND PHIL

My name is Gary Hall. My two students are Mary and Phil. They asked me to teach them how to read Black Poetry—that is how I became a teacher. At 10:30 every day I found myself having to chase them around our schoolhouse before they would come to class.

After arguing for a little while, they began to take part and participate. After nine weeks of going though changes, Mary and Phil are tired of hassling me. They are treating me like a human being.

I have been going around to a number of different schools saying what I feel about things in a poetic form. Phil has immediately taken an interest and has written some poetry. Now he is traveling around to the schools with Alvin Curry and myself.

Phil's character has changed a great deal and his reading of Black Poetry has improved. Mary's reading was all right when she first started coming to class—except that she ignored periods and stopped in the middle of sentences. I have tried to help her stop on periods and complete her sentences. Mary has improved during the time we have been working together.

I am fifteen years old and I like the job of being called a teacher.

### DARRYLE AND BETTY

After a year of working with Betty, she is now moving in a direction of self-pride and concern for herself and others. She, like so many others, was very heavily involved with dope. She had given up on school because of her long-established bad record and had turned to dope for comfort. Thus, my initial objective was not to teach her academic subjects but to help her understand herself and her emotions so that she would not want to destroy herself. I had to win her confidence as a teacher and friend. I had to accept her no matter what she did and not be quick to suspend her from school, call her parents, and generally show the world that I thought she was worthless and too much trouble to help. Naturally Betty started testing me, trying to learn at what point I would discipline her and reject her so that she could classify me with the rest of the people who handle her badly.

Betty is much better now, not perfect—but better. We are beginning to do regular school work and she smiles now. I worked hard with Betty for her sake and for mine also—I don't like to fail.

## ALTA AND TOM

Tom is a big, loud, hostile boy who barges into situations and carries many students along with him. He usually speaks only in slurs and threats and used to show no respect. As a staff member and as a woman, I was constantly offended by him and spoke no more civilly to him than he did to me. In October we all went to lunch at Giovanni's and he and I sat at the same table. I asked him for a bite of his steak and he gave me a piece as big as a hamburger. I was really touched, told him later that he frightened me and asked him if I needed to be so uptight. He said no, said he didn't remember hassling me and seemed generally noncommittal. But last week he came to poetry class and although he refused to participate for the first hour, he joined us in making a group poem. His contributions were quite funny and greatly appreciated by the other students. (Although he is an amazing artist, he rarely draws unless requested.)

Our next encounter was at the retreat; he was most helpful with my children and sang with some other students for our entertainment. He came up singing to me and I was so delighted I jumped up and hugged him. He laughed happily and said, "You're bad, sister, you're bad!"

## ALTA AND VIVIAN

Vivian is an extremely shy girl with no close friends. She mentioned that she had never had a real talk with anyone in her life, and at fifteen she had never written a poem on her own, painted a picture, or composed a song. She wandered in and out of classes, refused to say which ones she was in and expressed no enthusiasm for her subjects. In humanities one day we tried improvisational theater and Vivian started each of the improvisations! She immediately threw herself into the roles she assumed and, with no shyness, invented characters for two and a half hours. When I mentioned her boldness later she said "really."

The change has been as dramatic as her performance. She is an excellent gymnast and has also started dancing. She came to my house one day and read my book on Harriet Tubman aloud. It took her one and a half hours and she never slowed down! My daughter and I fixed and ate dinner, cleaned house, etc., and Vivian real aloud constantly, repeating the difficult words until she got them.

At her first poetry class, she refused to write anything, but in each class she has participated more and more. Three weeks ago she made the finest collage I have ever seen. It's about overpopulation and it now hangs in the Other Ways office.

## MICHAEL SPINO

The student and I met last year at McKinley School. At the time, I was drifting among McKinley, Other Ways, and Berkeley High. We made contact last year but we eventually lost each other.

For a while, we had contact. His moods, variances, and problems were not things that tore us from each other, but feelings we worked at with trust between us.

I am a long-distance runner; mornings find me breaking

through the fog. Something happened to me during the time that I could relate to this person. "Relate" is a bad word because it wasn't that he understood a new knowledge or found the wholesome life. At times we ran together and, I believe, both our eyes shone; we smiled, the day's weather went through us.

We spoke of writing, of history, and the youth movement. He was an idealist, a committed revolutionary. Yet he sulked when people from other cultures interfered with his desires and wishes. We enjoyed being with each other, but there were many things to do and little time. Lack of time led us to talk and read some things about the individual. We would jog the street talking about individuals, communities, how much a person can or should give of himself. It's been only four months; we've gone to cross-country meetings, read much Hesse and Mao. But probably most important, our friendship has been cemented. Not through words or books or high grades on essays, but because we have seen each other in a way that prevents self-betrayal.

### ALVIN CURRY

Don

> Was not originally one of my students
>     of poetry or Black Studies
> . . . His education is of "*Life.*"

And how to learn without worrying
About being "*Hip*" all the time.

It is vitally important for Don to be accepted by his peers.

> Because of this
> He has to prove how much alcohol he is
> Capable of soaking up at a given time.

Ending in being farther away from his goal.

I have noticed certain things and have tried to keep them in mind in persuading him to attend some of my classes.

I sincerely hope that I will be able to
Reach his pseudo-militant eyes
So he may see that he is his own center
Of attention instead of cutting his finger
And having to brag about how much
Senseless blood is pouring out of white veins
In a black audience.

Don comes to school with problems and I have tried to help him deal with them. Going home to uncaring parents is a drawbridge that Don has to cross.

I will try
My best to be there if he doesn't
Make it.

# LEAP: School Plus

## BY MICHELLE COLE

In 1963 Michelle Cole came to New York's Lower East Side and started working with the tough kids who live there. Out of this experience grew the Lower East Side Action Project and the LEAP School. The school, which has more than twenty students and is planning to grow to seventy-five, is located in what used to be an A & P grocery store. It is another example of how education can work for the kids failed by the public schools.

Michelle Cole, director of the LEAP School, formerly was director of the Lower East Side Action Project. She is co-author of *Ghetto Caravan*.

THIS IS the LEAP School, the stage on which a collection of actors came together with notions of failure, cultural deprivation, Summerhill, schools without walls, grades, curricula, compulsory attendance, remediation, anxiety, authority, Montessori and control, only to find that their real common bonds were their anger and their frustrated creative energy—their need to be. It was from these common threads that the fabric of a school emerged, a school in constant motion, not without a structure, but without limits.

I am going to try to get you there by putting you in the audience for a week of LEAP School theater. Every so often, I'll come out from behind the narrative and make some points that I think need making. Otherwise, what follows are segments of a week spent behind my eyes. A week of the LEAP School, New York City.

324

Kiki flops down on one of the chairs in my office.

"How'd things go today?" I make conversation. Of all the guys in the school, he's the least likely to be in my office or any other adult's.

"Okay." No effort at conversation, but he's not moving out of the chair, either.

I've been thinking about Kiki all week. The week before, for the first time, he asserted his anger in Group Rap. It usually comes out in sulking and mumbling. But there's a lot there. Probably the angriest guy in the school.

"I'm glad you came in." I interrupt his thoughts. "Been wanting to ask you how it felt to change the whole school."

He looks at me in complete bewilderment.

Ignoring the "what-the-fuck's-she-talking-about" look, I continue. "Because you came out with your feelings about having classes together with the second-unit guys, the whole school changed." He had complained that the two groups of guys should be separate because the new group of guys were disrupting the kind of classes he thought the first unit should have. Everyone agreed with him and the scheduling of the school completely changed.

"Oh, that." He's smiling.

"Yeah, that. You changed the lives of everyone in the school. Our days are completely different now—" I keep pushing it—"because of you."

"Hey, yeah. Shit. That's right." He's leaning back in the chair. Takes a long drag on his cigarette.

"Damn, Kiki. You've got so much power. I'm glad you're finally starting to use it. The school's running so much better now."

"Yeah, I like it better."

"How does it feel to change things the way you want?"

He gets up from the chair. Broad smile. "I'm going to make a lot of changes around here." He opens the door. "See ya."

I'm sitting with Gaywood. He's telling me about his math class and how turned on the guys were. The door opens suddenly. It's Nancy. Face pinched. She's mad about something.

"Spoon-fed. That's what they want. They want to be spoon-fed. I asked them what they want and what do they want? To be spoon-fed. Hector wants to be spoon-fed."

I'm still thinking about Gaywood's class. She's not really there, only the words "spoon-fed" are there. I'm looking at her and thinking about Gaywood—by now I've forgotten what we were talking about.

"Is that what they said?" I ask. Still, I don't know what she's really saying to me. I know the guys couldn't have used the words "spoon-fed." I know those are her words. I know she's telling me something negative. What was I just talking to Gaywood about?

"What do the guys mean when they say they want to be spoon-fed?" I ask. I'm not asking anything about the guys; I'm really asking her what pinched her up so much.

"They want information given to them. They don't want any dialogue. They just want a lot of information."

The room is silent. I don't know what Gaywood is doing or even how he looks. My mind is searching for the negative. I'm trying to figure out what's wrong with kids wanting information.

"You want dialogue." My statement stabbing at the problem.

"Yeah, I don't want to stand up there and just give them information."

She's going to hate me. I know she's going to hate me for this. But I'm going to say it anyway.

"How can you have a dialogue on a subject with a group of kids who don't have any information on the subject? I think the kids are right. They want more information. I bet after they have more information they'll want more dialogue."

She hates me. Oh, does she hate me. I continue. As long as she hates me, what's there to lose?

"I agree with the kids. They know what they want. Why don't you listen to them? We're supposed to be a responsive school. You've got to be responsive."

The door slams. She's as responsive to me as she was to the kids.

I look over at Gaywood. He gives me a look of perplexity. I know he's not perplexed. He's mad. He's pissed. But he doesn't want to take the time to go into it.

He continues, "Anyhow, Michelle, I think I might need an assistant with my class, because the guys are moving so fast. You know what they got into today? Dig on this . . ."

It's Tuesday night. Hector's come over to my apartment. He's just come back from his first photography lesson.

"Wow, did I have a great time. First time I ever took pictures with a camera with settings and stuff. Got some great shots." He's making himself a cup of coffee.

"Where'd you go?" Tony, who's teaching him, said he'd take him around the neighborhood.

"Well, Tony and I started out at Tompkins Square Park. I see this guy sitting on top of a cement pole. Just sitting there. On top of a cement pole. It's freezing, and he's just sitting there and—dig this—he's an Arab."

"An Arab sitting on top of a cement column in the park?"

"Yeah. I figure this has got to be a great shot. I start walking closer to him to get a reading on my light meter. He takes part of the sheet he's wearing and covers his face. Only his eyes stick out. I figure, 'You motherfucker, I can wait you out,' and I keep standing there with my camera all set and I'm waiting. Tony was getting some cigarettes and I was waiting for him, anyway. I'm standing there and this Arab is sitting there and we're staring at each other and not moving and Tony came back from the store. He rushes up to me and says, 'Don't take a picture of that guy!'

"It's my first great shot and Tony tells me not to take a picture of that guy. I ask him 'How come?' and he tells me that he's a crazy nut and he's been arrested a few times and it's always taken six cops to control him because he knows karate and shit and don't take his picture 'cause he might come at me. Tony and I walk across the street from him. Hell, I don't want to get beaten up. But when we get to the other side of the street, I can't resist. I turn around. I look at the Arab. He's still got the sheet over most of his face, but I figure 'what the shit' and I took his picture and Tony and I ran."

I'm wondering how a photography lesson can be so complicated, while Hector continues.

"Then we walk over to the Village and I take a bunch of pictures of garbage and shit, but when we walk back through the park in the Village I see another great shot. This time it's a guy talking to another guy and the guy who's talking is all dressed up as an Indian. You know, not the kind who wear feathers, the other kind. So I go up kinda close to him and I start to focus and figure my light meter. The guy is still talking to his friend. And then he sees me. And he puts on this bad face and starts to wave his arms around, like telling me to go away. But I figure, shit, I'm not going to miss two great shots on my first lesson, and I stay there and click his picture. And you know what he does? He comes right over to me and he starts yelling and saying I had no right to take his picture. I'm thinking to myself, 'I thought people liked their picture taken,' but I don't want the guy to grab the camera, so I tell him I was really taking a picture of the building behind him, and he says to me in that crazy kinda English they talk, 'I know you were taking a picture of me.' Tony says, 'Let's walk away slowly,' and we got out of the park."

Hector is still excited. He has a whole new perspective on photography. It's an adventure. It's dangerous. I'm wondering what Tony is doing tonight. Whether he's sorry he volunteered to teach Hector photography. What if he were taking a photography class in a regular school or college? Would he have such adventures in his first lesson?

"Well, after today, you think you want more lessons?" I'm teasing him.

"Damn right," he answers me as though I had really asked him a question. "Best decision I've made in a long time."

Gaywood, first one in my office. "Made a discovery today."

"What's that?"

"The first-unit guys want to know me. They want to go out with me and find out where I am as a man. We're going to see *Putney Swope* on Friday. Going bowling as a math lesson tomorrow. I thought all Thanksgiving vacation about LEAP and how different it is here and how hard it is and how nobody can understand what it's all about. And I also thought about my problems in teaching the first unit. I've been depending on the classic fight between student and teacher as a positive force for teaching my classes. They don't want to be classic students. They want to be on a man-to-man basis with me and to know what I know so we can discuss and not argue and hassle things out in class. I never had a group like that. Gotta think about how to work with them. How to get dialogue with them on a whole other level. It kinda scares me. They want to know me. Me, Gaywood. Not me Gaywood-the-teacher. It's weird. It's different."

"I'm glad you came in. Yeah, the first-unit guys are past all the teacher-student role fighting. Yeah, I guess it's scary. It's going to be interesting to see how it all works out." I pause, because I'm about to dump on him. "The thing I wanted to talk to you about is your math book. I don't understand a word of it."

Gaywood worked out a booklet on math that's been his teaching treasure. It condenses many of the successful things he's had with kids on paper. It explains how to teach various areas of math. He's been talking to me about it since he came to LEAP. It's something he wants to be published. He went to a publisher with it. It's his first attempt at breaking out of just teaching and breaking into the Kozol-Holt world of the teacher-expert. At the beginning of school I told him to type it up and show it to me and I would see if I could get it published. He finally gave it to me a week ago and I really didn't understand any of it, not just the math part—I didn't understand the sentences. I've been putting off talking about it. He hadn't asked me if I liked it, and all during the past week we've been staying away from each other.

"Well, let me explain . . ."

"No. If you've gotta explain it, it's not good. You won't be able to explain it to everyone out in the world who reads it. I wish I could tell you particular things I don't understand. But the true fact is I don't understand any of it."

"Oh, ssshhhhhhiiiitt."

I ignore the "Oh, shit." "Who are you writing this book for?"

"Whatcha mean?" He's still thinking oh, shit. He doesn't want to be in my office. He's sorry he gave the booklet to me. He wishes I wasn't there and that I'd shut up.

"I mean, are you writing this for a publisher? Are you writing this for any group in particular?"

He still doesn't want to talk to me, but he pushes out the words. "For teachers."

"Ah hah! For teachers. Gaywood, what do you think about teachers?"

God damn, he's still thinking oh, shit. C'mon, Gaywood, pull out of it. Get past it. Relate to me. I think I've got something to tell you that'll make you happy, that'll improve your writing.

"What do you mean, 'what do I think about teachers'?"

"Fuck. What the fuck have you been telling me you think about teachers? Since the first time I met you, you've been saying the same things about teachers."

He's back in the room. He heard what I said. He lights up. "They're the dumbest fuckin' group of people I've ever known. I hate teachers."

"So who are you writing this book for?"

He's laughing. He's gleaming. He knows. He knows what I'm getting to. "I'm writing the book for teachers."

I jump in—all the words I can think of—"So, here you are. You've taken all your successes and put them down on paper for a group of people you hate. You've put yourself out for people you can't stand. You don't want them to understand that booklet. You don't want them to know you that well. You don't want them to use you and what you know. You hate them. Of course you're going to make it un-understandable."

He's staring at me, smiling. I don't know whether I've made any sense, but it feels right.

"Those motherfuckers. They couldn't pull off good classes even with me explaining every single detail of a lesson to them. Even if I drew diagrams." He understood.

I venture into another area. "So, who else are you writing the book for?"

He's right in there with me. "For me."

"Fucking right. You're writing that book for yourself. You don't want to be another teacher. You want people to know you. You want to get yourself out there in the world with the rest of the people. You want to get out of the classroom-only bag. That's really why you're writing the book. For you. You want to make it, and in this case you thought you could make it by writing for teachers."

He's smiling again. "You fuckin' bitch, Michelle—God damn."

"How about writing the book for kids? One of the problems about the book is that you use so many big words, a lot of times in the wrong places."

"Well, those fuckin' teachers won't read anything that has just plain English. It's gotta have a lotta big words."

"So write it for kids and put in all the 'shits,' 'pisses' and 'fucks' you feel like putting in. Write a math book using the kids' and your own language—the real language, not book language."

He's excited and happy and I'm happy too, because I think we hit on something. I think he can write a fantastic book if he can only capture the same spirit he generates in his classes.

"Yeah, shit. That's what I'll do. I can always modify it afterwards, but I'll write it for kids. Shit, it's the kids I care about. Nobody writes for the kids." He's standing, smiling and leaving.

The door shuts. I look at my mail and there's a knock and I say "Yeah?" and Nancy comes in. I should say Nancy stomps in. She's mad.

"What's up?"

"That fuckin' second unit. Can't do a thing with the second unit. I don't think I want to teach them anymore. Just can't get anything across to them. That fuckin' Paulie keeps messing up the class. There's something between him and me. I keep asking him what's the matter and he just shuts up. But then he bombs my classes. This is the third day I'm explaining directions to that group and they're just about getting the meaning of direction and Paulie comes on saying, 'Why can't I say Eastnorth instead of Northeast?' I tell him that he can, but all the maps say Northeast and learning the directions the way they're put on the maps makes it easier to read a map. He says he wants to do it his way, and I tell him, 'Go ahead and do it your own fuckin' way,' and he says 'Why don't you like me?' and I tell him I do like him, but I don't like the way he acts sometimes—sometimes he just comes on like a snotty punk kid and I don't like that, and he keeps on insisting that I don't like him."

"Do you like him?"

"Yeah, I like him. I just don't like some of the things he does."

"Well, for the past two weeks you've been telling me that Paulie is out to fuck you up and to fuck up your class and he picks on you in the hall. Do you really like this guy who's always fucking you up?"

Silence. Audible silence. It's a sin for a teacher not to like a kid. Especially a humanitarian teacher. You can feel sorry for a kid. You can think he has problems, but you can't just plain not like a kid.

She begins repeating, "I don't know. I think it's not only Paulie. I don't think I can get through to the second unit. Three days explaining directions. *Three days.*"

She goes on, but I can't hear her. I just got in. Had a whole thing with Gaywood and I'm thinking about our permanent school building that was supposed to be renovated two months ago and that we won't move into until after Christmas vacation. And I'm worried about our chartering problems and can't move on those until we're in the renovated building. And the kids and the teachers are cramped. And classes aren't being taped and other systems are breaking down and there's a teachers' meeting this afternoon and I have a lot to say, but I have to organize it. And a fantastic teacher applied to work in the school and I don't have the money to hire her. And Ralphie got his draft papers and he's listed as 1A.

"Do you mind if I call Larry in on this? Maybe he can help."

"No, sure."

I buzz Larry, and he comes in and Nancy sits back in her seat and lets me explain what she's just told me.

Larry: "Well, I sat in on part of your class and I thought it was great."

There's pure surprise on Nancy's face.

"Really?"

"Yeah. What may be the problem is that you take the kids too seriously. You don't go along with their goofs. Why not tell Paulie, 'Sure you can call it Eastnorth. You can call it Yourmother, too. You can even find a word that no one's heard of and call it that.' Extend the goof."

"I thought you came into my class because the guys were making so much noise."

They look at each other blankly. Then Larry smiles.

"Oh, yeah?"

"Yeah, they were making an awful lot of noise."

"That *is* why I came into your class. It sounded like an awful lot was going on and I wanted to sit in on the fun. What's wrong with an awful lot of noise?"

"Well, the only time anyone of authority ever came into my class it was because something was wrong. And noisy kids are not what authority people consider a good class."

"I'm an authority figure?"

"Well, you're the Director of LEAP. Well, I don't know you very well. Well . . ."

Larry jumps a step. "I think you're afraid of the excitement you generate in your class. You're afraid it'll get out of your hands.

You're the one who's worried about noise. I thought it was a great class. The kids were so excited about directions—shouting out North, South, East, West—they were actually excited about learning directions. I think it was amazing."

She's thinking. "Yeah, I do take Paulie too seriously, and he rides me because of it. You're wrong, though, Michelle. I really do like him. I just hate some of the things he does, but I think he's a sharp kid."

She looks at Larry. "You really thought it was a good class?"

Larry smiles and leaves.

Nancy looks at me. "So I'll keep trying with the second unit."

She leaves as Kathy walks in.

"I started the Planning for Change program today. We started off with a film strip. The film strip is about a guy who wants to change things, how he tries, first in New York City and then in other countries' cities, to implement change."

"How did it go?"

"Well, they liked the background music."

Ralphie, Hector and I are having coffee. They want to talk to me about "something very important." Ralphie begins.

"The second-unit guys just don't understand that the teachers here aren't like the ones they used to have. They keep wanting to bag them."

I see a plan in their faces.

"Hector and I've been thinking. Maybe we should be in on their Group Raps. We could show them how to talk to the teachers."

"Yeah." Hector's holding onto his cup with both hands. "They keep wanting to impress the teachers. Just like it was a regular school. They don't understand yet."

My mind is wandering. Hector never used the word "impress" before. I'm thinking about the two of them at the beginning of last year. It took them three months longer to get to the point the second group of guys had already come to. The two boys sitting with me are young men. Their concern about the new guys in the school is as intense as mine. Their concern about the school has the same intensity. They're not students and I'm not the director.

I realize I've been staring at them. They're looking at me, waiting. "Well, who helped you learn to talk to teachers differently?"

They've been expecting this point of view. "Yeah, but look how long it took us."

"That's true. But you didn't have an older group of guys around you at all. At least the second unit sees you talking to the teachers. And I think they're going faster than you did."

"Not fast enough," Hector interrupts.

"But if you came in on their Group Raps, they'd try to relate to the adults through you, instead of directly. I think you'd provide a good cop-out."

Ralphie's pouring some more coffee. "Didn't think about that. Probably's true."

"Shit," Hector breaks in. "It takes so long to get through to them. It just takes too damn long."

"How did you wait so long for us to come around?" Ralphie asks.

I want to cry, but I smile instead. I could give them a good rap on patience, but that rap never worked with me.

"Who waited? We all just kept talking until we could hear each other."

The conversation over the second cup of coffee was about being a kid again.

Nancy's been teaching lecture-style for a week. We're at a teachers' meeting and she's talking about how bored she is and how bored the kids are.

"I decided to start with 1898, beginning with the Reform movement. But I've found in this past week that the guys really don't know anything. Nothing. They don't know names or periods of history. Nothing. I can't talk about reform without talking about what was being reformed—big business. They don't know what big business is. So I'm explaining corporations—the corporate structure. God, it's dull. Made a chart of the whole structure of a corporation. It took me three days to get across the concept of direction—on a map. Corporations should take about a month."

I see in her face the dismay she's been carrying for a week. She really has been spoon-feeding. She realized as soon as she got off of current social discussions that the guys really needed what they said they needed—information.

Gaywood picks up on her depression. "Why don't you use the guys' personalities to teach about corporations? I've done this in my math class. Each guy approaches math from a different perspective—Victor wants answers, Kiki is always questioning the premise. You could use this in teaching about corporations."

"Yeah, but it's easier to do that in math than in history where there's so much information to get across before the guys can project themselves into an historical situation."

Gaywood disagrees. "Take Hector. Who would he be in a corporation? Who would Ralph be? Who would Siggie be? Who would Carlos be? They all have certain personalities that fit differently into a corporation. Include them. Make them a corporation. They'll find out what kind of role each title plays."

"But they don't know the feeling of a corporation. They don't even know what it is. They don't know what it was in 1898. They don't have the information."

The discussion continues for a while. It stalemates. Then, somehow, all together, Nancy, Gaywood, Jill and I realize something. All at the same time. All in different ways. The composite of our realizations comes out like this: Big business is power. Reform and revolution are reaction and assertion. Within ten minutes we related the whole of American history to the whole of everyone's personal experiences in growing up. Of course the guys know what reform is. They want to reform their parents. Of course they know what big business is. They want power. They have experienced personally in their growing all the concepts of history. All that's needed is the translations.

The next day, Nancy's class is screaming and yelling. Hector has been assigned the president of a corporation. Ralphie has been assigned vice-president. Kiki has been assigned business manager. Victor had been assigned security officer. Charlie has been assigned union leader. All the kids have been assigned corporate roles relating to their approach to life. Hector, being the founder of the corporation, has 51 percent of the stock. The guys don't know yet what stocks are, but they do know that 51 percent is more than half and that means that Hector alone has controlling interest. Charlie, the union leader, and the same Charlie who is rebelling strongly at home, is calling a strike.

Gaywood is participating in the class. During the teachers' meeting Gaywood and Nancy decided to sit in on each other's classes. They found that they're crossing subjects. Gaywood wants to take the subject of stocks and bonds and averages and include them in his math class. Nancy wants to find out more about stocks and bonds herself. Nancy has assigned Gaywood a corporate role, too. He's not just sitting in on her class. He's a student. He's yelling as much as the rest of the students.

The guys are talking in the hall after school. They stop me as I'm walking to another office.

"Guess what?"

"What?"

"Gaywood and Nancy were in each other's classes today." I have the feeling they're uncomfortable. Somehow teachers don't do this. They don't learn from each other in front of the students.

"How'd it go?"

They're searching my face for disapproval. They see excitement.

"Dynamite."

It's Friday morning. Group Rap day. Pay day. Each student is paid a starting salary of $2.50 a week based solely on his attendance. Raises come once a month. The first unit of guys who were in school last year worked out a system for this year. The first six weeks of school is compulsory. No pay raises. After that, a student may take three cut days a month. The raise should be 75¢ per month if a student isn't absent at all. But if he takes his cut days, he gets docked for the day plus he gets a pay raise of 50¢ instead of 75¢. If he's out more than that, no raise.

They presented this system to the adults and the second unit of guys. We all agree to their system. Now they want the teachers to keep the records.

Hector is on the spot. Gaywood's addressing him. "Where were you on Tuesday?"

"Whatcha mean? I took a cut day."

"I don't think that cut days come up yet."

Victor cuts in. "You're the ones who keep attendance. Don't you even know if school's been going six weeks or not?"

Ralphie: "Your records are all fucked up anyway. I don't know what's the matter with you people, but you can't even keep your records straight."

Kiki: "Yeah, I'm down for being late more than Hector, and that's bullshit."

A whole argument begins around attendance and pay. It develops into a student-teacher confrontation. The students feel that the teachers aren't paying enough attention to the attendance form. The teachers feel that their records are accurate. The students ask to see the forms from the beginning of school. They're shown the forms. They still don't agree with what's been put down. They accuse the teachers of waiting till the end of the day and then writing in who was and wasn't absent or late. They contend that the teachers forget by the end of the day. The teachers eventually admit that they haven't been strict about taking attendance.

It wasn't until this Group Rap that the teachers really took the attendance duty seriously. The kids have been very serious about it because it involves money. Those who have been in school every day want their pay raises. They don't want to see a guy who has missed a couple of days getting the same raise. For most of them, this is the first time they want teachers to take accurate attendance.

The argument about attendance, salary and raises ends with Gaywood. "I've been mad at you, motherfucker." He's talking to Hector. "You've been coming in late."

Hector is in the process of taking a picture of himself. Everyone laughs.

Gaywood continues anyway. "I talked to you last week. I said, 'Why are you comin' to school late? Why have you been fuckin' off?' You know what you told me? 'So what. Whatcha gonna do about it?' That shit made me mad."

Ralphie: "Hector's gonna do the same thing he did last year. He was always comin' in late. And he always said, 'Whatcha gonna do about it?' If you just make a joke out of it, he'll keep doin' it, until you really get mad at him and then fuck him up. Then maybe something will happen."

Kathy: "No one really ever gets mad at Hector. The other morning Kiki called and was real mad before he called. And then Hector got on the phone and Kiki gave the phone to Charlie. And all Charlie did was ask Hector why he wasn't in school. Not mad. Just asked him."

Hector: "Charlie was absent and late much more than me. I checked the attendance book. No one came down on Charlie. So why are you comin' down on me?"

Gaywood: "You were really mad about Charlie, so why are you doing the same thing? Why?"

Michelle: "Well, no one came down on Charlie. And now no one is coming down on Hector, so why shouldn't he?"

Gaywood: "The same thing is happening in my class. You told Victor to shut up—'You talk when I say talk,' you said. Nobody attacked him [Hector] for that."

Ralphie: "You cop to his shit, that's why. He plays a game and everybody falls into it. I told you people, leave him alone."

Michelle: "How does that happen?"

Ralphie: "Like when he comes into class and you tell him to read and he says 'I don't want to read,' and you say, 'Aw, come on, Hector, read. Come on Hector, read.'"

Nancy: "Yeah, that happened in my class. It was your turn to read and I asked you to read."

Hector: "Yeah, and you fell into it. You fell into it. You started begging and shit."

Nancy: "We ignored you."

Ralphie: "After I told you not to play into his shit."

Everyone's talking about Hector, how much control he has over everyone, how much control everyone lets him have. Methods of dealing with him are yelled out. Even Hector is talking about how to deal with himself. Then we all discover that Hector has had the complete attention of this Group Rap. Again, he's been in the middle of everything.

Something else. The Group Rap turns into an adult-against-Hector session. The guys have been goofing with each other for the last fifteen minutes of the argument and none of us notices.

Michelle: "Hey, where are you guys?"

They all laugh.

Michelle: "Ooooh, you guys put out all this shit about Hector. You guys are mad at Hector. You want the adults to go down on the line with Hector. And you want to watch a fight between Hector and the adults."

Hector doesn't want the argument to end. "Gaywood, you always crash on me."

Gaywood: "Oh, no."

"You always do that, Gaywood."

Gaywood reverses. "Why?"

"You're the one who's crashing. You must know why."

"I crash on everybody."

"Not like with me."

"I crash on Kiki."

"Not like with me."

Kathy: "Maybe there's a reason."

"That's what I'm saying. I want to know what it is."

Gaywood addresses the rest of the guys. "Do I crash on him more than anybody?"

Ralphie answers. "Most of the time you crash on him."

The whole group of guys agree that Gaywood crashes on Hector more than on anybody else.

Kiki: "Gaywood crashes on everybody."

Michelle: "But is it different when Gaywood crashes on Hector?"

Gaywood comes in with an "Oh shit!"

Gaywood continues. "That's bullshit. That's bullshit."

Silence.

Gaywood: "It might be true."

The whole room is laughing.

Gaywood is talking to Hector. His voice is completely different. "You know, we developed a goddamn relationship. We went to that IBM thing together. I came over to your house. We went to see Ike and Tina Turner. So I really have an investment in you, man."

Now everyone's singsonging "Aaaaaaaaahhhhhh."

Michelle: "All right. So you know him better than you know the other guys, so when you crash on him it's in a more personal way."

Gaywood: "When I went bowling with Hector and the other guys, it was beautiful, because I've always been doing things with Hector. So this time everyone went. Then I got a chance to go out with the other guys." His voice changes again. "So what might have happened, I might have put him in that position. I was fighting him. And all the other cats were fighting him too."

Jill: "So maybe you're crashing on him a lot so he won't be the favorite."

Gaywood: "Yeah, that might have been the thing."

Hector is smiling. "Right, that's right."

Gaywood: "I don't want these cats to think I like Hector more than I like the rest of them. 'Cause that's not true."

Michelle: "Ah, but the thing is that you have more contact

with Hector. The reason that anybody has more contact. You have a whole guilt thing about having more contact with Hector outside of the school. But really, if anybody else wanted to have more contact with you on the outside of school, they would have done it. Why should you feel bad?"

The first-unit Group Rap ends with a discussion around who is responsible to make relationships. Should it always be the adult? Should it ever be the student? There are no decisions. Only reflections. Everyone knows that Hector has put himself out more to get to know Gaywood. They know that if they put themselves out they would know him better, too. And Gaywood is laughing at his feeling guilty.

The second unit begins with Paulie yelling at Gaywood because his classes run overtime. "You made a schedule. Now you keep your schedule." The whole session is about class time. The guys want more class time. But they also want the teachers to stick to the schedules they made or change them, but not ignore them. Gaywood's class runs overtime according to the schedule. The kids decide to extend all class time and to work with the teachers so classes can run "until we're tired."

Gaywood's sore from his math class.
"How can you be sore from a math class?"
"We went bowling."
"Bowling? For a math class?"
"Yeah, the alleys are parallel lines, the pins are triangular, the angle of the ball going down the alley—bowling's all math."
Only Gaywood. Only Gaywood. He's still talking, making the comparisons and the liaisons between bowling and math. I'm not listening to him, I'm watching him. Watching him be excited. Completely engrossed. There is nothing else on his mind but bowling and math. The room is filled with his excitement.
"Not only that—" I've tuned in again—"but I've found a way for the guys to do drill work through bowling. Keeping score—it's all addition and subtraction and division and averages. Drill work in disguise. So I've made up these . . ."

He takes out small booklets he's made for each student. The booklets are score sheets for bowling, and on the top of each sheet is the person who's doing the bowling and another student who's helping with the scoring. Two people responsible for the scoring.

"They chose who would work with who. And they chose well —in each team there's one who's more proficient than the other. They know. I didn't have to pair anyone up together."

If only I had had a math teacher like Gaywood. "Gaywood, I wish I had a math teacher like you."

He's not interested in compliments. He's too engrossed in bowling and math. "I've got a lot to do."

I leave him alone to work.


A news commentator is watching one of our Group Rap sessions. Afterward he asks me questions.

"What's going to happen to these kids when they get out of the LEAP School?"

I think he's asking whether we're a college-bound program or a vocational-bound program. "I don't know."

"Do they know?" He expects some sort of definitive answer. He's used to getting answers.

"Some of them. Not many."

"Would you like them to go to college?" He *was* asking what I thought he was asking.

"I think some of them would be able to go to college. Some would enjoy college. Some would be killed by college." I lean back while he writes notes.

He looks up. "What do you think will happen to them?" Still looking for answers. I wonder where he's been educated.

I try to answer the question, try to make him feel better. "Well, I think that Kiki will go into music. Hector will go into photography. Carlos is working as an apprentice to an architect." I'm doing a public-relations job and I can't continue. "I can't really tell you what they're going to be doing. The guys in the school are sixteen, seventeen and eighteen. No one asks middle-class kids what they're going to do at this age. I don't ask poor kids. Some are exploring and some are just happy to feel, for the first time, that they're learning."

"Do they ask you what you think they will be doing?"

"No, but they do ask what good a high-school diploma is."

"And what do you tell them?"

"I tell them it doesn't mean a thing sometimes and sometimes it's crucial, depending on who they are. I tell them the truth. Some exceptional people without diplomas have 'made it' in the world and some with diplomas are pushing dress carts on Seventh Avenue. It really depends on them and how they learn to use their resources."

"Do they understand that?"

"They not only understand it, they know it before I tell them anything. They usually ask the question just to see if I know what the world is all about."

He's satisfied. He, too, knows about diplomas and success. He also knows that our school is not molding individuals into a common goal after graduation.

He continues into something else. "Do you think your school is a good alternative for public schools?"

"Yes. *An* alternative. Not *the* alternative. Just as there's no one answer for the population of LEAP students' futures, there's no one alternative to public schools. I would like to see many different schools. Not only different from public school, but also different from the LEAP School. We're not *the* alternative for kids who don't succeed in public school. In fact, public school is better for some kids than the LEAP School."

He didn't expect to hear what he just heard. Silence. He writes some more notes.

Now he goes into something else. Another standard question, "Do you think that you can implement change in public schools?"

"I don't think so. I'm not interested."

His face is puzzled. How can we not be interested?

I'm mad. Somehow, just because we have started an innovative school that is working, people try to put the impossible burden of "changing the public school system in the United States" on us. No fancy private school is asked to do this.

"If the public schools were really interested in changing themselves, they would have found us and asked us how we work and what we're doing. They're the ones who will come to us, if they're interested. As it is now, public-school people are busily fortifying themselves against any change. They take innovative programs and modify them into the context of regular public-school programs. They try to crush schools like ours that are emerging all over the country. I'd be a fool to attempt to convince them that they can be successful with students like ours. It would take too much time and would be futile. Changing the public-school system means changing themselves, and they're just not interested in that kind of commitment. They want to extend their power, their control, not their humanity."

He understands completely. "Aren't you still having problems getting your state charter?"

"Yes, we are. You know, they make those decisions based on a whole arbitrary thing: for example, providing what they call 'an equivalent education'—equivalent, that is, to the schools our kids left behind. So right from the start we're forced to be like or play like the system we all know has failed."

"But that sounds absurd," our newsman guest responds. "It's maddening."

"Only if you're rational," I'm quick to add.

"An equivalent education," he thinks out loud. "Wow."

# BIBLIOGRAPHY

## RADICAL SCHOOL REFORM: THEORY AND PRACTICE

Altshuler, Alan A., *Community Control: The Black Demand for Participation in Large American Cities.* Pegasus, 1970.

Ashton-Warner, Sylvia, *Teacher.* Simon and Schuster, 1963.

Berg, Ivar, *Education and Jobs: The Great Training Robbery.* Frederick A. Praeger, Inc., 1970.

Berube, Maurice, and Gittell, Marilyn (eds.), *Confrontation at Ocean Hill-Brownsville.* Frederick A. Praeger, Inc., 1969.

Birmingham, John (ed.), *Our Time Is Now.* Frederick A. Praeger, Inc., 1970.

Brown, George I., *Human Teaching for Human Learning.* Viking Press, 1970.

Bruner, Jerome S., *The Process of Education.* Vintage Books, Random House, Inc., 1960.

Clark, Kenneth, *Dark Ghetto.* Harper and Row, 1965.

Cole, Lawrence, *Street Kids.* Grossman Publishers, Inc., 1970.

Coles, Robert, *Children of Crisis.* Delta Books, 1968.

————, *Teachers and the Children of Poverty.* The Potomac Institute, 1970.

Danforth and Ford Foundations, *The School and the Democratic Environment.* Columbia University Press, 1970.

Dennison, George, *The Lives of Children.* Random House, Inc., 1969.

Dewey, John, *The Child and the Curriculum.* University of Chicago Press, 1956.

————, *Experience and Education.* Crowell Collier and Macmillan, Inc., 1963.

————, *The School and Society.* University of Chicago Press, 1915.

Dewey, John, and Dewey, Evelyn, *Schools of Tomorrow.* E. P. Dutton and Co., Inc., 1962.

Divoky, Diane, *How Old Will You Be in 1984?* Avon Books, 1969.
Emerson, Ralph Waldo, *Emerson on Education.* Teachers College Press, 1966.
Fantini, Mario, Gittell, Marilyn, and Magat, Richard, *Community Control and the Urban School.* Frederick A. Praeger, Inc., 1970.
Fantini, Mario, and Weinstein, Gerald, *The Disadvantaged: Challenge to Education.* Harper and Row, 1968.
Featherstone, Joseph, "School Managers." *New Republic,* February 8, 1969.
The Freestone Publishing Co., Rasberry Greenways' Exercises: *How to Start Your Own School—and Make a Book.* The Freestone Publishing Co., 1970. (Write: The Freestone Publishing Co., c/o New Schools Exchange, 301 E. Cañon Perdido, Santa Barbara, California 93101.)
Freire, Paolo, *The Pedagogy of the Oppressed.* Herder and Herder, Inc., 1970.
Friedenberg, Edgar Z., *Coming of Age in America.* Vintage Books, 1965.
———, *Dignity of Youth and Other Atavisms.* Beacon Press, 1965.
———, "The Hidden Costs of Opportunity." *The Atlantic,* February 1969.
———, *The Vanishing Adolescent.* Dell Publishing Co., Inc., 1962.
———, "What the Schools Do." *This Magazine Is About Schools,* Toronto.
Gattegno, Caleb, *Toward a Visual Culture.* Outerbridge & Dienstfrey, 1969.
———, *What We Owe Children: The Subordination of Teaching to Learning.* Outerbridge & Dienstfrey, 1970.
Gibson, James M., and Hall, James C., *Damn Reading: A Case Against Literacy.* Vantage Press, 1969.
Goodman, Paul, *Compulsory Mis-education.* Vintage Books, 1962.
———, *Growing Up Absurd.* Vintage Books, 1960.
———, *The New Reformation.* Random House, Inc., 1970.
Green, Robert L. (ed.), *Racial Crisis in American Education.* Follett Education Corp., 1969.
Gross, Ronald (ed.), *The Teacher and the Taught.* Dell Publishing Co., Inc., 1963.
Gross, Ronald, and Gross, Beatrice (eds.), *Radical School Reform.* Simon and Schuster, 1970.

Gross, Ronald, and Murphy, Judith, *The Arts and the Poor*. U.S. Government Printing Office, 1968.

———, *The Revolution in the Schools*. Harcourt, Brace and World, Inc., 1964.

Hart, Leslie, *The Classroom Disaster*. Teachers College Press, 1969.

Hedgepeth, William, and Stock, Dennis, *The Alternative: Communal Life in New America*. The Macmillan Co., 1970.

Hemming, James, *Teach Them to Live*. Longmans, Green and Co., 1957.

Henderson, David, with Barbara Christian and Carol Walton, *Black Papers on Black Education*. Other Ways, Berkeley, California, 1968.

Henry, Jules, *Culture Against Man*. Vintage Books, 1963.

Hentoff, Nat, *Our Children Are Dying*. Viking Press, Inc., 1967.

Herndon, James, *How to Survive in Your Native Land*. Simon and Schuster, 1971.

———, *The Way It Spozed to Be*. Simon and Schuster, 1968.

Hilsheimer, G. von, "Is There a Science of Behavior?" *Humanitas*, 1967.

Holt, John, *How Children Fail*. Dell Publishing Co., Inc., 1964.

———, *How Children Learn*. Pitman Publishing Corp., 1967.

———, "Letter From Berkeley." *Yale Alumni Magazine*, November 1969.

———, "Summerhill and Beyond." *Summerhill: For and Against*. Hart Publishing, 1970.

———, "To the Rescue." *New York Review of Books*, October 8, 1969.

———, *What Do I Do Monday?* E. P. Dutton and Co., Inc., 1970.

———, "Why We Need New Schooling." *Look Magazine*, January 13, 1970.

———, *The Underachieving School*. Pitman Publishing Corp., 1968.

Illich, Ivan D., *Celebration of Awareness*. Doubleday and Co., 1970.

———, *Ciclo Lectures Summer 1970*. (CIDOC Cuaderno No. 1007), Centro Intercultural de Documentacion, 1970. (Order from CIDOC, Apdo. 479, Cuernavaca, Mexico.)

Jerome, Judson, *Culture Out of Anarchy*. Herder and Herder, Inc., 1970.

Koch, Kenneth, *Wishes, Lies and Dreams*. Chelsea House Publishers, 1970.

Kohl, Herbert, *The Open Classroom*. Vintage/*New York Review of Books*, 1970.

———, "Teaching the Unteachable." *New York Review of Books* pamphlet, 1967.

———, *Thirty-six Children*. New American Library, Inc., 1968.

Kozol, Jonathan, *Death at an Early Age*. Houghton Mifflin Co., 1967.

Lauter, Paul, and Howe, Florence, *The Conspiracy of the Young*. World Publishing Co., 1970.

Leonard, George, *Education and Ecstasy*. Delacorte Press, 1968.

Levin, Henry M. (ed.), *Community Control of Schools*. Brookings, 1970.

Levy, Gerald, *Ghetto School: Class Warfare in an Elementary School*. Pegasus, 1970.

Libarle, Marc, and Seligson, Tom (eds.), *The High School Revolutionaries*. Random House, Inc., 1970.

Lindenfeld, Frank, et al., *Directory of Free Schools*. Alternatives Foundation, 1970. (List of free schools across the country, plus essay by Lindenfeld, "How to Start a Free School." Order from Alternatives Foundation, Drawer A, Diamond Heights Station, Sebastopol, California 94131.)

Lurie, Ellen, *How to Change the Schools: A Parents' Action Handbook on How to Fight the System*. Random House, Inc., 1970.

McLuhan, Marshall, *The Medium Is the Massage*. Random House, Inc., 1967.

Macrorie, Kenneth. *Up Taught*. Hayden Book Co., 1970.

Marin, Peter, "The Open Truth and Fiery Vehemence of Youth." *The Center Magazine*, January 1969. (Order from *The Center Magazine*, 2056 Eucalyptus Hill Road, Santa Barbara, California 93103.)

Maslow, Abraham, "Some Educational Implications of the Humanistic Psychologies." *Harvard Educational Review*, Fall 1968.

Neill, A. S., *Summerhill*. Hart Publishing, 1960.

———, *Talking of Summerhill*. London: Victor Gollancz. (Order from the British Book Center, 996 Lexington Avenue, New York, N. Y. 10021.)

New Directions Community School, *How to Start a Free School* (3rd ed.). Order from New Directions Community School, 445 Tenth Street, Richmond, California 94801.)

Oettinger, Anthony G. *Run, Computer, Run.* Harvard University Press, 1970.

O'Gorman, Ned. *The Storefront.* Harper and Row, 1970.

O'Neill, William F. *Selected Educational Heresies.* Scott, Foresman and Co., 1969.

Lady Plowden, et al. *Children and Their Primary Schools.* 2 volumes (The Plowden Report). British Information Services, 1967. (Order from British Information Services, Sales Section, 845 Third Avenue, New York, N. Y. 10021.)

Postman, Neil, and Weingartner, Charles, *The Soft Revolution.* Delacorte Press, 1971.

————, *Teaching as a Subversive Activity.* Delacorte Press, 1969.

Provincial Committee on Aims and Objectives of Education in the Schools of Ontario, *Living and Learning.* Ontario Department of Education, 1968.

Rathbone, Charles, *Open Education: Selected Readings.* Citation Press, 1970.

Read, Herbert, *Education Through Art.* Faber & Faber, 1958. (Order from British Book Center, 996 Lexington Avenue, New York, N. Y. 10021.)

Reimer, Everett, *An Essay on Alternatives in Education.* (CIDOC Cuaderno No. 1005.) Centro Intercultural de Documentacion, 1970. (Order from CIDOC, Apdo. 479, Cuernavaca, Mexico.)

Resnik, Henry S., *Turning on the System.* Pantheon Books, Inc., 1970.

Richardson, Elwyn S., *In the Early World.* Pantheon Books, Inc., 1969.

Rogers, Carl, *On Becoming a Person.* Houghton Mifflin Co., 1961.

Rosenthal, Robert, and Jacobson, Lenore, *Pygmalion in the Classroom.* Holt, Rinehart and Winston, 1968.

Rousseau, Jean-Jacques, *Emile: or, Education.* Everyman, E. P. Dutton and Co., Inc., 1932.

Rubinstein, Annette T. (ed.), *Schools Against Children: The Case for Community Control.* Monthly Review Press, 1970.

Russell, Bertrand, *Education and the Good Life.* Liveright Publishing Corp., 1931.

————, *Education and the Social Order.* Humanities Press, 1967.

Schoolboys of Barbiana. *Letter to a Teacher* (with postscripts by Robert Coles and John Holt). Random House, Inc., 1970.

Scribner, Harvey, "Make the Schools Work for All the Children." *Staff Bulletin,* N.Y.C. Board of Education, 1970.

Silberman, Charles E., *Crisis in the Classroom*. Random House, Inc., 1970.

Stein, Maurice, and Miller, Larry, *Blueprint for Counter Education: Curriculum, Handbook, Wall Decoration, Shooting Script*. Doubleday and Co., Inc., 1970.

Student Rights Project of the New York Civil Liberties Union, *Student Rights Handbook for New York City*. New York Civil Liberties Union, 1970.

Summerhill Society, *A Bibliography for the Free School Movement*. (Order from The Summerhill Society, 137a West 14 Street, New York, N. Y. 10011.)

Taylor, Harold, *Students Without Teachers*. McGraw-Hill Book Co., 1969.

————, *The World as Teacher*. Doubleday and Co., Inc., 1968.

Tolstoy, Lev Nikolaevich, *Tolstoy on Education*. University of Chicago Press, 1967.

Urofsky, Melvin (ed.), *Why Teachers Strike*. Anchor Books, Doubleday and Co., Inc., 1970.

Vermont Department of Education, *Vermont Designs for Education*. Vermont Department of Education, 1969. (Montpelier, Vermont.)

Wasserman, Miriam, *The School Fix, NYC, USA*. Outerbridge & Dienstfrey, 1970.

Weinstein, Gerald, and Fantini, Mario D., *Toward Humanistic Education*. Frederick A. Praeger, Inc., 1970.

Whitehead, Alfred North, *The Aims of Education and Other Essays*. The Macmillan Co., 1929.

Woulf, Constance, *The Free Learner*. (Survey of experimental schools in the San Francisco Bay area. Order from Constance Woulf, 4615 Canyon Road, El Sobrante, California 94703.)

Wright, Nathan, Jr. (ed.), *What Black Educators Are Saying*. Hawthorne Books, Inc., 1970.

## SOURCES OF INFORMATION ABOUT RADICAL SCHOOL REFORM

*About Education*, 219 Broad Street, Philadelphia, Pennsylvania 19107.

*Anarchy Magazine*, Freedom Press, 84A, White Chapel High Street, London, England.

Arts and Humanities Program, U. S. Office of Education, Room 3137, 400 Maryland Avenue, S. W., Washington, D. C. 20202.

*Big Rock Candy Mountain,* Portola Institute, Inc., 1115 Merrill Street, Menlo Park, California 94025.

CIDOC (Center for Intercultural Documentation), Box 479, Cuernavaca, Mexico.

*Change,* 59 East 54th Street, New York, N. Y. 10022.

*Edcentric,* Center for Educational Reform, (National Students Assoc.), 2115 S Street N. W., Washington, D. C. 20008.

Humanitas, Box 606, Orange City, Florida 32763.

Idea Exchange, Education Assoc., Inc., Upward Bound, 1717 Massachusetts Avenue, Washington, D. C. 20036.

Institute for Community Studies, Queens College, 153-10 61st Road, Flushing, N.Y. 11367.

Libertarian Teacher, 36 Devonshire Road, Mill Hill, London NW7, England.

*Manas,* P. O. Box 4173, Woodside, California 94062.

*New Schools Exchange Newsletter,* 301 East Canon Perdido, Santa Barbara, California, 93101.

Ortega Park Teacher's Lab, P. O. Box 4173, Woodside, California 94062.

Project Follow Through, Education Development Center, 55A Chapel Street, Newton, Massachusetts 02160.

*Psychology Today,* P. O. 60407, Terminal Annex, Los Angeles, California 90060.

"Radicals in the Professions," Newsletter of Radical Education Project, P. O. Box 625, Ann Arbor, Michigan 48107.

Schools for the Future, specialized seminars, 821 Broadway, New York, N. Y. 10003.

The Summerhill Society, 6063 Hargis Street, Los Angeles, California 90035; and 137a West 14 Street, New York, N. Y. 10011.

Teacher Drop-out Center, School of Education, University of Massachusetts, Amherst, Massachusetts 01002.

Teachers and Writers Collaborative, Pratt Center for Community Development, 244 Vanderbilt Avenue, Brooklyn, N. Y. 11205.

*This Magazine Is About Schools,* P. O. Box 876, Terminal "A," Toronto 1, Ontario.

*The Whole Earth Catalog,* Portola Institute, Inc., 1115 Merrill Street, Menlo Park, California 94025.